SOOCH!

SOOCH!

Sports writing by Joe Soucheray of the Minneapolis Tribune

Published by the Minneapolis Tribune
Minneapolis Star & Tribune Company
425 Portland Av. / Minneapolis / Minn. 55488

First Printing

Library of Congress Cataloging in Publication Data
Soucheray, Joe.
    Sooch! : sports writing of Joe Soucheray of the
Minneapolis Tribune.

    Includes index.
    1. Sports--Addresses, essays, lectures.
I. Title.
GV704.S6   070.4'49796   81-11322
ISBN 0-932272-07-X   AACR2

Copyright © 1981/Minneapolis Tribune

Design/Michael Carroll
Illustrations/L. K. Hanson

Dedication

For all my family and friends

Introduction

The collection of writings gathered here will take the reader back over the last half dozen years or so, a time period that might or might not be the most telling in the development of sports as a national obsession. That is for the reader to decide.

But just as often as not these columns and stories should inspire some laughter; I am not a great fan of obsession.

In some instances, the 1980 Olympics, for example, the columns are offered sequentially, so the reader might be reminded of his own involvement in an event that held him from beginning to end.

Other events — the World Series, the Super Bowls, the important prize fights — are highlighted by a selection of pieces from over the years.

Dates on columns indicate the times of publication in the Minneapolis Tribune. When action took place outside Minneapolis, the sites are indicated in datelines.

These columns are offered as they first appeared, incidentally, usually written under the pressure of the newspaper's deadline. Taken together they are my record of a time.

Joe Soucheray
September 1981

Contents

1/Winter Olympics, 1980	**1**
2/World Series	**29**
3/Super Bowl	**45**
4/Boxing	**59**
5/Boston Marathon	**71**
6/Women's Open, 1977	**81**
7/Kentucky Derby	**91**
8/Joe goes fishing	**103**
9/Athletes, past and present	**117**
10/The Minnesota Twins	**141**
11/Calvin Griffith	**173**
12/The Dome	**187**
13/The Minnesota Vikings	**203**
14/Around and about sports	**247**

1 / Winter Olympics, 1981

February 13, 1980

Lake Placid. N.Y.

By nightfall Tuesday the Almighty had absolved nature from any further embarrassments connected with the XIII winter Olympic Games.

Snow fell yesterday in large, wind-driven flakes and there was no mistaking it as a gift. Shopkeepers along Main St. in the village of Lake Placid stood in the wet street so that snow could fall into canisters that were quickly capped, labeled and sold as the official snow of the winter games. Honest.

"I was wondering," a man said to a shopkeeper, "if there is an official Olympic match?"

"No," she said and she made her lips into a straight line, "but there is an official Olympic bathroom."

No one from above or below this mortal valley will ever be able to absolve the Olympic organizers of conduct unbecoming the operators of even the crudest sideshow carnival. The games are so fat with politics and the streets so clamorous with the exchange of money that the athletes have become pawns, virtually expendable according to the whims of the International Olympic Committee (IOC).

Before the first ski race, or before today's official opening ceremonies, the IOC has been simultaneously burdened with President Carter's request to move, postpone or cancel the summer games scheduled for Moscow and the lawsuit brought against the IOC by Liang Ren-guey, a skier from Taiwan who wishes to march under the flag of the Republic of China.

Burdened would be the IOC term. The lords, noblemen, counts and other pompous fools in the IOC are not accustomed to dealing with such grave matters so close to the cocktail hour.

Last night the IOC unanimously voted to uphold its decision to hold the games in Moscow as planned. The IOC theoretically disavows itself from any political maneuverings, which makes the case of Liang so immediately suspect and confusing. The IOC had ruled last year that athletes from Taiwan could no longer call themselves representatives of the Republic of China, could not bear that flag or hear that anthem.

The ruling was coincidental to mainland China's entering the winter games for the first time since 1949. Mainland China is big, powerful and now friendly with the United States. Taiwan is a small country. When the athletes from Taiwan showed up here last week, they weren't admitted.

"You are to call yourselves the Taipei Olympic Committee," they were told.

"But we are the Republic of China," they said, "and have always competed under that name."

On behalf of his teammates, Liang filed suit. A New York State Supreme Court judge named Norman Harvey understood Taiwan's plight and ruled that the IOC had indeed acted with discrimination. The IOC appealed.

Lo, the appellate division of the state supreme court ruled Monday in favor of the IOC, deciding that it was not a matter of individual rights, but a sovereign matter. To blacken matters further, the appellate court said that any nation that participates in the games "shall accept the supreme authority of the IOC". The implications of such a ruling are frightful; what if the wife of an IOC member dislikes the way an American boxer combs his hair?

The United States has shown the world its scar on this matter as well. Because the United States supports mainland China in its efforts to enter the games without embarrassment, our government dispatched a Department of Justice attorney to the scene. Mark C. Rutzick wanted everyone to know that the United States recognizes and believes in the IOC authority in Olympic matters — this on the heels of the United States begging the IOC to pull out of Moscow.

The State Court of Appeals upheld the IOC yesterday, clearing the way for mainland China's participation. The Taiwan group said after the decision that it was considering a further appeal to the U.S. Supreme Court, but even they must realize that such a gesture would be hopeless bravado.

A day or so in an Olympic village is long enough to become familiar with the way the IOC operates. Because the committee has dealt so rarely before with such pressing matters, the IOC press conferences have been traditionally attended by perhaps three or four people.

Now, when the IOC and its decrees are at the forefront of world news, still only three or four people are allowed within the IOC conclaves. It turns out that one must be separately accredited to attend IOC press conferences, but because there was never much need to in the past, few people filled out the proper forms years in advance. Not only is the IOC ponderous and dictatorial, but anachronistic as well. It neither bends nor moves forward. It exists.

The snow provided a pleasant walk yesterday across Mirror Lake to the ancient lodge where the IOC is gerrymandered, the Lake Placid Club. A man had come just to see how the ruling body lives. Inside, the polished wood floors creaked and the high-ceilinged rooms and halls smelled of leather. The lodge is so completely self-contained that an IOC member can post his mail, cash a check in any currency, shop, dine, drink and dance in one glorious setting overlooking Mirror Lake.

Counting the main lodge rooms, the adjoining cottages and apartments, the Lake Placid Club could accommodate close to 1,200 souls, all within walking distance of the hockey arena and speed skating oval and equidistant from the ski slopes and bob runs.

The 1,400 or so athletes who make it all possible (it's tough to make an exact count when the IOC bumps a delegation here and there) are quartered 10 miles from town in an Olympic Village that will become a prison when the games are concluded.

The lodging is backward. But it will always remain so when the premier athletic events of our time are entrusted to men who condone the sale of snow, not to mention the humiliation of Liang Renguey.

February 14, 1980

Lake Placid, N.Y.

Even as the chorus sang the cantata and 2,000 doves fluttered into the cold sky during Wednesday's opening ceremonies of the XIII winter Olympics, those citizens of the world encamped in the Adirondacks might have created another event not listed on the agenda.

Because a shuttle-bus system in and around the village has been unreliable and often nonexistent and because streets have been rerouted so circuitously that even lifelong residents cannot get to the drugstore, Lake Placid has become a walking village.

If this truly will be "an Olympics in perspective", as suggested in welcoming remarks yesterday by the Rev. J. Bernard Fell, president of the Lake Placid Olympic Organizing Committee, then hoofing it through the snow will be as pleasant a way as any to make fast friends with Boris and Per and Heidi.

"Without competition," Fell said, "and without communication, there is chaos." Approximately 20,000 witnesses to the opening ceremonies in the horse show grounds just south of town had a laugh on the good reverend and made as much noise as is possible through muffled mittens. Communication has broken down in many cases in Lake Placid and fans, press and even some athletes may not be able to get from here to there. But more importantly yesterday, no one cared.

"Many people wonder," Fell continued, "just what an Olympics in perspective means. It means that we should revert and yield the games to the athletes. Let these games signal the beginning of a new understanding around the world."

And if these games are the last conducted in a manner that is both grand and perhaps unmanageable, then they were introduced in style. Regrettably, the athletes from Taiwan did not enter the grounds, even though the International Olympic Committee (IOC), as well as the United States, offered to harbor the group under the IOC banner or the American flag.

On Tuesday a New York appeals court upheld the IOC ruling that the 27 Taiwan athletes could not march under the flag of the Republic of China. While they passed up the opportunity to stand outside for a couple of hours yesterday with the 1,600 athletes from 35 other nations, the Taiwan athletes still can compete in the games, so long as they don't get the notion that they are who they claim to be.

A further dilemma may have been created by the harsh treatment of the Taiwan athletes. Must the Taiwan manufacturer of the official Olympic lapel pin disclaim credit for his work?

Just as the clients were beginning to turn purple with chill, army-brown helicopters chattered into view and deposited Vice President Walter Mondale onto an adjoining field. The governor of New York, Hugh Carey, had already delivered his version of a welcome, so Mondale and Lord Killanin, president of the IOC, kept their tongues remarkably in harness.

Notes of Mondale's speech were unnecessary. He used just one sentence: "On behalf of the president of the United States and the American people, I am pleased to declare officially the opening of the XIII winter Olympic games held this year in Lake Placid." It did serve to confirm the belief that on this occasion, at least, everyone was where he or she was supposed to be.

The march of the athletes made for a warm glow, although there are some who attach significance to the way Mondale ignored the waving Russians and still others who attach more significance to the way one poor dove, who appeared to suffer a heart attack upon its release, never did get airborne and crashed among the boots of the assembled, and quite startled, Russians.

All in all, a client got his ticket's worth, even at $50 a crack. The Golden Knights U.S. Army parachute team managed to land on the grounds without impaling themselves, and the Olympic Orchestra and Chorus from the Crane School of Music of the Potsdam College of Arts and Sciences were brilliant, considering that with frozen lips it is nearly impossible to make music from a tuba.

The Olympic torch was lit, of course, and Eric Heiden of the United States delivered an oath of fair play for athletes and there were prayers and more tunes and the flight of hot-air balloons.

But there was no mistaking the cold and the wind that whistled through the Adirondacks yesterday. Most affected were the members of the Old Guard Fife and Drum Corps of the Third U.S. Infantry, who wore authentic Revolutionary War costumes that were somewhat less warm than a fur coat. One poor fifer, departing the grounds, was nearly in a trance when a state trooper offered him a cup of coffee.

"Now that I look at you, son," the trooper said, "you want something stiffer than that?"

February 17, 1980

Lake Placid, N.Y.

Bob Kane, president of the U.S. Olympic Committee, was having coffee with his wife, Ruth, on Saturday morning in the Whiteface Inn, the old lodge overlooking the lake that gives Placid its name.

New snow was falling and the forested shoreline of the mountain lake came in and out of view, a cabin in the distance, a pine tree bending in the wind. The couple rose and looked at each other and they knew that this was one more day they would be robbed of time together.

Like a guy on the subway or at a breakfast counter, Kane has been stunned by the world news in the last few months. The Russians invaded Afghanistan. Kane knew that. He was not prepared for what came next, when the president of the United States, without first consulting Kane, made the U.S. Olympic Committee (USOC) a tool of foreign policy.

Jimmy Carter had vowed that U.S. Olympians would not compete in the summer games in Moscow unless the Soviet Union withdrew its invading forces by Feb. 20. And suddenly Robert Kane was on the front page of newspapers trying to get himself untangled from his call to patriotism and his call to the Olympians.

He was upstairs in his suite now, Kane was, kissing his wife goodby. He is a fit man, 67 years old, with hair as white as snow and a tough, leathery face. His tenure as USOC president began in the spring of 1977 and will conclude in April 1981 and he should be enjoying himself during the XIII Winter Games.

But again he has been forced to the front of world news. He carried Carter's request to the board of the International Olympic Committee (IOC), told the IOC it was wrong for holding the games in Moscow, but he was shot down and a little more age crept around his eyes.

"I was president of the Eastern College Athletic Conference," Kane was saying, "and I have served as a vice president of the National Collegiate Athletic Association, but nothing could quite prepare me for what I've had to face lately. I've tried not to get shaken up, you have good days and bad. But we weren't even consulted by the government until five days after Carter informed the world that our Olympians might not be able to compete in Moscow. What was I supposed to think? We are the custodians of American athletes for the International Olympic Committee. We are private. We don't get one dollar from the U.S. government. I'm torn, really torn."

"Do you wonder," a man asked, "if foreign policy based on the appearance or nonappearance of American athletes is wise? Isn't the real issue about bombs and warplanes and fighting troops?"

"I've asked myself the same questions," Kane said. "I've tried to put myself in Carter's shoes. Like him, I guess I would use any weapon, including Olympians. But what worries me is that if the use of us as a tool is successful in getting the Soviets out of Afghanistan, what if that result comes too late to send our athletes to Moscow? We go unrewarded."

"Have you ever met Carter personally?"

"He shook my hand a few weeks ago when we both appeared in Washington at a national council on physical education. He shook my hand and walked past me."

"Do you want to meet him?"

"You're damn right I do," Kane said, "and I better meet him."

Bob Kane is a tough man. He was born and raised and still lives in Ithaca, N.Y. His father was a salesman who could not afford to send his son to Cornell, which is the center of life in Ithaca. Kane worked his way through Cornell and was in law school there in 1936 when he tried to become an American Olympian as a sprinter and quarter miler.

"I was disqualified," Kane said. "I was considered a professional because I had accepted money to help coach track and field at Cornell. I dropped out of school then to earn some real money so I could come back and finish law school, but I never came back."

Kane never returned to the classroom and he never became a lawyer. He was named assistant athletic director at Cornell and, at age 26, acting athletic director. In 1940, Cornell had the No. 1 football team in the nation and was working on an 18-game winning streak when they were forced to give a victory to Dartmouth after films showed that Cornell scored the winning touchdown on a play that was actually a fifth down.

"That was a famous thing, the fifth-down play," Kane said, "but you're too young to remember it. By 1943 I was head athletic director at Cornell and I remained in that position until I was elected USOC president in 1977."

Very early in his career, Robert Kane was singled out for the Olympic movement in this country. In the 1952 games at Helsinki, he was manager of the men's track and field team. By 1960 he was secretary to the USOC, a second vice president in 1964, a first vice president in 1972. And now as the chief he has caught a bad turn of the wheel and it couldn't have come at a worse time.

The American Olympic programs have improved remarkably under Kane's leadership. As early as 1962 he had been campaigning for the national sports festivals that became a reality four years ago. Fund-raising has never been more lucrative.

"We are at the pinnacle of the movement in this country," Kane said. "I'd like to think I help to put us there. At Cornell, we had 22 sports for men and 18 for women, more than any college in the country. We are engaged in programs now in this country that boost our women athletes."

Kane closed his eyes and rubbed his face. He clearly does not know what to do and admits it. He suffers no illusions; sports is a business, he calls it that, and his business is crashing around him because a foreign army is having its way in Afghanistan.

"How did this come to be?" Kane was asked. "How did it come to be that Olympic competition has become so big, so political, that it can dominate the news and put you in such a confusing position?"

"We could have seen this day coming by studying history," Kane said. "In 1952 there were 52 nations in the games. Now there are 141, virtually the entire world. The IOC wanted this, they wanted world participation. And the medal counts began and television brought the games to billions of people. And the Eastern bloc countries began to use the games and the medal counts to make themselves look good.

"We used to dominate the games, not the Eastern Europeans. We had the college and high school programs that produced the best athletes in the world, not the Soviets. So the Soviets look at our system and they create one of their own, a better one, a broad-based one with as much emphasis on canoeing, for example, as on basketball. We got left behind. And now we try to play catch-up. We won a medal in basketball in 1976. That's one medal. The Russians won eight gold medals in canoeing alone."

The nations of the world know each other now and there seems to be no satisfactory way, save games, to prove superiority. The Americans and the Russians can kill each one of us 17 times over with bombs, so what good are they? Robert Kane has devoted his life to the business of sport and he doesn't know what to do.

"It will be shameful and it will be outrageous," Kane said, "if our athletes are used to make some peace in the world and then we don't get to compete. That's the message I have to take to Carter. I need to talk to him. I need to meet him personally."

Robert Kane deserves more than a handshake. Like the rest of us, he needs to know what is going on in this world that seems determined to rip itself apart.

February 18, 1980

Lake Placid, N.Y.

The Minnesota franchise in the elegant world of Alpine skiing slid down Whiteface Mountain Sunday forenoon in 1:39.69, which might as well be the speed of light to a civilian.

But when Cindy Nelson, who wears the decal of her family's Lutsen resort on her black racing helmet, came across the finish line she knew that her time would never hold for a medal against the Olympic field. As she skidded to a halt at the base of the run, Nelson lifted her arms in a gesture that could be read two ways, because her time had moved her into third place, exactly where she finished at Innsbruck four years ago.

"That wasn't elation," Nelson said after the run, "that was dismay. I was lifting my arms as if to say, 'Oh Lord, what next for me?' I knew that if I made the run of my life I could have won the gold."

Annemarie Moser-Proell, Austria's six-time World Cup champion, had already been posted at 1:37.52 for first place and Marie Theres-Nadig, the Swiss who had won all but one World Cup downhill this year, at 1:38.36 for second. Nelson held the bronze position for exactly 1:38.22, or the time it took for Hanni Wenzel of Liechtenstein to bust across the finish line, bump Nadig down a notch and claim the silver medal for herself.

And Nelson kept slipping down until she was off the board and in a tie for seventh place with Ingrid Eberlie of Austria, behind Heidi Preuss the 18-year-old from Lakeport, N.H., and Cathy Kreiner, a Canadian.

Counting Holly Flanders of Deerfield, N.H., who finished 14th, the Americans had more women in the top 15 of yesterday's Olympic downhill than any other country. But as good as the Americans have become, they are still driving station wagons to the supermarket compared to the race-car performances of the Austrians and the Swiss.

Moser-Proell's time yesterday was four seconds faster than the fastest training run recorded on Whiteface. Nadig proved that she hasn't lost much speed since winning the gold in the same even in 1972.

"I feel obliged to get this gold medal," said Moser-Proell, a pretty woman of 26, with blue eyes and short-cropped brown hair. Yesterday's gold medal performance was her first. She was a disappointing third in the 1972 games and did not compete in 1976 because she was taking care of her dying father. Yesterday the frustration ended.

"I knew I could win it," she said, "and I was certain I had it won after Nadig's run."

This was a remark that could have burned a hole through Nelson, who wore bib No. 11 yesterday. Nadig was No. 9 out of the gate. And yesterday was to have been Cindy Nelson's day for gold.

Morning broke clear and bone-chilling cold, with 40-mile-per-hour gusts blowing across Whiteface from west to east — Nelson's weather, Minnesota weather. There was even rumor that the race would be canceled because of the wind, but having already paid $28 a ticket and having managed to con a ride to the area, more than 20,000 clients marched up the slope through deep snow to witness one of the glamor events of the carnival. Some of the spectators wore mink, but then again some children were bounding about in tennis shoes.

"The course was perfect," Nelson said. "The wind had blown the flats free of snow and the course was fast. I knew that I could ski the upper part of the course as well as or better than Moser-Proell. But I didn't. I know I'm one of the best in the world, but I didn't ski like it."

There was a touch of irony in Nelson's remarks. At 24, tall and not as bulky as most women ski racers, Nelson regards herself as the leader of the American Alpine team. She has worked hard all her life, said she wouldn't be up on the mountain if she thought she couldn't win a gold.

But now she was flustered and confused. Even her 18-year-old teammate had surpassed her on this day.

"I don't know Heidi that well," Nelson said, "I don't know her psychological makeup. I can warn her that things only get tougher from here on out. She's only reached a certain level. Just wait until she has to maintain it."

A month ago Nelson was considering retirement. But after yesterday's run she said she hasn't reached her potential yet and that she won't consider making any such decision until after the giant slalom and slalom events later this week.

"I'm more hungry than ever now," she said. "I dislike getting beaten. I was bouncing around up there today and my skis were crossing, out of the groove. I didn't have my feet under me, it was as if I was skiing with my mind a little bit behind me. I ski best when I anticipate, but today I was thinking about what I was doing, rather than what I would be doing in a fraction of a second."

Because she made mistakes of concentrating in the upper, twisting reaches of the course, it was impossible for Nelson to gain ground over the last 15 seconds. The windswept and icy final approach was equally favorable to all contestants.

If this sounds hopelessly technical, or if Nelson sounds full of despair, she should remember that what she does bears absolutely no kin to the way we ski on weekends. As of right now she is the seventh best woman in the world at throwing herself down a mountain.

February 19, 1980

Lake Placid, N.Y.

There is a brown log warming shack for sledders up top and the squeaky spring noise of its door is startling. Only the silence of the deep woods can be heard up here, where the mile-long Olympic bobsled run begins its twisting course down Mount Van Hoevenberg. The run looks like sewer pipe that was sliced in half, flooded with water that froze slate gray, then left unburied on the forest floor.

Monday was the first day of final training for the four-man sleds that will compete next weekend. The final sled off the top yesterday was U.S.A No. 1, driven by Bobby Hickey, who grew up 10 miles across the ridge in the Keene Valley.

Workers in blue coats lifted Hickey's sled onto the iced grooves at the start of the run. The warming shack door sprung open and out came Jeff Jordan, who rides the second seat; Willie Davenport, who rides the third, and Jeff Gadley, the brakeman in the final seat. Davenport and Gadley are the first blacks ever to compete in the Winter Olympics, but the two of them kid each other because Davenport, by virtue of his more forward seating in Hickey's sled, will be the first black ever to complete a Winter Olympic event.

Hickey exhaled air and looked down the run. He made the sign of the cross quickly and nodded, and the four men began the slow rocking rhythm that exploded into a sprint. The four ran madly, until that last moment when the red sled would have shot ahead without them, and then they lowered themselves onto the tiny seats as softly, Davenport said, "as a man would set himself down on a bag of eggs".

There hasn't been a bobsledding death on Mount Van Hoevenberg since Feb. 21, 1966, when an Italian named Sergio Sardini, racing that day on a Canadian sled in the International Diamond Trophy Race, was killed in the zig-zag portion of the course.

"Sardini always wore a helmet about five sizes too big for his head," said a man named Steve Duprey. Duprey, middle-aged, with a thin, drawn face, was hanging around Mount Van Hoevenberg yesterday the way an ex-fighter might hang around the gym. Duprey remembers the date of Sardini's death because he was there that day, as a competitor on a sled from nearby Saranac Lake.

"He lost that big helmet when the sled hit the lip in the first turn," Duprey said. "The helmet flew off. When the sled ran high into the zig-zag, he hit his head on the wall and died instantly."

Mount Van Hoevenberg has been completely redesigned for these XIII Winter Olympics, but it follows the same path it did in 1932. Only now it is narrower than before, to contain the speeding sleds, but since it opened in December there have been more than 60 accidents, spills, flips and turnovers.

Hickey's U.S.A. No. 1 team holds the track record in 1:01.32, remarkable considering that two of its members, Davenport and Gadley, rode a bobsled for the first time Dec. 8; remarkable because Davenport, a superb hurdles and sprint man, had never before spent any more time outdoors in the winter than was necessary.

"How did Willie react after his first ride?" Hickey was asked at the bottom of the hill after the team's training run yesterday.

"He went and changed his pants," Hickey said.

Hickey is 27, with long sideburns and a mustache. His father, John, a retired forest ranger, and his older brothers, Jim and Bill, raced bobsleds before him. Bill Hickey was on a four-man sled that finished sixth at Innsbruck in 1964.

"I grew up with the sport," Hickey said. "This is the only area in the country where you can. I have a job, too. I'm a guide and a caretaker in the Ausable, a private reserve in the Adirondacks."

"Married?" he was asked.

"Separated," Hickey said. "Everybody in bobsledding is. When I went to Europe the last time, for seven weeks, she said don't go. I told her I had to and I went. Hey, I gotta go now, OK? I gotta take the sled to my father's house in Keene. I want to take it apart and put it back together again."

It may or may not go against protocol, but Hickey's team has been assembled without any input by U.S. team Coach Gary Sheffield. Hickey's team was assembled for him by a friend, Al Hachigian from Plattsburgh, N.Y., who was a member of a U.S. four-man team that finished third in the world in 1969. Hachigian is the money man and he was the middle man between Gadley and Davenport and Hickey, and Hachigian will tell those who bother to ask that he is acting as the unofficial coach of U.S.A. sled No. 1. Davenport won an Olympic gold medal in the hurdles in 1968. Gadley, 24, was a decathlon champion in New York's Empire State Games. By winning a medal in this carnival, Davenport could duplicate Eddie Eagan, the boxer and bobsledder who was the only man ever to win medals in both the summer and winter games.

"I met Willie at an Athletes Advisory Council meeting of the Amateur Athletic Union," Hachigian was saying. "Willie didn't know me and I didn't know him. We talked. I got him here. There is a real companionship developing on that sled."

Davenport was peeling an orange in the lodge at the foot of the run. He wore a blue U.S.A. sweater with red lettering. At 36, he is in his fifth Olympics, working for his third Olympic medal over-all, and the glamor has worn off for him. He has refused invitations to go downtown to speak to the journalists of the world, but out here on the course he will sign autographs for anyone and tell everyone he meets how much he hates the cold.

"My wife and child are back in Baton Rouge, Louisiana," Davenport was saying. "My wife wished me good luck and told me she loved me, but she said it was too cold for her."

"People think you're just here to lean," somebody said.

"Hey," Davenport said, "we just don't get on the damn thing and ride. Bobby chews us out. He wants pressure on the upper runners at all times. We turn right, he wants pressure on the left runner. We've got to push a 700-pound sled faster than a man should be able to. And then we got to sit ourselves down in that thing as softly as sitting on eggs. It ain't easy. I don't even know if it's fun."

Davenport is not kidding about the cold. He wants to make arrangements to have his medal presented to him — there are no ifs with Willie Davenport — right away after Sunday's final run.

"I've got my car here," Davenport said, "and on Sunday I'll have my bags packed and I'm heading straight out. We'll keep in touch, the guys on the sled, but old Willie is going home."

He will drive straight home, passing through Warren, Ohio, to see his parents, and then on to Baton Rouge, where he is in business selling pumps and pump supplies. Finally, Davenport will take off his U.S.A. shirt and hang it in the closet. He said he will be through with games forever.

February 20, 1980

Lake Placid, N.Y.

And on the eighth day of games Tuesday, with a whiff of spring on the wind and the snow on Whiteface Mountain slick and a bit wet, Ingemar Stenmark of Sweden drove himself through the giant slalom gates in 1 minute, 20:25 seconds to win the Olympic gold medal he was certain to receive.

Sweden's King Carl Gustav, Queen Silvia and the Swedish ambassador, Wilhelm Wachtmeister, had wrapped themselves in royal garments and crawled up the hill to be there when Stenmark came flying across the finish.

"The king said congratulations to me," Stenmark said afterward. This amounted to a long speech for Stenmark. The best skier on earth is not the most talkative, although he knows many languages and speaks splendid English. The best skier on earth remains the most mysterious man of the mountain, any mountain. By winning his first Olympic gold medal yesterday, Stenmark now has won every conceivable loving cup in circulation and he has not lost a giant slalom race since 1977. But Ingemar Stenmark has never said more than hello, thank you and good-by.

There is no telling what mass despair would have crept over Sweden yesterday had Stenmark lost. He entered the second and final run of the giant slalom in third place, trailing Andreas Wenzel of Liechtenstein, Hanni's brother, by three-tenths of a second, and Hans Enn of Austria by a little more than a tenth of a second. At least 25 times in his more than 40 World Cup victories, Ingemar Stenmark came from behind to win and he did so again yesterday, beating Wenzel by a full second and Enn by a fat two.

"How could this be?" he was asked afterward. "How could you be so sure of victory?"

It was not easy on Whiteface yesterday. The wind was snapping flags. Piero Gros of Italy, the slalom gold medalist at Innsbruck in 1976, fell. Valeri Tsyganov of the Soviet Union crashed through one gate on one leg and rolled through another, the gate pole whipping across his rib cage.

"I had to win," Stenmark said. This was his second speech. He stood under hot lights in a lodge at the base of Whiteface and he squirmed. He is 23 and his handsome, square face was blank against those people who pressed him for details of his skill.

"I can't explain," he said in his third speech. "I was very nervous and I knew I had to ski fast. Impossible on that snow, on that machine-made snow."

"How will your country react?"

"I don't know," Ingemar Stenmark said.

He must know. He must know that the Expressen of Stockholm will headline his victory as though war had been declared. He must know that he is more popular than Bjorn Borg. He must know that the most popular movie celebrity with Sweden's young people now is John Travolta, but that if Travolta and Stenmark walked down the street, the clothes would be torn from Stenmark's back.

He knows all of this and more. But he will not share himself. Phil and Steve Mahre, the Americans who had the best chances for a medal yesterday but finished 10th and 15th respectively, are in awe of Stenmark.

"He is the best technician on the slope," Phil Mahre said yesterday. "He cuts corners better than anyone; he follows a line better than anyone and it is probably inevitable that he wins. But I don't know him."

Kurt Karlsson, Expressen's correspondent in New York City, was dispatched by his paper to the Olympic games. After yesterday's race he said he would send 12 pages back to Stockholm, 12 pages on Stenmark. Kurt Karlsson said that all of Sweden would be in an uproar and he recalled his own youth when he worked in Tarnaby, the tiny town of 500 souls where Stenmark was born and raised and still lives.

"Stenmark could live anywhere," Karlsson was saying yesterday. "But he remains at home in Tarnaby, very near to the Arctic Circle. So close to the Arctic Circle, there are only a few hours of daylight in Tarnaby in the wintertime. The people heat their homes with wood stoves there and even with all of Ingemar's success, his family has only made improvements on the home. They heat with wood."

They piled more logs on the fire in Tarnaby last night and they stayed up late, to talk and celebrate Ingemar Stenmark. The town lies in the shadow of the mountain called Laxfjallet. It is not a big mountain, which is one explanation for Stenmark's refusal to enter downhill events; he has not had the practice.

As a child on Laxfjallet he was a slalom expert. He once won a Donald Duck race, one in a series of races sponsored for children by a publisher of children's books. It is possible to imagine many things about Stenmark, but it is impossible to picture him in Mickey Mouse ears.

"There is only one road in to Tarnaby," Karlsson was saying. "And up there they have six or seven months of snow a year, with temperatures that go to 30 below. Maybe I am helping you understand the boy's shyness? I have never seen him with a girl, or take a drink, or have a smoke."

It was easier to understand now why Stenmark left the mountain without stopping to talk after Monday's first run in the giant slalom, the run that left him in third place and worrying. He spent Monday evening watching television and worrying.

It's easier now to imagine that one day when he was younger — Stenmark has been skiing competitively since 1967 — a man, or perhaps a group of men, might have come to Tarnaby and told him he should go into the world and become a star.

Stenmark's father now works in the tourist industry for Sweden. It is unknown what employment he had before his son gathered such fame on so many glamorous mountains of the world. Experts joke about the way skiers become millionaires while retaining amateur status and people wonder how Stenmark has salted his away. They are only certain that he has.

Ingemar is a common name in Sweden. Stenmark, broken into two words, means stone and turf. Like the country he comes from, the best skier in the world is hard, unforgiving and silent. He is a rock, and if he doesn't repeat as gold medalist in the coming slalom event, King Gustav will probably call for an inquest right there on the mountain.

February 22, 1980

Lake Placid, N.Y.

Before he is canonized for his patriotism, and before his players become millionaires at the hands of agents and scouts who lurk in the shadows, Herb Brooks and Team U.S.A. must play the Soviet Union this evening in a hockey game.

But it is more than a hockey game. ABC was on its knees Thursday begging the Lake Placid Olympic Organizing Committee to switch the face-off from 4 p.m. Minneapolis time to 7:30.

"We will not attach any political significance to the game against the Russians," Brooks said yesterday afternoon after his team practiced in the Olympic Arena before hundreds of international correspondents. "I guess Russia is mad at the Americans and maybe we are mad at the Russians, but this team should be capable of forgetting that on the ice."

"Should the game be switched," Brooks was asked, "to prime time?"

"If we start later tomorrow," he answered, "then I can drink more beer tonight."

When Brooks says the Russians are mad at the Americans and that Americans are mad at Russians, he is not talking about ice hockey. Brooks is talking about the political climate on earth. But when the puck is dropped this evening, the people from ABC have said, they could attract a viewing audience even larger than for the Super Bowls.

"Maybe we shouldn't show up," Brooks said. "Maybe we should set our own deadline of 4 p.m. tomorrow. If we don't show up, the rules say we can lose by only 1-0. Then we go into the second game of medal play down by just a goal. What do you think? Would they kick us out of the tournament for that?"

The air around Brooks and his players was supercharged with electricity yesterday. No other game in the world will be able to parallel America's anger with the Soviet Union for its failure to withdraw from Afghanistan; no other game in the world will provide the Russians with such a forum to display their strength.

Even the best of athletes and coaches begin to joke and talk nonsense when the magnitude of their task is overwhelming, and Team U.S.A is about to engage in perhaps the most significant political confrontation of the year. It is not just a game. When young American hockey players wearing red, white and blue uniforms go against veteran Russian hockey players wearing red, and when a medal in the Olympic Games is at stake, it is not just a game.

America is not a hockey country. But from Alaska to California and from Florida to Maine, people will become hockey fanatics in front of their television sets tonight because America is going against the Soviet Union in the most understandable political maneuver short of dropping a bomb.

"Hey," Buzzy Schneider said after practice, "if we thought about all the political stuff that people are talking about, we'd go out there tied into a knot. Once the game starts, we must play. We won't have time to be thinking politics."

"It's a miracle situation to be in," Brooks said. "I don't have to talk to my players about it. They know. This game has nothing to do with coaches, managers or guys who smoke cigars. Team U.S.A. is self-motivated. We don't need to make things complicated."

Team U.S.A. — so named subsequent to its success at Lake Placid — is the hottest attraction of these Olympic Games. Eric Heiden is wonderful, but he skates around in circles. Figure skating is beautiful, but figure skaters are pampered children who are surrounded mostly by women. The men and women who slide down mountains are daring and courageous, but who can identify with them?

As boring as professional hockey might be, and as undernourished as college hockey might be compared with basketball, the game of hockey is still the only legitimate game being played in Lake Placid. Schneider has the puffy lips to prove it.

As the coach, Brooks has had furious run-ins with the press in Lake Placid. Some people are angered that Brooks will not display his players for interviews after games. Brooks has been doing all the talking, and when he perceived that people were dissatisified with that arrangement, he twice dispatched his assistant, Craig Patrick, to field questions.

This has upset many people who have been exploring a sport they rarely see or talk about. Team U.S.A. might have been involved in sport back when it played Sweden or Norway, but it isn't involved with sport any longer.

"All I know," Jim Craig, the goaltender, said yesterday, "is that I have to be careful when I raise my head after lacing up my skates. So many reporters, and so close, that I'm liable to bump them in the head."

Wave the flag and stand back. When Team U.S.A. meets the Soviet Union tonight, the teams will be fighting for the bragging rights to the planet. Maybe that is the wrong way to look at it. But no other way comes to mind, because this will be more than a hockey game.

February 23, 1980

Lake Placid, N.Y.

All that America wants and ever hopes for its young people was displayed on the hockey rink of the Olympic Field House in the village of Lake Placid Friday night.

America's team beat the best hockey club in the world, the team from the Soviet Union, by 4-3 and America's people would not leave the arena until after they had sung and chanted America's name.

America's people would not leave the arena until Mark Johnson tossed his stick to a fan. America's people would not leave the arena until they had stopped laughing and crying and dancing in the aisles. A fan crawled over the boards and he paraded America's flag around the rink. America's people chanted the initials of this country until they were hoarse and they kept on chanting as they streamed from the building and into the cold streets.

Olympic workers in the adjacent Lake Placid High School pushed open windows and screamed America's name. And down on Mirror Lake, where nightly Olympic medal ceremonies have been held, the first boom of the evening's fireworks display shook the air and people stopped in their tracks because something magical was happening. Fireworks were bursting in air and strangers were hugging each other in the streets.

America works. America's team proved that.

They are children for the most part and they have not played as a team for even a full year.

The Red Army team of the Soviet Union carried six members who were playing in their third Olympics, and the Russians had not even been beaten in Olympic competition since they lost to a Czechoslovakian team in 1968. The team America's team beat last night to keep alive hopes for the Olympic gold medal had beaten the All-Stars of the National Hockey League last season. The team America's team beat last night beat these same Olympians 10-3 two weeks ago in Madison Square Garden. The team America's team beat last night had won every Olympic gold medal in hockey in the last 24 years, except one, in 1960, when the fathers of America's team were children themselves.

"This is a difficult time for me," said the Soviet co-coach, Vladimir Yurzinov. "This was the best game of the tournament. The merit should be given to our opponents."

America's president, Jimmy Carter, was at that moment calling Herb Brooks in the locker room of America's team. When Herb Brooks finally entered the Lake Placid High School, he was smiling and fidgeting with his tie and he looked forward to his sparring with Vladimir Yurzinov.

"The president," Herb Brooks said, "invited us all down to the White House Monday for a couple cases ... of Coke."

Herb Brooks then pulled a piece of paper from his pocket and held it in the air and he said that his entire pregame speech was written on that piece of paper.

"We had a meeting at noon," Brooks said. "We talked some Xs and Os. Then before the game we had another meeting in the locker room. I can tell you exactly what I said. I said, 'You were born to be a player, you were meant to be here. This moment is yours, you were meant to be here at this time.'"

When Herb Brooks was speaking to his players in the hour before last night's game, America's people, at least those who could afford the $67.20 ticket, had begun to file into the arena. Many of them had purchased American flags from a vendor outside who said, "Let them be seen all over the world." Inside the arena the flags of the world hung still from the blue and white ceiling. The balconies were festooned with real flowers that had begun to wilt after 11 days of games.

And then the noise began, and though it rose and faltered again, the noise was a solid thing in the third period and a rule of decorum was broken in the press box. There was cheering in the press box last night. There was the shredding of notes and paper and there was cheering in the press box.

"We played with a style of hockey that American kids don't grow up with," Herb Brooks was saying now. "And you saw tonight how we sometimes reverted, how we forgot to weave and keep control of the puck. When the Russians beat us at Madison Square Garden (10-3) we were in awe of them. I knew we were in trouble that night because our players were applauding the great Russian players. Tonight I turned our players loose. I told them to be creative and to play with poise. I had been asking them to play an adult game against the Russians two weeks ago and they weren't ready for it. They had too much pent-up anxiety. Tonight we turned all that loose."

Herb Brooks was again asked last night why he wouldn't bring his players to be interviewed. At first Brooks shoved the microphone away and then he retrieved it.

"We don't have stars on our team," Brooks said. "I've tried to create a family of 20 people and I will not single anyone out as a star. It's my rule. I'm not coaching in the National Hockey League. I'm coaching the Olympians and I work for the Olympic Committee. When I'm finished here I return to the University of Minnesota and I have the same rules there."

Buzzy Schneider scored first, Mark Johnson scored twice and Mike Eruzione scored the last one last night, a goal that you could see coming from every corner of the rink, a goal that had America's people on the edge of their seats. Mike Eruzione shot the puck over Vladimir Myshkin's left shoulder into the corner of the net.

"We didn't want to get into a muscle game with the Russians," Herb Brooks was saying now. "There isn't any politics on the Russian team and there isn't any politics on our team. We wanted to play hockey."

America's team played hockey so well last night that the Russians pulled their famous goaltender Vladislav Tretjak, after one period and inserted Myshkin.

"Tretjak," Yurzinov said, "was made nervous."

America's people can do that to an opponent. America's people could not be quieted last night. Because America's team was proving that America works.

February 24, 1980

Lake Placid, N.Y.

Eric Heiden raced around a circle of frozen water 25 times Saturday morning without getting dizzy and won his fifth Olympic gold medal, this time at 10,000 meters, or approximately 6.2 miles.

In doing so, in shifting his will and spirit into overdrive in the final

— and longest — speed skating event of the Winter Olympics, Heiden established a world record time of 14:28.13, more than six seconds better than the mark held by the man Heiden was paired with yesterday, Viktor Leskin of the Soviet Union.

Perhaps President Carter made another attempt to connect his name with Olympic glory by calling Heiden — Carter called Herb Brooks on Friday night — but Heiden has long since disconnected his telephone. He is now in that caliber of people who take messages.

"It would be neat," Heiden said after the race, " to go back to the village and find a message from the president."

Neither the weather nor those skaters who train specifically for such a marathon distance gave Heiden much of an edge for victory yesterday. Light snow had frozen to the resurfaced track, dulling its finish. And only one other skater besides Heiden, Hilbert Van Der Duim of The Netherlands, had been in the field at all five distances.

The rest of the contestants were frisky and eager to knock Heiden off the board. But there was Heiden, in bib No. 71, dressed in the gold skating suit that made him look like a frogman. There was Heiden, chasing down the record fifth medallion that will go in a bureau drawer in his mother's room with the rest of his hardware.

"Gold medals are nice," Heiden said afterward, "but what can you do with them? I'd just as soon get a nice warmup suit, or something I can use. But then maybe if I ever need the money, I can sell the medals."

Altogether, his medals — each containing six grams of gold plated over 10.34 ounces of sterling silver are worth about $2,290 at current commodity prices.

Never before in the history of either the summer or winter carnivals had a man swept the card in his event. Mark Spitz won seven golds in warm water in Munich, but three of those were claimed as a member of relay teams. Jesse Owens won four golds in 1936, but one of those in a relay. Ard Schenk won three golds in four events at Sapporo, Japan, in 1972 and Lydia Skoblikova of the Soviet Union swept the female speed skating card at Innsbruck in 1964, but there were only four distances.

Heiden stands alone now, as the best speed skater in history and maybe as the best Olympic athlete ever. He won at every distance, 500, 1,000, 1,500, 5,000 and 10,000 meters. Only a swimmer, with a chance at 11 individual events, could ever break his record.

Heiden did not expect such fortune, or such a fast track yesterday. But when distance specialists Mike Woods of Milwaukee and Tom Erik Oxholm of Norway went off first in 14:39.53 and 14:36.60 respectively, Heiden knew as well as anyone that he could work the track for speed. Oxholm eventually claimed the bronze with Piet Kleine of The Netherlands sneaking in at 14:36.03 for the silver.

"I was scared when those first two had such good times," Heiden was saying now. "That was the last world record I ever expected to break. I didn't think five golds were possible, which made this race the best of all. I was going against the best-trained athletes in the world. I think the racers at shorter distances don't train as hard; maybe they do."

"Was it painful?" Heiden was asked. To a speed skater, 10,000 meters is considered to be a foot racer's 26 miles.

"Yeah," he said. "For the first five laps, I was looking at the lap cards and that's something you don't want to do so early in the race. By the last five laps, I had to stand up a little in the turns to keep from stumbling. I didn't have a very good morning, either. I overslept and I had time to grab three pieces of bread before I drove to the track."

The inevitable question for Heiden is whether he will become a perpetual Olympic personality, in the manner of Spitz or Bruce Jenner. Heiden insists that he will study for a year at Idretps, a sports college in Norway, and then he will try to get into medical school at the University of Wisconsin, in his hometown of Madison.

But he insists as well that he will not be taken advantage of, though he has already managed to sneak a few breakfast cereal brand names into his conversations and his attorney, Art Kaminsky, was present yesterday in the role of agent.

But Heiden competes in speed skating, a sport that appeals to perhaps 300 people in this land and even Heiden doubts that his Olympic accomplishments will do much to popularize the sport.

"People in America are turned on by big-money sports," Heiden said. "They like contact sports, they like the blood. I don't think the number of speed skaters in this country will grow because of what I've done here. I don't think any new tracks will be built. It's a fun sport and I like to skate, but I don't think I could watch a 10,000-meter race. How could those people sit there? It was boring to them."

"But is your accomplishment the best you know of in sports?" Heiden was asked.

"The biggest accomplishment I ever saw was when the U.S. beat Russia in hockey Friday night," Heiden said. "I'd like to have been out there. I thought it was great."

Heiden, who is 21 and quick-witted, said there is time for him to compete in one more event before these games conclude today and the athletes of the world head for home. Heiden wants to take his skates to the luge run at Mount Van Hoevenberg. He wants to skate down the luge run. No stop watches, no medals at stake. Just Heiden and a few of the guys. Just for the hell of it.

February 25, 1980

Lake Placid, N.Y.

The XIII Winter Olympic Games narrowed to a close Sunday afternoon with a freeze-frame of America's team in the act of celebration. Freeze that moment when 20 boys on the road to manhood came together in a jumble of dark blue jerseys on the ice of the Olympic Fieldhouse in the tiny village of Lake Placid. Freeze that moment and remember it in the rough times.

There was no way that yesterday's hockey game against Finland could have been as good, or meant as much, as Friday's game, when America's team defeated the Soviet Union. But on Friday night America's team wasn't playing for itself.

On Friday night America's team gave a medal in heart and soul to everyone in this land. Yesterday America's team played for the gold medal and they won it 4-2, and they did it for themselves. That was the difference yesterday and it made the game every bit as good as Friday's.

And after yesterday's game, America's team came out of the fieldhouse in full uniform. They stood in the falling snow on the avenue above the speed skating oval. They stood there with America's people and something good was happening again because that was real and it was a moment that was earned.

America's team moved on through the snow, through the doors of the Lake Placid High School, now the headquarters of the world press. This place had been off-limits to America's team because America's coach, Herb Brooks, had forbidden any player to go on display in interview sessions. America's team was a family without individual stars, Brooks had been saying, but he introduced them all yesterday.

"This team has startled the athletic world," Brooks said, "not the hockey world, but the athletic world. Whatever you people write, remember that these players are deserving. Any father or mother will know how much I love these players."

America's team was on the stage of the high school auditorium. They were mugging for the cameras and there was a lightning storm of flashbulbs. Mark Wells of St. Clair Shores, Mich., and Ken Morrow, the bearded defender from Davison, Mich., put towels over their faces.

Mike Eruzione, the team captain from Winthrop, Mass., took one of the high-backed leather chairs in front of a microphone. Eruzione, whose father is a sewage plant worker when he isn't tending bar at Santarpio's in east Boston, was the first to speak.

"We'd like to stay together," Eruzione was saying. "We'd like two weeks off first, but we'd like to stay together. We came from all over the country, with different backgrounds and different ethnic beliefs, and we jelled into the kind of team that no one thought was possible. The saddest thing in the world is that we are splitting up now. We are going our own way now and who knows if I'll ever see John Harrington again, or Mark Pavelich, or any of them."

There was a commotion in the rear of the room now because Jack O'Callahan was late in arriving. O'Callahan came down the aisle with a bottle of beer in his hand. And then O'Callahan, whose smile is missing some teeth, stood on the table in front of Eruzione and he led a cheer.

"I'm from Charlestown in Bahston," O'Callahan said, "right in the shadow of Bunker Hill. The Americans won at Bunker Hill and they won here today."

"The Americans didn't win at Bunker Hill," somebody said.

"Hey," O'Callahan said, "I don't want to hear that. They won there. We won too."

Oh, it was something. It was beautiful in this room because history was being made and because it was impossible for these 20 players to hide the admiration they felt for each other. The goaltender, Jim Craig, gave a speech of his love for the backup goalie, Steve Janaszak, and how Janaszak had made him a better person by always pushing him to do his best.

"I want to thank Steve Janaszak for making me a better man," Craig said. And then Janaszak got out of his chair and he walked across the stage with his arms open for Craig and Herb Brooks's family realized that they were leaving each other much too soon.

"When we got on the ice out there," Mark Johnson of Wisconsin was saying, "everybody knew that we would never have another 60 minutes together. We knew we would never have another time like this."

America's team faced off at 11 a.m. in Lake Placid, not so early that the building wasn't jammed with nearly 10,000 souls. It wasn't so early to keep Vice President Walter Mondale away. He took a seat behind the American bench and Mondale stood and screamed with one finger in the air. Mondale was on his way to New Hampshire and more politics, but he said that nothing was going to keep him away from yesterday's game.

It was not easy yesterday. The Finns were tough. They led 2-1 going into the last period, but the Americans remembered that this was their last 20 minutes together. They did not yield. This one was for them. At the end, they stormed the ice and they threw their sticks into the air and then they lined up to shake hands with the Finns.

Nobody saw the fan come over the boards. Nobody saw the fan with the American flag until he had walked up behind Craig. And then everybody saw the guy because he draped the flag over Craig's shoulders and Craig wore it like a robe.

It looked good. When was the last time it looked better?

February 27, 1980

Reflection only enlarges the moment. It cannot change it.

The American victories over the Soviet Union and Finland for the gold medal in hockey during the Winter Olympic Games were probably the most stirring sports dramas of our time. But the drama needs to be put into perspective.

From a newsman's standpoint, the Olympic Games were difficult. Because of tremendous mismanagement by the Lake Placid Olympic Organizing Committee, thousands of spectators never got closer to a speed skating event or a preliminary-round hockey game than a bus stop at Saranac Lake, 10 miles outside town. In many instances it seemed as though newsmen were the only witnesses to the games, and newsmen make bad customers; they're too busy trying to be smart. Besides, most sports writers found it impossible to regard the sport of luge seriously. Same goes for bobsledding or Alpine skiing.

Lake Placid was full of guys looking for Willie Stargell or Terry Bradshaw. After about 10 days of games, Lake Placid was full of guys who were going stir crazy for spring training or a basketball game, something with some meat on it.

Figure skating did not begin to fill this order, either. Figure skating might be beautiful and its participants might be among the most dedicated athletes in the world, but figure skating was the biggest shill of the XIII Winter Games. How can you take figure skating seriously when one of the most important people connected with the sport is the team hairdresser? This is truth. Figure skaters have team hairdressers.

And figure skaters skate to music that sounds like the music they play in shopping center malls, or music that sounds like theme music from old Marx Brothers films. And then, some doll comes out and skates to something with a beat, her hair might be mussed or the judge from Yugoslavia might be blowing his nose and miss the all important triple camel, double toe, loop over or whatever Dick Button dreams up to call the stuff.

We are creating perspective here, remember. You've got an arena full of guys lonesome for Willie Stargell and these guys are watching some 15-year-old girl worried about the team hairdresser. Maybe the mothers of figure skaters understand how the results are determined, but guys who are lonesome for Willie Stargell wanted to kill the umpire. There was no consistency at all in the way a performance was judged. Gump Worsley could have gotten good marks from some of the judges they had down there at rinkside.

All these guys who were lonesome for Willie Stargell felt the same way about luge, which is practiced by people who apparently have escaped from someplace other than normal surroundings.

Biathlon was another beauty. This is a sport that requires a contestant to ski for a while and then stop and shoot a rifle before skiing on again. In other words, biathlon closely resembles the actions in a bank hold-up, where the contestants run, shoot, and then run some more.

Now, out of the corner of their eyes, all these frustrated smart newsmen are keeping track of the American hockey team, a hockey team that was supposed to get bounced out of the tournament on the first round.

Pretty soon, this team is being called Team U.S.A. and the next thing you know, this team is being called America's team. This was because hockey was the only normal game in the Winter Olympics. People understand hockey. Guys lonesome for Willie Stargell or Terry Bradshaw can go to a hockey game and at least see something familiar.

What America's team really became was the newsmen's team. America's team had the stories. America's team had normal guys who didn't need a team hairdresser. America's team played hockey and there was no way that nine judges could sit down there at rinkside and determine the outcome by writing down numbers on a card. America's team didn't have Dick Button and American's team didn't skate around in circles or carry target rifles and America's team did not grow up on the slopes of some ski resort that newsmen couldn't spell.

The newsmen had something with meat on it in America's team. We are talking every kind of newsman here, but especially the cynical, suspicious, hard-talking columnists from every big city in the country.

But then, something magical happened. Not only did all these guys lonesome for Willie Stargell have something to write about, but they began to care about the U.S. hockey team. This is the part that reflection cannot change. Maybe it was subconscious. Maybe all the tough-guy newsmen embraced America's team for the way it bailed them all out of an impossible situation.

Ingemar Stenmark is an impossible situation, OK? Ingemar Stenmark is a great skier, but he says "yumpin' yimminy" three times and he disappears. You cannot behave that way around cynical newsmen from New York or Chicago or Los Angeles or Minneapolis.

America's team players drank beer and they fought and most of them had fat lips from going into the corners where no hairdresser could save them. So the newsmen let the magical happen. We let ourselves care and we cheered in the press box. All of us. Guys who would not be caught dead cheering in a press box, they were cheering. Some of them were crying. When we shook hands in the press box after America's team beat Finland, those handshakes were tight and they were genuine.

And down on the rink, America's team, the Yankee Doodle Dandies, they were draped in the flag. It should have closed like that, with some music and some flag waving.

If the president had to get into the act to boost his campaign, that's his problem, that goes on his conscience. If some people in this country think that capitalism defeated communism on that rink in Lake Placid, then they are fools, that goes on their conscience. As for me, I don't apologize for a thing. I will never forget what America's team did for me. I will never forget.

2 / World Series

October 17, 1976

Cincinnati, Ohio

The best third baseman in the Ohio River Valley opened the World Series Saturday afternoon with the savage fury of a gorilla.

When he couldn't range far enough left on a bullet by Roy White, Pete Rose lunged on all fours and got enough of his paw on the ball to steer it to his shortstop, Dave Concepcion. The next time up White hit a line drive that was a weapon on the rise. Pete Rose leaped and winced as the ball lodged in his glove. His mouth made a pained "O" as 54,826 customers at Riverfront Stadium went "ah." Devastated, White salvaged a hit in the eighth.

"That's the toughest one-for-four Roy White ever had," Rose said in the celebrators' locker room.

The Cincinnati Reds whipped the Yankees 5-1 yesterday and even though Rose went hitless he supplied the decisive second run on a sacrifice fly that sent Mickey Rivers into the gray wall in center.

Pete Rose ticks like a metronome for the Reds. In the year of the third baseman — the Yankees' representative there, Graig Nettles, led the American League in home runs, Kansas City's George Brett led the American League in hitting and Rose led both leagues in hits with 215 — Rose established himself yesterday as the best of all of them. Not a ball got by him yesterday and he caught Elliot Maddox's last effort to send the Reds to celebration.

"We hit more line drives for outs than they did for hits," New York Manager Billy Martin said.

Not only were the Yankees whipped on the field, they were humiliated off it when Bowie Kuhn ordered Yankees scout Clyde King out of the press box, where he had been installed with a walkie talkie to help Martin position his outfielders.

"Were they using CB radios?" a character wondered. "Hello good buddy, this is Flycatcher."

"I was told it was legal for me to use the walkie talkie setup," Martin said. "I got permission. But I suppose they backed out because it hasn't been used for 100 years like everything else in this game."

"I have no comment on walkie talkies," Reds manager Sparky Anderson said. "I didn't know we had them in baseball. Geez!"

Rose padded about the locker room in a red T-shirt that had the picture of a gorilla on it holding a baseball bat.

"Walkie talkies," Rose said, "ain't that something? What the hell is this, football? The Yankees might end up needing those things. We're gonna play good baseball and we don't need them."

Rose is a baseball purist, of course, and he delights in backfired chicanery. He especially delights in victory and points out continually that the Reds are the best team in the world by virtue of winning 102 and 108 games in the last two seasons. Before yesterday's game Rose leaned on the dugout steps and moved his hips as a swing band on the field played "Cherokee" and "Eager Beaver".

"What goes through your mind before a World Series game?" Rose was asked.

"It's impossible to tell what goes through a man's heart or his mind," Rose said. "It's just pure excitement, raw. I'd play four World Series games a day if I could."

After the only one he was allowed in yesterday, Rose stood in front of his locker and swung his bat.

"We played a sound game but weren't nearly as aggressive as we could have been," he said. "Alexander (Yankees starter Doyle) isn't a strike-out pitcher; that's why I am so glad to have a chance to drive a man in."

Concepcion tripled off Alexander to lead off the third inning. Rose came to the plate and dug in low with his feet close together. He watched some offerings and then belted the long fly that scored Concepcion. It was all Don Gullett needed.

"A hitter's delight, that was," Rose said. "Alexander let me hit the ball, he let all of us hit the ball."

The only Yankees' run was Nettles's doing. His sacrifice fly scored Lou Piniella. But in the field, Nettles, whom Martin called the best in the game at third, was not nearly as destructive as Rose. Tony Perez doubled down the third-base line and George Foster whizzed a single under Nettles's glove. Pete Rose, the gorilla, would have eaten those hits.

"And I ain't that fancy," Rose said. "I'm just so damn delighted to be here, I'll do anything to stay."

October 14, 1977

Los Angeles, Calif.

The New York Yankees assembled for a workout at Dodger Stadium Thursday, where the World Series, tied at a game apiece, will resume tonight. The Yankees were ill-humored and surly, reminiscent of the last American League nine to challenge the Dodgers at the Palace Elysium, the 1974 collection of Oakland A's.

Billy Martin wouldn't go beyond Mike Torrez, who will oppose Tommy John tonight, in naming his starting lineup, but he promised there wouldn't be any surprises. That might or might not mean that Paul Blair will supplant Reggie Jackson in right field.

Reggie was in one of his "I-brought-my-glove-and-hope-to-play" aloof moods and Blair had no comment on the situation. Billy was mad at Reggie because Reggie thought Billy made a dumb move pitching the erstwhile marvelous Catfish Hunter in game two.

"In case anybody's wondering," Billy said, "I didn't pitch Ken Holtzman because he has a stiff neck. I pitched Catfish because he was throwing well in the bullpen. Reggie isn't a coach. Reggie Jackson is having a difficult time playing right field. We didn't think it was necessary to ask him what he thinks."

Folks seem to think that was Billy's way of saying Blair will start. Besides, Blair is right-handed and John is left-handed. Elsewhere on the grounds the Yanks were ribbing each other in a customary fashion. Graig Nettles called Mickey Rivers a "tankhead" and Rivers retorted with, "what do you know?" Chris Chambliss is bored with interviews and Thurman Munson said he couldn't believe the amount of refuse he has heard this year concerning himself and his friend Jackson.

Munson has had contract squabbles with team owner George Steinbrenner but has generally stayed out of the Martin-Jackson feud. However, he stood up for the manager yesterday.

"We have a chance to win the World Series," said Munson. "And there's another guy out there second-guessing the manager. I wouldn't be second-guessing the manager. I think it's just a little heated argument. You know Reggie has not been doing all that well. He's been doing OK, but not all that well ... and he wants to.

"I guess Billy just doesn't realize that Reggie is 'Mr. October.' I read that somewhere."

Munson said there has been so much feuding on the Yankees that he's grown accustomed to it. "I used to know what was going on," he said with a smile. "But I've quit stirring the drink. I'm subdued. There have been so many things going on this year that I just laugh at them now. Of course I have been guillotined five times myself this year by George in negotiations, by Reggie in spring training."

The absence of laughter was beginning to make itself felt when Sparky Lyle rescued the proceedings by chasing a news photographer from in front of the batting cage.

"I wouldn't of warned ya if it was just me in there battin'," said Lyle. "I couldn't hurt ya none with a bat. It's these other guys who could take your head off."

Lyle speaks with great difficulty in uniform but that's because his words are fighting their way through a pack or two of Red Man chewing tobacco lodged in his left cheek along with his tongue.

"Yessir," Lyle said, after taking his warmup bunts, "there's only one thing better than a good chaw and that's a . . ."

Never mind. Albert Walter Lyle, 33, out of Reynoldsville, Pa., never said he would make a good after-dinner speaker. He is all he wants to be, the premier relief pitcher in baseball. The 6-foot-l, 208-pound left-hander appeared in four of five playoff games with Kansas City and the two Series games to date and he is the winner of New York's last three victorious games.

His ERA for the last nine days work is right around one and if he ever feels depression or pressure he is keeping it a secret.

"Can't feel pressure because I don't know what it is," Lyle said. He had finished his work on the field and was one of the few Yankees in the clubhouse. He also was chawless and one almost expected his left cheek to be floppy without support. "And I've never been depressed, either."

"Then you've never been pickpocketed," a man said.

"Oh yes I have," Lyle said, "but I beat the hell out of the guy that did it."

Before Sparky Lyle became a reluctant hero he worked at the Jackson China Company in Reynoldsville. He was a mold runner, hustling pottery plate molds around the plant in 160-degree heat. He said he got up early and went to work and the pay was $58 a week.

"Was college ever in your plans?" a man asked him.

"I got a scholarship offer someplace, can't remember where," Lyle said. "It was for football. I was an end in high school. My dad handled all that. When my dad told me he had a scholarship lined up I told him to shove it. But I said it kind of polite like. I didn't want to go to college."

Reynoldsville is 90 miles from Pittsburgh. Lyle's father is a contractor. Sparky wanted out of town on a baseball contract — he was pitching for a beer league team called the Dubois Rockets. In 1964 he was drafted by the Boston Red Sox from Rochester, a Baltimore farm club, but he didn't make the Red Sox for keeps until 1967.

"I had great years there, too," Lyle said. "I learned the slider for one thing and it's done a little for me. It seems like a turning point in my life came when I got traded to the Yankees in 1972. Nobody ever heard of me in Boston. They've heard of me in New York. I wanted to go to the Yankees because I wanted to play for Ralph Houk. I love that guy. He never lied to a player."

Lyle established a major league record for most saves in a lifetime — 159 — last season. He has had honors and awards and fat contracts but he has never misdirected his fame into arrogance. He is simple. On the matter of playing with pain, he pointed out that he has received one cortisone shot in his entire life.

"Just ask those guys in the training room," Lyle said, "how many times I've been in there. Hardly ever is what they got to tell ya."

His teammates even mellow around Sparky. One time Nettles went to comfort Lyle on the mound because enemy runners occupied every base.

"The bases are loaded, Spark," Nettles said.

"Yeah, I know," Lyle said. "They ain't extra infielders."

"The only only thing I ever hear on the mound when Sparky's pitching," said Bucky Dent, the shortstop, "is a joke or two."

The Yankees need Lyle's laughter. A sulfurous pall descended on the Los Angeles basin yesterday and it was thick enough to reduce visibility and sting a man's eyes. Lyle had run awkwardly through the outfield, shouting that the smog was getting him, choking him, stinging him blind. Billy laughed, then Yogi laughed, and pretty soon all the Yankees stepped out of character and laughed because Albert Walter Lyle was having fun again.

October 15, 1978

New York, N.Y.

The mysteries, and ceremonies of brilliance, repeat themselves in the baseball series now captivating partisans of the Yankees, who evened the championship with the Dodgers at two victories apiece Saturday in the damp twilight of Yankee Stadium.

Familiar confrontations — the Autumn Child, Reggie Jackson, vs. the kid, Bob Welch — recurred, but we had buffoonery with our baseball yesterday, a good old-fashioned rhubarb and a bellyful of laughs.

For the books, the Yankees came from three runs down to beat the Dodgers 4-3 in 10 innings yesterday. There was excellent, spellbinding pitching by both clubs, but subsequent developments by fielders and batters made the game memorable.

Go back for a moment to the critical sixth inning, with the Yankees trailing the Dodgers and Tommy John 3-0. Peel back the developments of this inning, like the skin from an onion, until we reach the punch line.

Paul Blair struck out. Roy White singled. Thurman Munson walked. Jackson appeared for his turn and the crowd erupted with a celebration of paper scraps and the rhythmic chanting "Reggie, Reggie, Reggie!" The night was getting on and if the Yankees were to strike, the appropriate Yankee employee was in position.

Jackson lashed a single to right, scoring White with the first New

York run. Lou Piniella, who would win the contest with his extra-hours single, ripped a line drive to Bill Russell at short. Russell dropped the ball.

Munson consulted himself in full flight to third, jammed on the brakes, returned to second in time to see Russell drop the ball and immediately reversed field, all the way to home plate with the second run.

Jackson, meanwhile, rumbling toward second, was stricken with anxiety and halted dead center in the roadway. He headed back to first — "No, no," the shouts from his bench informed him, "Russell dropped the ball."

"Yipes," said Jackson, reversing his field just in time to block Russell's throw to first (Piniella was not forgotten by Russell) off his right hip. Jackson was out, forced at second, with Piniella safe at first on what could only be called a fielder's choice.

The dust didn't settle there. Dodgers Manager Tommy Lasorda, his cheek bulging with a furious chaw, demanded an audience with second base umpire Joe Brinkman and first base umpire Frank Pulli. The umpires proved themselves tolerant gentlemen, considering that Lasorda reconstructed the development in a spasm of violent gestures.

The questions were these: Did Russell intentionally drop Piniella's hit? For if so, the ball would be dead, the batter called out and Munson would have remained a captive at second.

Secondly, did Jackson intentionally interfere with Russell's throw to first? Had he done so — and it was the judgment of Pulli, the umpire, that he had not — he would have been automatically out.

Graig Nettles, incidentally, halted the theatrics of the inning by grounding out meekly to second base. But the Yankees had scored, and in the aftermath of a dramatic extra-inning victory the principals in that vaudevillian episode were brought front and center before interrogators in the basement of the House that New York Taxpayers Rebuilt.

"Well, it was like this," said Pulli. "Lasorda wanted interference called on Jackson. It wasn't interference. Jackson didn't go out of his way to hinder the throw of the ball."

At this point Jackson had sneaked into the room behind Pulli and — could it be? — winked.

"And Russell," said Brinkman of the American League, "did not intentionally muff the catch." Here Jackson and his manager, Bob Lemon, exchanged mirthful glances.

"Could either of you," it was asked from the floor, "check the other fellow out on your respective decisions?"

"I was watching the bag to see that Russell stepped on it, to force Jackson," Brinkman said. "I didn't see Russell's throw."

"And Reggie blocked my view of Russell's play," Pulli said.

The umpires quickly developed the look of men who would rather be elsewhere and removed themselves from the room.

"Well, boys," Lemon said, "I think we can go seven games now. You know I'm always pretty confused about things but I saw that sixth-inning play as clear as day. I did realize something odd happened because something odd always happens around Jackson." Here, turning to Jackson, Lemon said, "Take it away, motormouth."

Jackson quickly gulped the remainder of his beer, scratched his belly and strode to the microphone.

"Lou hit that ball sharp," Jackson said, mugging for cameras. "I got caught is all. I froze in the road. He threw it in my road."

Vindication can be comical. Merriment returned to the Bronx, and with it, a brand new baseball series that will burrow still further into autumn with its beautiful plays and pleasant memories.

The Dodgers took a 3-0 lead in the fifth inning off a three-run homer by Reggie Smith, the other Reggie, into the right-field porch. Only another miraculous entertainment by Nettles at third prevented additional Dodgers scores. Davey Lopes had led off the Dodgers third with a weapon of a hit aimed to the left field corner, but Nettles timed his leap and sucked the ball back to earth on his backhand. Nettles also screwed himself into the earth on his foul line in the ninth, catching Bill North's pop-up for an important out.

It is Jackson's series as well and he, like Nettles, continues to drift in and out of the various developments. It came down to Jackson in the sixth and he delivered. He reappeared in the eighth and was hit on the right wrist by a Terry Forster pitch.

He surfaced again in the 10th, his wounded wrist bandaged, only to face Welch, the youngster who had struck him out in the ninth inning of the second game back in Los Angeles. He muscled a sharp single to right, with Roy White holding at second. There were two outs when Piniella appeared and lined a single to right-center. Jackson and Piniella, two of the most gregarious and engaging Yankees, celebrated in a bearhug as White raced home with the winning run. The fans remained in their seats, drenched with rain, with private joys, with hope.

"It was supposed to be a good series, wasn't it?" Lemon said.

The comedy and the merriment were a bonus.

October 9, 1979

Baltimore, Md.

It was cool, clear and russet-stained on the Chesapeake as the two winningest teams in baseball this season convened in Baltimore on Monday for today's start of the 76th baseball championship of North America.

But even before the Pirates and Orioles repaired to Memorial Stadium for workouts, a cluster of players was displayed showcase style in a downtown hotel ballroom.

It would have been a largely meaningless exercise, this concession to the herd school of journalism, were it not for the presence of the huge and jovial Willie Stargell, the Pirate's first baseman and spiritual leader.

After a dissection of the starting pitchers, Pittsburgh's Bruce Kison and Baltimore's Mike Flanagan, Pittsburgh shortstop Tim Foli was being interviewed in the front of the room when he was asked about his team's aggressive style of play.

"I play a lot better when I'm bleeding," Foli said.

From the back of the room came a war whoop, then a barking sound. It was Stargell, waving his cowboy hat in the air and whooping it up before turning on his boot heels to disappear as suddenly as he had arrived.

Foli may have sung an advance tune for this World Series, a rematch of the 1971 entertainment won by Pittsburgh in seven games, but Stargell will hum the pitch. Willie is 38 now, coming off a season of 32 home runs, 82 runs batted in and a .281 batting average, or nine points better than the Pirate team average and a whole lot better than the Baltimore aggregate.

Those are Willie's best numbers since 1973, when he launched 44 intercontinental ballistic missiles. Stargell is the only player ever to hit a home run clear out of Dodger Stadium, which he did twice, and the only player ever to hit a home run into the upper deck of Busch Stadium in St. Louis. The prospect of watching this happy man rise up once again in the autumn of his own youth will be something to treasure.

"Is that true what Foli said," Stargell was asked later yesterday in the Pirates' locker room, "about playing hard and letting the blood flow? You guys would bleed for each other?"

"Oh, a lot of it is just woofin'," Willie said, "you know, making noise. But the Pirates are a family. We believe we're unique. Well, just look here."

Willie took a man by the arm and gave him a tour of the clubhouse, meanwhile noting the birthplace of every Pirate, demographics that range from New Jersey to Panama. "And Madlock," Stargell said, making sure Bill Madlock heard him, "Madlock is from Sing Sing."

"And Stargell?"

"Earlsboro, Okla.," Stargell said. He became serious for only a moment, smiling, with memory in his sad, droopy eyes.

It was still early in the day, and, while hundreds of groundkeepers had worked over the Memorial Stadium turf, Stargell had spent the afternoon in the clubhouse playing cards. No reason, he said; he just figured he ought to be around early. The Pirate concept of familial togetherness is endorsed and nurtured by Stargell, the keeper of the cloth gold stars that are dispensed to teammates for good pitching, good hitting and good fielding.

The stars show up in the most unlikely places — on vests, on attache cases and travel bags. You want Willie's approval. You want Pop looking your way with a smile.

After Stargell came out of Earlsboro, he signed with the Pirates as a free agent. He in turn was nurtured and taught his lessons — the same way he counsels young Bucs now — by Roberto Clemente.

There is a story told about Willie and his wife, Dolores. She suffered a cerebral hemorrhage in 1976. Willie was asked if he wanted to go on the disabled list, to get time off to spend with his wife.

"Naw," Willie said, "it wouldn't be an honest D.L."

When his wife recovered and made a visit to Three Rivers Stadium in Pittsburgh, she received a standing ovation.

"From everyone except me," Willie said. "I stood out at first base and cried myself into a heap."

Willie was pulling on his ominous black uniform now. Other Pirates began filtering into the room, and the music was turned up loud, and pretty soon Willie Stargell was dancing, all 225 pounds of him twirling around the room on his tiptoes.

Across the way, the Baltimore Orioles were behind locked doors in a long and secretive meeting in which their super scout, Jimmy Russo, revealed a battle plan that moved Flanagan to call Russo Inspector Clouseau. But Willie Stargell was dancing.

"He's always like that," Bert Blyleven was saying. "I've seen him strike out three times in one day and come back the next day and hit two home runs. I've seen him play in pain, terrible pain, and I've never seen him get down. When I pitch poorly, hang a curve ball or something, Willie will walk over to the mound and tell me he wishes he could be hitting against me. You gotta have fun when you're around Willie."

"The key," Stargell said, "is that I never want to be too sharp or too flat. I want to be in the middle, just natural all the time. My mother taught me that. Really, she did. The reality of life is the way you feel, not what you do or what you do to other people. You need feeling."

"You gonna tell the press about your contract?" Madlock said.

"Yeah," Stargell said. "I'm playing out my option. Gonna play goalie for the New York Rangers."

Willie Stargell put on a stocking cap then and walked out into the late afternoon. A chill had set in, and the wind was blowing in stiffly from the west, and in the retreating sunlight Willie Stargell flexed his muscles and made his war whoop.

October 15, 1980

Philadelphia, Pa.

No matter what else happens in the tournament to produce this year's best professional baseball team there will exist forever a small scar on the psyche of Darrell Porter and another notch on the gun Pete Rose aims at his opponents.

Go back to the third inning in the opening game Tuesday night in the chill glare of Veterans Stadium. The Kansas City Royals and the Philadelphia Phillies had been brought together on this clear October evening to establish a new era for the old game. For the first time in Series history, both teams feature artificial playing surfaces and the Royals had never before advanced to the big show, the Phillies just twice previously, in 1915 and in 1950.

If the participants are foreign to the Classic, nearly everyone has heard of Porter, the Royals catcher who earlier this season admitted his addiction to drugs and alcohol and then turned himself over to medical authorities for help.

And Rose.

You have heard of Rose, the man-child of 39 who races around the bases with his elbows cocked and his spikes flashing. The two of them figured in a third-inning tableau last night that as much as anything enabled the Phillies to take the opening game victory 7-6.

With the Royals leading 4-0 on two-run home runs by Amos Otis and Willie Mays Aikens, Porter came up in the third against rookie Philly pitcher Bob Walk. Porter walked and took second when Otis beat out an infield hit. Clint Hurdle singled to left field. Porter was off at the crack of Hurdle's bat and steamed around third toward home when it suddenly became evident that Lonnie Smith's throw to Bob Boone would arrive at the plate in sufficient time to nail Porter.

Most of the Royals would have relished this moment, to go in at Boone hard, with spikes high. Hal McRae would have forced a collision, same for George Brett and Hurdle. We know what Rose would have done. He would have smashed the catcher the way he smashed Houston's Bruce Bochy in the face in the eighth inning of Game 4 in the splendid National League play-off series. Even millionaires must play hardball at World Series time.

We know what Rose would have done. Rose would have taken that same play and bent it to his liking.

Darrell pulled up. He stood up straight is what he did, like a spooked horse and he might as well have kissed Boone as he applied the tag. End of that half inning.

"I hate to see a man go in there and just take a tag," Kansas City Manager Jim Frey said afterward. "I'd have preferred to see Darrell slide, even though he was out by a long way.

"But, then, if Porter knocks Boone into the seats, Porter could have gotten hurt, too."

"I'd have run into him," McRae said. "Boone was gonna roll back and he would have had to make a tag. Hit him."

"I think it psyched them up," Otis said.

Porter said he had no idea where the ball was. "And my timing was off coming around third," Porter said. "I wanted to slide but my footing was all wrong."

Now you've got the Phillies up in their half of the third and it is wise at this point to remember that the Phillies play "Jailhouse Rock" at the seventh-inning stretch. The Phillies didn't get their first hits off Dennis Leonard until this inning, but a couple of singles and a double had produced two runs when Rose came up with two out.

Annoyed at the inordinate amount of time spent by Leonard studying him, Rose timed his retreats from the batter's box to coincide with Leonard's delivery. An eerie mind game was developing here. Rose urging Leonard to get on with it and then stepping out to adjust a phantom wrinkle in his batting glove.

Leonard glared back. Rose crouched over. Leonard fired low and inside and caught Rose square on the right leg. Rose threw down his bat and took a wide arc past the mound on his way to first. Whatever Rose said loosened something in Leonard's spirit, for the subsequent batter, Mike Schmidt, was walked and then Bake McBride belted a home run that bounced off the upper and recessed portion of the right-field wall and back onto the playing field.

Phillies 5, Royals 4, and you immediately had to wonder what would have happened had Porter not tried to dance with Bob Boone.

"All I said to Leonard," Rose was saying in his clubhouse now, "was that I wasn't gonna steal on him. I told him to watch out for Schmidt cuz Schmidt could tie it up with one swing."

"And the Porter play?" Rose was asked. He needed no explanation.

"I think Porter made the mistake of thinking he was safe," Rose said.

Leonard lasted another inning after Rose unglued him and then he was gone. The rookie, Walk, went seven innings before giving way to Tug McGraw. Rose never did score another run in the game and he didn't reach base again after the third. But Peter Rose won this initial game for the Phillies because Pete Rose never makes the mistake of taking anything for granted on a ball diamond. Real grass or fake.

October 19, 1980

Kansas City, Mo.

The Kansas City Royals have issued a directive of sorts to the Philadelphia Phillies, advising the National League champs that if they want to make an issue of character in this World Series, they will be obliged to do so until the final game.

The Royals beat the Phillies 5-3 Saturday afternoon at Royals Stadium, squaring the tournament at two games apiece and ensuring a return to Philadelphia for at least a sixth game Tuesday evening.

On this bright Saturday Willie Aikens connected for two home runs, Dennis Leonard and Dan Quisenberry combined to protect an early lead and George Brett almost fell victim to some vicious chin music arranged by Philly reliever Dickie Noles. The Brett incident, in the fourth inning, may have sustained whatever ardor the Royals had accumulated from the first inning, when they scored four runs off Larry Chistenson in one-third of an inning.

Brett tripled in the first, and he is hot, hitting close to .500 in the Series. Brett is regarded in Kansas City with the same consideration given the late Harry Truman, born in Independence, Mo., just beyond the Royals Stadium center field fence. All of this becomes important in the fourth.

The Royals, behind Leonard, were leading 5-1 when Brett came up against Noles with one out in the fourth. The count went to 0-2. The next pitch was a fast ball, clearly aimed at Brett's prominent chin. Brett dived and spun out of the way, looking to the mound as he pulled himself together. It was impossible not to recall a statement made by Pete Rose before the game, that Brett's health problems had been exaggerated, the implication being that the Phillies regarded Brett with somewhat less affection than Kansas Citians.

Brett's manager, Jim Frey, rushed from his dugout and tried to get at Noles.

"It looked to me like a knockdown pitch," Frey said afterward. "You've got a good hitter at the plate and a count of 0-2 and the next pitch comes at his head. That's a knockdown. I hollered at Noles to stop it, I didn't want a battle of head-hunting just because we were hitting so well. I've seen guys get almost killed because of the so-called brushback pitch."

Noles stayed on the mound. Rose, meanwhile, intervened and conversed with Frey.

"Rose told me to get off the field," Frey said. "I don't remember what I said to him."

"Brett was the guy who should have argued," Rose said later. "I just told Frey it was a hell of a thing for a manager to come out and yell at our pitcher. Brett wasn't saying anything. It was really a weird thing."

"I didn't say anything because the brushback happens," Brett said, "and when it happens, it happens. I got out of the way. I was lucky, too."

As a moment of confrontation it was indecisive. But the Royals held the lead and when they trooped into their clubhouse after the game Willie Wilson could be heard in a sing-song voice. "Let them tell us about character, now," he chirped. "Who's got the character now?"

The Royals, probably. According to Clint Hurdle, Wilson, Brett and the others, the Royals are an awesome ball club when they play all loosey-goosey. Yesterday they mashed nearly every pitch Christenson threw and he threw just 23 and the damage was over. Wilson led off the game with a single and took third when Christenson's pickoff throw headed toward Nashville. Brett tripled. Aikens drove a home run ball into the fountains in right field. Hal McRae and Amos Otis cracked doubles.

Noles relieved Christenson at this point and calmed matters, closing the inning by taking a throw from Rose to nail Wilson speeding down the line.

"I have no excuses," Christenson said. "I felt 100 percent. I just went out and pitched the worst game of the year."

The Phillies chipped back here and there, scoring a run in the second when Larry Bowa's single scored Manny Trillo. But the Royals added a fifth run in the same inning, when Aikens rerouted a Noles curve ball into the Kansas City bull pen. Aikens stood at the plate and watched that one, and 42,363 customers were beside themselves with the joy of a hero in the making. One more dinger and Willie Aikens ties Reggie Jackson's record for five home runs in a single World Series.

"If you have a book on Willie Aikens," Philly Manager Dallas Green said afterward, tilting his cap far back on his gray hair, "please let me see it. Because we apparently don't have the guy figured out."

The Phillies added a run in the seventh. With one out, Trillo doubled and took third on a Bowa single. Bob Boone then launched a Leonard pitch that might have been a home run in Philadelphia, but Wilson ran down the ball and made the catch.

He could not prevent Trillo from tagging at third and scoring, but he certainly saved two runs. The Phillies added a final run in the eighth when Rose, who had doubled, scored on a sacrifice fly hit by Mike Schmidt off Quisenberry.

"Without a doubt," Schmidt said, "the play of the game was the ball Wilson caught off Boone. If it goes through, it's a double, it puts us in a position for a big inning. Wilson's catch took us right out of things."

"We'll win this thing on speed and defense," McRae said afterward, then nodded at Aikens. "And with power, too."

"If Aikens keeps hitting two home runs a game," Rose said, "we're going to have some World Series."

3 / Super Bowl

January 8, 1977

Los Angeles, Calif.

Bud Grant arrived for the last of his Super Bowl XI public speaking engagements through the side door of a Jet Ranger helicopter that had transported him from Costa Mesa, Calif., up the coast to Los Angeles.

He was dressed in a purple sweater over a yellow shirt and black trousers and was wearing a pair of Hush Puppies that looked like old friends. He walked like a tired hunter. He had an NFL henchman at his elbow and a trail of machine gun photographers in his wake as he waded through a river of cords and wires attached to microphones and tape recorders on the podium.

Few politicians or football coaches, if that is a position without distinction, ever attracted such a sparkling and expensive array of electronic gadgetry.

Grant gave it all a bemused look, placed his hands on the lectern and said that he had only one announcement to make, that his starting line-up will be the same as listed in the Super Bowl program. Like an experienced teacher he held a copy of the program aloft to all corners of the Grand Ballroom in the Marriott Hotel. Then he fell silent. He indeed had only one announcement. As he studied his audience he was saying to them with his eyes, "Ask me something, that's why I'm here."

Despite his reputation as an iceman, and that is largely the creation of dimwits, Grant is a warm and open public speaker. People are not satisfied with that, especially on the eve of Roman Numerals. Speculation runs high that because Grant smiles infrequently or is tight with jokes he must be masking some great wisdom or humor that he will share with appropriate intimates only at the appropriate time.

The speculators would do better to study Grant more carefully in group assemblies. He is the same here as he is on the trail stalking deer or whatever it is he stalks in the wilds surrounding Gordon, Wis. What you see is what you get.

Grant is far too honest for the sudden little shifts in temperament or personality that other coaches have come to rely on. He will answer any and all questions and if you aren't careful he'll slip a one-liner into the stream and follow it with his blue eyes.

Phyllis George once asked him to smile for her. "Say something funny," Grant replied. He had most of his constituents believing him when he said he would have the team practicing "on a hill in Duluth" following Minnesota's loss to San Francisco. His delivery is cold, not his intentions.

He was asked about the weather, of course. Rain has pounded Los Angeles for days.

"When we practiced Thursday," Grant said, "the rain stopped when we went on the field and started up again as we left the field." The blue eyes flickered.

"You should have saved that miracle for Sunday," somebody said.

"We can always hold off the rain," Grant said.

He was asked what had been his favorite question during the week.

"Let's see, oh what was it?" Grant said. "Something about losing three Super Bowls, I think."

He laughed with the group then and they warmed to him just a little bit more. They inquired about his wife and children who were waylaid on their cross-country journey to California by a snowstorm in the high country. They arrived safe and sound, he said. He was asked if Chuck Foreman's contract talk had disrupted his camp.

"Of course not," he said. "All week long we're probably asked too many questions and you give out too many answers. You get tired of hearing yourself talk. Our spirit is good. Good Lord, it better be. We're here and we're healthy."

Never once did Bud Grant hesitate with an answer, never once did he camouflage his response and never once did he belittle an interrogator for a question so stupid he had to bite his lip to keep from laughing. If an extremely stupid question is asked, he replies with an extremely human answer.

Asked if the Vikings would try to block any of Ray Guy's kicks, Grant said, "We're thinking of using a helicopter, just swoop down on him and pick it out of his hands."

Sanity radiates from Grant, which should be expected because one of his basic tenets is not to worry about what you cannot control. He cannot control the weather or his opponent or Chuck Foreman's money problems or his wife's snowstorm or the barrage of flash bulbs and microphones. Therefore, gentlemen, there will be no controversy.

At the conclusion of his appearance Grant waded through the crowd in his tired hunter walk and stopped to chat with anyone who cared to stop him. Out in the hallway, alone, he was approached by a newsman from New York who apparently was not familiar with Grant's life style or his demeanor.

"What do you do?" the newsman said.

"Work," Grant said.
"When?" the newsman said.
"Nine to five," Grant said.
"I mean, what do you do after work?" the newsman said.
"What do you mean?" Grant said.
"To relax," the newsman said.
"We have a summer home that we also use as a winter home. We go up there."
"Do you hunt?"
"There's not much to hunt in the summer. I fish."
"Are there lakes nearby?"
Grant's eyes rolled imperceptibly.
"Almost as many lakes as the swimming pools I saw flying in here," Grant said.

January 16, 1978

New Orleans, La.

The money championship of professional football was awarded the Dallas Cowboys Sunday evening when they eliminated Denver 27-10 in the Louisiana Superdome. Super Bowl XII proved a number of things about life in America, but mostly it proved that Denver's storied heart and emotion could not overcome stupidity and clumsiness.

What was supposed to be the premier football game ever waged for cash on this planet featured as its main attraction 10 fumbles and four interceptions, both new and dubious Super Bowl records. Denver surrendered four fumbles and Craig Morton, the born-again Christian who apparently has discovered inner peace, threw into the hands of the enemy four times. He was seen talking to his maker in the quiet Denver locker room.

Ordinarily, a team that is handed eight gift opportunities will provide an evening of exciting entertainment. But the Cowboys scored just once after grabbing a Denver turnover.

"We obviously should have more points," Dallas Coach Tom Landry said. "But we were so high at the start of the game that we couldn't do anything effectively. When it settled down, and it did, it became a more normal game for us."

The teams convened before 76,400 clients in a building about the size of Duluth. And because it was the Super Bowl and a certain amount of premium was placed on live attendance, the game sustained interest even as the teams on the field stumbled about like nervous schoolboys. Great waves of orange-shirted Broncomaniacs, who put such stake in the tale of Cinderella, were still present at the conclusion, assuring their Broncos that, if they weren't No. 1, they were at least still loved.

The Cowboys, billed as hardened and computerized, entered the game with virtually every statistical advantage and they left that way, but not before they took an emotional half-lap of the carpeted arena with one finger aloft in the universal sign of superiority.

"We were more emotional than any of my three previous Super Bowl teams," Landry said. "When the other team is emotional, you have to throw that into your game plan as well."

"I knew they were better on paper," Denver Coach Red Miller said, "but I didn't see turnovers on paper."

Interesting matches that were anticipated never developed. Morton and Roger Staubach are old Dallas teammates, but Staubach proved Landry was right when he elected to let Morton seek his living elsewhere in 1974. Morton was unparalleled in stupidity when, in the death grip of Randy White, he threw an inexcusable pass that was intercepted by Randy Hughes on the Broncos' 29. Dallas went in to score and take a 7-0 lead.

Morton was intercepted a second time on the next series when his pass was tipped by Bob Bruenig and scooped up by Aaron Kyle. Morton was establishing a dangerous pattern that caused his removal in the third quarter.

"They took away everything we had," Morton said, "and I'm disappointed. But the way I look at it, nobody expected us to be here and we're a blessed team because we were here."

After Efren Herrera kicked a 43-yard field goal early in the second quarter for a 10-0 Dallas lead, the Cowboys forced five consecutive Denver turnovers. Broncomaniacs sagged in disbelief, but the Orange Crush defense limited Dallas to three field goal attempts and Herrera missed every one of them in a variety of directions.

The Dallas tally sheet at the end of the second quarter read: Two interceptions and three recovered fumbles as well as field position on the Denver 40, 27, 28 and 35. But Denver still was miraculously in the game.

"I was uneasy at the half," Staubach said. "Can you imagine what Miller must have been saying? Nobody remembers a Super Bowl loser. We were thinking about the way Denver is supposed to own the fourth quarter."

"It was a great season," Tony Dorsett said, "but only because we finished it with a bang."

The third quarter was remarkably free of turnovers and Denver enjoyed a sustained opening drive that resulted in Jim Turner's 47-yard field goal. But with the score at 13-7, Dallas snapped out of the lethargy that had masked its usually brilliant execution.

Staubach struck back with a 35-yard scoring pass to Butch Johnson, whose pretty stretch and dive for the ball at the goal line stirred even the quiet and confident Cowboy fans.

"I thought it was about time somebody got behind their linebackers," Staubach said.

Rick Upchurch took the ensuing kick-off and ran for 67 yards to the Cowboys' 26. Morton, who by now had set his record with four interceptions, was about to be sacked by Harvey Martin when he dumped another pass into the middle of silver and white. When the ball went in and out of the hands of Ed Jones, Miller had seen enough. He dispatched second-year quarterback Norris Weese, who engineered Denver's only touchdown, a 1-yard run by Rob Lytle.

"I'm still thinking we've got to win the fourth quarter," Landry said.

Slipperiness returned for the final 15 minutes. Rubin Carter recovered a Staubach fumble, fracturing Staubach's finger in the process. Dallas held, but then Weese apparently inherited Morton's jitters, fumbling to Kyle. Still, the $18,000 per man winner's share was not secure until Landry ordered a touch of flair. Robert Newhouse went to his left in the backfield and passed 29 yards to Golden Richards for the Cowboys' final touchdown.

"It took two great plays to separate us," Landry said. "Butch Johnson's catch and the fullback pass. It was the time for the Newhouse play."

The betting establishment must have been relieved and Dallas was pleased to have retained its cool and analytical image. But the Broncos' fans, who turned this playpen orange with love, were a sad lot of harlequins when they left. They're No. 2 now. For them, it's a stigma.

January 22, 1979

Miami, Fla.

In the frantic aftershouts of the money championship of professional football Sunday, Terry Bradshaw stood squinting into the klieg lights in the basement of the Orange Bowl. His receding hairline was plastered with sweat and he mopped his brow with a club of a forearm.

Bigger than life he looked and bigger than life he felt in this moment when the pride came out of him. His Steelers had just become the first three-time Super Bowl winners in history by beating the Dallas Cowboys 35-31.

"Whooooweee," Bradshaw said, "you all better put that one down as exciting. I'm not all caught up in the glory yet, but by God it was exciting."

Terry Bradshaw had proven beyond doubt that he is the shrewdest quarterback in football. What Brand XIII came down to yesterday was not a battle between Bradshaw and his Dallas rival, Roger Staubach, but Staubach's mouthpiece and coach, Tom Landry. Terry Bradshaw, who once was called dumb and too countrified for big-time football, ignited the Super Bowl by throwing four touchdown passes.

It was Terry Bradshaw against the computer and Terry Bradshaw won.

"And look here now," Bradshaw said, depositing a clump of chewing tobacco in his cheek, "I didn't call an audible all day. Those were set plays that I called in the huddle."

It was the best of Super Bowls because of Bradshaw. He established personal and championship records for touchdowns thrown and passing yardage. Bradshaw was 17 of 30 for 318 yards and so swift was his mission that in the first half, when he threw for 253 yards, he eclipsed Bart Starr's 1967 game record of 250 passing yards.

"The thing I didn't want to do," Bradshaw said, "was change what got me here. I was determined not to let the Super Bowl dictate to me. I was going to throw long. I was going to throw play actions. I was going to leave happy, win or lose. I never thought I'd pass for 300 yards, but I didn't change what got me up here. None of us did."

Chuck Noll, the Pittsburgh coach who is not a mouthpiece, stood across the room, too hoarse to speak. He managed in a scratchy way to salute his receivers and to tip his cap to his quarterback.

"We didn't think there was any way," Noll whispered, "that Benny Barnes or Aaron Kyle could cover Lynn Swann or John Stallworth in man coverage and we still feel that way. Our veterans wanted this game very badly."

Millions of people might have anticipated a defensive war yesterday, what with both clubs leading their conferences in the stingy department. But it was a Super Bowl measured by air, by gambling, blitzing defenses and by brilliant play in the Pittsburgh receiving corps.

It was a typically nifty affair off the field as well, if you like balloons and hoards of Steelers fans who wave something called a "terrible towel" in lieu of cheerleaders. Miami police antiterrorist teams never even had to suppress any riots or run for the helicopters they had stashed within seconds of the Orange Bowl. It was a football game that somehow managed to live up to its absurd advance billing.

Bradshaw came out firing and mesmerized the clients. He hit John Stallworth in the first quarter with the first of Stallworth's two touchdown catches. The play was established when Drew Pearson dropped the ball on a reverse and Pittsburgh's John Banaszak recovered.

"The same play that would go to Lynn Swann later," Bradshaw said. "He faked inside and then ran out and away from the coverage."

Dallas tied the game at the close of the opening quarter when Hollywood Henderson nailed Bradshaw behind the line. Mike Hengen reached down and in a version of the hidden ball trick stole the ball from Bradshaw and scored on a 38-yard run. Bradshaw was never the same after that play. He was better, despite injuring his left shoulder when he crashed to the ground under Henderson.

"It ached," Bradshaw said, "but it wasn't the time to worry about it."

Stallworth spun Aaron Kyle around a second time and hauled down a 75-yard touchdown pass early in the second quarter and after two passes to Swann for 30 and 21 yard gains, Bradshaw spotted Rocky Bleier in the end zone. The two were running in opposite directions when the 5-foot-11 Bleier leaped over the 6-1 D.D. Lewis. Bradshaw had been running to his right and lofted a floating pass to his left.

"And Bradshaw told me I made an excellent adjustment," Bleier said. "What about him?"

"The Bleier touchdown," Tom Landry said, "was the play that turned the momentum around."

The game settled momentarily into a defensive struggle in the third quarter as Dallas crawled back. A sentimentalist might remember that just before Rafael Septien's 27-yard field goal Dallas tight end Jackie Smith dropped a certain touchdown pass that would have tied the game at 21. The 38-year-old Smith, a veteran of so many years with the St. Louis Cardinals, was playing in his first Super Bowl game in what most likely will be his final season.

When Bradshaw wasn't good, he was good and lucky, a killer combination. In the fourth quarter, a pass interference call on Benny Barnes gave Pittsburgh the ball on the Dallas 23. Franco Harris then scored Pittsburgh's only touchdown by land.

On the subsequent kickoff Pittsburgh's Dennis Winston recovered Randy White's fumble. It took one play for Bradshaw to go to the man who destroyed Dallas in Brand X in 1976. Bradshaw hit Swann in the end zone and Swann responded with a leaping 18-yard reception as the Steelers had scored twice within 19 seconds.

"Now there's 6:48 left in the game," Bradshaw said, "and our guys are starting to celebrate with a 35-17 lead. That made me mad. I've been in this game too long. I know what can happen in six minutes, especially in a Super Bowl game. I was going around on the bench telling guys to shape up."

C'mon, Terry, the Steelers only looked like they were in danger. Just because Billy Joe DuPree and Butch Johnson pulled down touchdown passes in the closing moments was no cause for alarm. It was still a test of a man who called his own shots against a team that runs by computer.

"You know what I think?" Noll said. "I don't think we've peaked yet."

Then the rest of us better hope Terry Bradshaw and the Pittsburgh Steelers return to the Super Bowl next year. It would have been a dreadful affair without this gang.

January 21, 1980

Pasadena, Calif.

It will always be remembered for what it wasn't. Super Bowl XIV was not a blowout. It was not an embarrassment to either the party of the first part, the Pittsburgh Steelers, or the party of the second part, the Los Angeles Rams.

The Steelers are again the champions of professional football, for an unprecedented fourth time in the carnival of excess that has become an American showpiece. But beating the Rams 31-19 Sunday in Pasadena's ancient Rose Bowl was not easy for the monsters in black and gold.

The Rams fulfilled the contractual obligation most often overlooked in Super Bowls. They made for a good game. The Rams made for such a good game that they led at half time 13-10, led again 19-17 at the end of the third quarter and trailed by just five points with two minutes remaining when a pass interference call in the end zone went against Pat Thomas of the Rams.

The Steelers occupied the ball at that point on the Los Angeles 1-yard line and, after two plays, Franco Harris scored and grabbed the brass ring.

Only then could the customers from back east stand up and whip their Terrible Towels in a frenzy. They knew a nifty job when they saw one and so did the Steelers. There in the twilight, with sun glinting in purple shafts off the San Gabriel Mountains, the Pittsburgh Steelers could proclaim themselves the best team in the history of football.

"I don't have to say that," Chuck Noll said over the din of his players. "I won't say that. But I will say the facts speak for themselves. It wasn't that tough. We've been working on. . .what do you call it, deja vu?"

It will always be remembered for what it was. Super Bowl XIV was a game of big plays, none larger than Terry Bradshaw's 73-yard touchdown strike to John Stallworth with 12:04 left in the game to put the Steelers up 24-19. Like a maneuver of war, the play needs explanation.

Because it was also the roughest Super Bowl ever played, Steeler receiver Lynn Swann went out of commission late in the third quarter. He already had caught a 47-yard touchdown pass from Bradshaw at 12:12 of the quarter. But he was later upended by Thomas. Swann landed neck down on the turf and never returned to the game, complaining of double vision.

When Bradshaw attempted to connect with Jim Smith, Swann's replacement, he was picked off for a second time, by Eddie Brown. Bradshaw threw another interception early in the fourth quarter. Consider that bettors were beginning to get serious about the Rams's chances, when Bradshaw uncorked the Stallworth bomb from a third-and-eight situation from his own 27.

"A younger Bradshaw," his center, Mike Webster, said afterward, "would have sat and sulked after throwing three interceptions. The older Bradshaw comes back with the big play."

"Big plays sustained the drama of the game," Rocky Bleier said. "The Stallworth play was actually called by Mike Kruczek (a Steeler backup quarterback). Stallworth was lining up in a slot and usually double-covered because the Rams were doing all sorts of goofy things on defense. Kruczek figured how Stallworth could get only one man on him."

"A hook and go," Stallworth said in another part of the damp and close caverns under the Rose Bowl. "I stuttered once and the safety took the fake. He stayed in. That left me alone on Thomas."

And all Thomas could make of it was a last futile dive. That play said more than anything about the Pittsburgh Steelers and their desire to fight back. They are not a dumb ball club, or, as Bradshaw said, "Any fool who believed that we were 11-point favorites was crazy." The Steelers were so convinced that they would have to win the game by special team play that they had a special half-time special-teams meeting.

The wedge already had sprung Larry Anderson for kickoff returns of 45, 38 and 32 yards. In the second half, Anderson, a second-year man from Louisiana Tech, had returns of 37 and 10 yards.

"The way things were breaking for me up front," Anderson said, "we thought we'd have to win it on something special. There was no way we were thinking blowout."

Beginning with Swann's touchdown catch in the third quarter, and the way he threaded between Thomas and Nolan Cromwell, Super Bowl XIV was a game of sustained excitement. The first half wasn't bad and a record crowd of 103,985 clients enjoyed the clear skies and 67 degrees while they waited for the game to take form.

But Swann's remarkable catch was followed in succession by a 50-yard pass from the brash and dashing Vince Ferragamo to Billy Waddy; by Ferragamo's handoff to Lawrence McCutcheon and the subsequent 24-yard TD strike to Ron Smith that put the Rams up by two; by Swann's head-first and incapacitating dive into the field, and by two more Bradshaw interceptions before the redeeming missile to Stallworth.

"We've never played in a dull Super Bowl," Bleier said.

"We've never played in a rougher Super Bowl," Webster said.

"Probably the most physical Super Bowl we've ever been in," Noll said. They fooled me alright, fellas," Bradshaw said. "Everybody's shootin' for us fellas. I'm tellin' ya, everybody's shootin' for us. Everybody says we'll blow 'em away. Well, that was quite a remarkable game and to repeat as champions next year will be the toughest thing we've ever done."

"The Steelers are a proud bunch of people," Fred Dryer of the Rams said. "They deal with their problems."

They do. And there was one more big play that proved it. Trailing by just five points, with more than five minutes remaining, and having a first down on the Steelers' 32, Ferragamo threw an interception. The kid wasn't perfect. The guy who picked it off was Jack Lambert, a big, toothless hulk who didn't manage to intimidate the Rams much — until he needed to, really needed to.

"I should have dumped that pass off," Ferragamo said, "but I had it in me to go deep. I should have dumped it off."

"He threw it right to me," Lambert said through the spaces in his mouth. "He never saw me sneaking around."

And with that the Steelers began their final scoring drive in the game of big plays. They began it from their own 30 and they marched down the field to the accompanying whooshes and flappings of thousands of those Terrible Towels.

You know what a Terrible Towel is. A Terrible Towel is what Rocky Bleier and Franco Harris and Mike Webster and Joe Green and John Stallworth and the rest of the black and gold monsters use to wipe the blood from their grins.

January 26, 1981

New Orleans, La.

One of the shiniest creations ever tooled by a silversmith is the Vince Lombardi Trophy, awarded Sunday afternoon to the Oakland Raiders, champions of professional football. It was lugged into Oakland's clubhouse in a bolted and padlocked wooden crate, lugged in with a full three minutes left in the ball game and the Raiders out there in the haze of the Super Dome, beating the Philadelphia Eagles in the money game of the year.

Al Davis went through the doors next. He had spent the pre-game period on the sidelines but now he had descended from a private box.

Davis is the renegade managing general partner of the Raiders and yesterday he was dressed for the role. Davis wore a white v-necked shirt piped in black. A silver chain flashed on his wrist and his patent leather shoes gleamed in the light. At the same moment the commissioner of football, Pete Rozelle, entered the quarters through a side door and positioned himself in the growing bedlam.

Rozelle had to present Davis with the trophy that symbolizes the unity of a league fat with its own wealth. But Davis runs things his own way and just two days earlier Rozelle had called him an outlaw because Davis wants to move his team to Los Angeles without league approval.

The gun sounded at last and the Raiders stormed through the gates, drunk with victory and weary from the long pull against bad odds. And now in the clubhouse that Davis runs like a saloon, the commissioner and the outlaw stood together on a beat-up gray training table in the middle of the action.

It was hard to hear them. The players all stood on stools around the perimeter of the room and even they only heard snatches of what went on.

"They didn't bark at each other," said linebacker Randy McClanahan. "They were too cool to create a scene. It was all very formal and handled well."

Rozelle slipped out his own entrance and then suddenly the joint was alive. Somebody cranked up a stereo box, got Kool and the Gang up real loud. There were shouted demands for a beer. The Oakland Raiders had won the 15th Super Bowl by 27-10. The Pirates had overtaken Camelot.

Directly across the hall in the Eagles locker room the walls had been plastered with hundreds of telegrams from the people back in Philadelphia. The paper was tattered now and the names of the faithful had been ground into the floor under spiked shoes. The Eagles were silent, as though scolded.

The Lombardi Trophy, meanwhile, was never secured. The wooden crate was kicked aside and the silver treasure was passed around the locker room like a bottle of rum. Soon it was marked with 45 sets of fingerprints. It couldn't even shine brightly in the light. There was some goo on it from the mitts of Lester Hayes; a drop of sweat, a tear stain and grime. The trophy was shared in these wild moments, by Jim Plunkett and Bob Chandler, by Cliff Branch and old Gene Upshaw, by John Matuszak.

If Matuszak played for the man across the hall, for Dick Vermeil, who coaches the Eagles, he would have been deprived of this game. Matuszak cruised the joints on Bourbon Street the other evening and was fined for his late dance at the Old Absinthe House. Vermeil would have dumped him on the spot, Vermeil said earlier in the week. And here was Matuszak now, a big, happy thug.

"If Vermeil was my coach," Matuszak said in his growl, "I'd send him home."

"What will you do now?" Matuszak was asked.

"I think I'll take only one or two days off," Matuszak said, "and then I'll start lifting weights to get ready for next season. We only have five months to prepare. Let's go!"

This was theater, you understand. Vermeil's club probably will only get a day or two off and then begin packing for this journey again. Matuszak, like his boss and the rest of the Raiders, had played the game his way.

"I don't think the Eagles thought we were capable of the way we played," Matuszak was saying now. "Like Dick Vermeil said, we weren't prepared and he's — what — coach of the year?"

And then he was serious, for at least a moment before the silver treasure came his way.

"Jim Plunkett," Matuszak said, "is the story of the game, the story of the year. A down-and-outer, man. He was just like me. Came to Oakland and got some new life. People don't realize — maybe they realize now — that Plunkett was burning up when he played behind the snake (Kenny Stabler) and Dan Pastorini. He's a stud. We're all studs. We're the Oakland Raiders and we belong in Oakland."

Plunkett was among the obvious Oakland stars who were elbowed out of the madhouse by policemen and taken to an interview room with carpeting. The locker room was left to the pirates who either would not go or were not wanted. Odis McKinney, a cornerback, had just placed his prints on the treasure and passed it along and now he was kind of talking to himself.

"For a team so young," he was saying. "We've got 24 ballplayers with less than four years' experience. So young we go all the way and now I'm makin' money and I'm gonna have a Super Bowl ring."

The young Mr. McKinney swooned at the prospect of life ahead. As did Hayes, he of the sticky fingers. There was goo on his equipment, goo in his hair and on his lips. He was a human piece of fly paper and he had left his gooey smudge on the silver treasure.

And in the corner of the room, sweat on his brow, his voice dry and cracked, stood Davis. A small gathering surrounded him and he had the curious habit of reaching out and touching the notebooks of those who were interrogating him, as if he wished to check the accuracy of his remarks.

"All along," Davis was saying, "we haven't been winning with owners and coaches. We've been winning with these remarkable players. I knew it could happen because at the beginning of the year I didn't see one super team in football."

"Are you surprised," someone said, "at the warmth your players have for you?"

Davis leaned forward and peeled back a notebook.

"We have a warmth," he said, "we've always had it in Oakland."

"But your players are giving you the credit," somebody else said.

"They're just being emotional," Davis said. "They should give themselves credit for attacking, for attacking on offense and attacking on defense. It was a splendid game plan."

And now a linebacker named Jeff Barnes held the treasure.

"Look at that," he said. "It's fine. Heavy, too. And we get to keep it. It's heavy. I won't drop it. I won't."

4 / Boxing

Norton-Bobick

May 12, 1977

New York, N.Y.

Ken Norton and Duane Bobick met in the prize ring at Madison Square Garden Wednesday night and gave nearly 10,000 clients who paid $250,000 a savage show that lasted exactly 58 seconds.

Norton came at Bobick with a wicked grin on his face and introduced his intentions by dropping his right hand for a fake body punch. Norton watched Bobick's eyes, and when they dropped to follow that hand, Norton came overhand and landed a right to the jaw with the power of a baseball bat.

Bobick was stunned, but he drove forward, and a Norton right landed on the head. It stumbled Bobick and he tottered backward, vulnerable to Norton's decisive blow — another right that came crosscourt and clipped Bobick's chin with a smack.

Bobick went down and stumbled back to his feet before the count hit nine. He fell into the arms of referee Pete Della, tried to brush the official aside and was finally waved to his corner. Bobick tried to walk to his corner, tried to explain to his trainer Eddie Futch what had happened, tried to tell his brother LeRoy and his parents at ringside what had happened, but Duane Bobick couldn't talk.

The punch that did him in was the middle one in that series of three, and it drove his Adams apple to the back of his throat. Suddenly Bobick had difficulty breathing, and the sting of the punch brought such a flood of tears to his eyes that he could no longer see properly.

"I could think clearly, and I wanted to have at him," Bobick said afterward in a raspy voice, "but it was such a shock to be hit in the throat that it distracted me. I remember everything about the fight. There's just not that much to remember."

Norton was the first to enter the darkened ring, and he was made to wait while Bobick fought his way through a scuffle near the fighter's entrance.

With both fighters finally in the ring, the house lights came back on, and Bobick squinted and blinked. Already there was sweat in his eyes, already he was teary and distracted. Upon his introduction he was greeted by unanimous cheers, partly because he is, or was to be, the new hero of boxing.

Norton was introduced as the unofficial heavyweight champion of the world, and if he isn't, he certainly earned the next shot at Muhammad Ali's title. There already is talk of that match for September in Rio de Janeiro. Last night Norton earned his $500,000 at the rate of $9,800 a second, and he never looked meaner in a boxing ring.

"At first, I was going to wait and see what Bobick was going to do," Norton said. "He waited outside for me to attack, so I made a move with my right hand. I lowered it like I was going to wind up and when his eyes followed my hand I turned that punch into an overhand right. I was surprised to connect so well that early. Then I came in with an uppercut that was lucky to catch his Adam's apple. That isn't a planned punch any more than cutting a man is planned. It just happened.

"I had a solid body punch in there for good measure. I kept shifting my eyes from his knees to his eyes, to see if he was wobbly. I had no idea the throat punch brought tears to his eyes. He went down when I caught him with another looping right," Norton said.

When Bobick went down for the nine-count it was the first time he brushed the canvas as a pro. And it was his first defeat in 39 fights. It was not the fastest destruction ever committed by Norton, however. On March 4, 1975, he knocked out Rico Brooks in 47 seconds of the first round, and he proved again last night that if he sets his mind to it early, he can shut up the people who insist that he tends to fall apart in the late rounds. Last night he didn't give anybody a chance to find out.

"And nobody really found out about me, did they?" Duane Bobick said. "Not yet anyway. Norton just came out bombing and he nailed me. I'm a slow starter to begin with, but this was ridiculous. I didn't have a chance to fight my fight at all, he came out so hard. I can't admit that those right hands hit me square on the chin. I thought one of them hit me behind my left ear."

"What did Joe Frazier have to say to you?" he was asked.

"Joe said it was OK," Bobick said. "He just said it was OK. He said we can't speculate. We can't speculate what would have happened without that throat punch. We just can't speculate. That's what the next fight is for, and I'll be back for more."

Bobick tried to talk in a steamy locker room in the bowels of the Garden. He was surrounded by all the friends from Bowlus, Minn., he bought tickets for so they could come to New York and watch him become a legitimate contender for the most prestigious prize in all sports — the heavyweight title.

Now he had to listen to the whispers and the laughter from people who kept saying, "I told you so," who kept saying that Duane Bobick would crumble in a prize ring when he fought a big man with experience.

"When are you leaving New York?" he was asked.

"When's the next train to Philadelphia?" Duane Bobick said. "I think there's one at midnight, and I'd like to be on it."

Ali-Spinks

Sept. 16, 1978

New Orleans, La.

Muhammad Ali reestablished his reign over the boxing world and over millions of his followers Friday night by winning back the heavyweight title from Leon Spinks.

The brief and turbulent stewardship of Spinks ended at approximately 10:30 p.m. under the glaring lights of the Superdome when referee Lucien Joubert and judges Ernest Cojos and Herman Dutreix awarded Ali a unanimous 15-round decision that enabled Ali to become the first man in history to win the heavyweight title three times.

For the first time in recent history Ali kept a prefight promise. He danced the route of the entertainment and seemed to grow stronger at the conclusion. Spinks, without a battle plan and with his corner in disarray, never injured Ali in the bloodless affair. Spinks fought on the instincts of enthusiasm in his first and only title defense since he won the belt last February over a much slower and less profound Ali.

Ali boxed a prudent match. He never relied on the ropes, he never wasted energy with his usual gossip and he never allowed Spinks to cut off the ring. Ali, in turn, also didn't injure Spinks but displayed on numerous occasions the flurries and jabs of his prime. It wasn't until the 11th round that Ali spun Leon's formidable and defiant jaw with right-left combinations that stunned him. But Spinks was a victim by then. As early as the fifth round, his chief strategist, George Benton, walked away from Spinks' corner.

"There's 10 guys in there," Benton said. "What could I do?"

What Benton and Spinks' trainer, Sam Solomon, wanted Spinks to do was nail the elusive Ali to one spot and then overpower him. Ali was in such superb condition — given that his admitted age is 36 — that he lured Leon around the ring in a futile round-by-round pursuit that exhausted the 25-year-old erstwhile champion.

"How could I pick how Ali would fight the fight?," said Spinks afterward. "I didn't fight the fight I wanted to; I tried, but I didn't fight my fight."

Asked about the effect one of his corner people leaving had on him, Spinks said: "There was no confusion in my corner. Did it look like I lost my cool? I'm asking you, did it?"

The contestants entered the ring during the height of one of the most stunning peacock walks in the history of the sweet science. The affair was presided over by such notable boxing writers as Lillian Carter and Liza Minelli and Jerry Lewis. Sly Stallone was there to light the cigarettes for his female admirers and Lorne Green rode in from Bonanza or wherever he is now. The helmeted police almost had as much trouble clearing a path for John Travolta as they did for the combatants. Ali entered the ring first, dressed in satin white trunks. He was solemn faced and remained so.

Spinks came into the ring wearing red trunks that matched his complexion when he saw what trouble he was in. Ali was merciless on his feet, bobbing and weaving like the Ali of a decade ago.

Purists will argue that neither Spinks nor Ali earned their $3 million-plus purses if payment is commensurate with blood drawn. But the exhibition staged by Ali proved that he probably is the greatest of all time, particularly in the department of wits.

Spinks enjoyed a left-right flurry that drove Ali into the ropes in the third round. Ali began to retaliate with his sticking left jab, an essentially harmless weapon that developed the force of a jackhammer. In the fifth round the estimated 70,000 clients in attendance picked up the chants of "Ali, Ali, Ali." Ali did not recognize the cheers but they drove him to become the clear aggressor.

In the sixth round Ali had momentary trouble with the referee, Joubert, who warned him about holding in the clinch. Spinks won the seventh round on most cards with an explosive left-right-left flurry exchanged at the sound of the bell and through it. Ali disdainfully performed an impromptu rendition of his famous shuffle.

Ali landed right uppercuts in the eighth, connected with a roundhouse left in the ninth and in the 10th seemed to obtain an unthinkable second wind. He never stopped his dance, never. Spinks was bewildered. A dozen voices cried out from his corner, but only the voice of his bodyguard, the bald Mr. T., could be heard. "Don't lose your gusto champ. You're losing your gusto."

Another right by Ali spun Leon's jaw in the 11th round and again the chants rose into the smoky air. In the 12th Spinks defeated himself by running into Ali's lowered right hand. Ali cocked it at waist level and waited for Leon to rise up out of the clinch. Spinks launched a right hand in the 14th that would have caused destruction if Ali had tired. Ali backed off imperceptibly and let the punch slip by.

Muhammad Ali, four months shy of his 37th birthday and fighting his 59th professional bout, did what he promised in the way he promised he would do it. He outthought his opponent.

LeDoux-Holmes

July 8, 1980

Minneapolis, Minn.

Hit him again, Larry Holmes. Hit him again because he's tough and he can take it. He's Scott LeDoux and he will stand there and take it until they come for him with sirens and white coats and stitching needles the size of plank spikes.

Hit him again, Larry Holmes. It doesn't hurt. Scott LeDoux wanted to stay all night Monday at the Met Center. He wanted to stay in the ring and win the heavyweight championship of the world from Larry Holmes. That's what Scott LeDoux told the ringside doctor, Gerald O'Brien, in the sixth round last night. Scott LeDoux told the doctor that his eye didn't hurt, that he could see just fine and would the doctor please mind his own business.

He said this, Scott LeDoux did. He caught an errant thumb, the aftermath of a Holmes left jab in the sixth, and tears filled his left eye. He couldn't see and mouthed the words of blindness to his corner. The corner cooled him down, told him to take the count of eight. The doctor examined the eye.

"It was only puffy and swollen," O'Brien said. "It was not cut at that point."

LeDoux has been thumbed before. It's part of the trade. He was thumbed in the fifth round of his fight against Ken Norton, but that injury cleared up. Last night LeDoux paid for the aberrations of the trade. Around the two-minute mark of the seventh, LeDoux bulled into Holmes and banged into the champion's shoulder. The eyelid split open. The eyelid began to tear itself away from LeDoux's skull. End of fight. Referee Dave Pearl stopped it right then.

Out in a hallway afterwards, LeDoux's wife, Sandy, put her arm around her husband.

"You did fine, honey," she said. Tears clouded her eyes. If she felt relief at the referee's decision, she could not admit it.

"It was just a damn thumb, Sandy," Scott LeDoux said.

"It's nothing, Ma," LeDoux told his mother, Mickie, in his locker room. "He got me with a thumb is all. It's nothing."

Mickie LeDoux, who cannot stand his trade, put her hands to her son's face and examined him.

"It's just puffy," she said.

"Ma," he said, "he never laid a hand on me."

Gerald O'Brien had himself another look and pleaded with LeDoux to see an ophthalmologist on the morrow.

"Do I need stitches?" LeDoux said.

"Not now," O'Brien said, "but please see an ophthalmologist."

His son, Joshua, was thrust into LeDoux's arms and the big man with the red and green working around his eye tried to comfort the boy.

"Papa isn't hurt, son," LeDoux told him. "Don't be scared."

LeDoux's locker room was crowded with people who could not believe this fight was stopped. They stood there wrapped in their disbelief, as if the potential loss of an eye was no reason to stop a fight. People came up and told LeDoux they loved him. These people might as well have been urging Holmes to hit him again.

Hit him again. He's Scott LeDoux and he can take it. This was LeDoux's fight plan: He was willing to absorb hundreds of Holmes's left jabs, waiting for that point in the later rounds when Holmes would have tired. LeDoux threw just one million-dollar punch per round. He missed with seven of them. It was his feeling that he would have connected with a million-dollar punch later in the fight.

And then they stop it because he got a nick on his eye.

"Nobody put a gun in my back and told me to enter the ring," LeDoux was saying now. "I fight of my own free will. What I do is my responsibility."

"Even if it costs you an eye?" somebody said.

"Even that," LeDoux said. "What did it cost me to get this far? It cost me plenty. An eye would have been worth the trouble. A thumb ain't gonna kill you. I been around long enough to know that a thumb ain't gonna kill you."

But a left jab can kill you. Hey. Face it. LeDoux might have had a fight plan, but it was an ugly one. He took dozens and dozens of left jabs from Holmes and they hurt.

"They did not," LeDoux said. "I was slipping that jab. He never caught me. He was surprised by how tough I was."

It's the business that jobbed him. LeDoux is convinced of that. A boxer named Cleveland Denny just died after injuries suffered in a fight June 20. LeDoux is convinced that the business is too touchy now.

"People who paid $200 for a ticket didn't even get to see a fight," LeDoux said. "I was willing to continue. The referee never even asked me if I could see. He didn't hold up his fingers for me to count. He didn't ask me a thing. He just stopped the fight. That's what they do now."

Ma. He never touched me. Joshua. He never touched me. "And our plan would have worked," the manager, Joe Daszkiewicz, was saying. "Holmes wasn't connecting with that short jab. It was a short jab. And Scott is throwing that big right always to the body and pretty soon Larry would have looked for it at the body and — boom! — we hit him in the head with it. Our plan was working."

What a plan. Hit him, Larry Holmes. Hit him until your arms fall off from exhaustion and then we move in and bop you. What a plan. Muhammad Ali at ringside was so bored that he sat there eating junk food. Occasionally he burped and then began shadow boxing between rounds. Holmes had enough energy left to mock fight Ali in the hallway after the fight, a mock fight that was so spontaneous, the two of them waited until the television cameras could record it. Larry Holmes had all kinds of energy left. The plan didn't work that well on Larry Holmes.

And just down the hall, where the words "Scott LeDoux, the Fighting Frenchman" were taped to the door, just down the hall the excuses were flowing. He never touched me. We'll be back. Oh, God, Ma, it was just a thumb, he never touched me.

Don't be scared, Joshua.

Don't be scared, Sis.

Oh, Ma. Ma. It was just a thumb.

Leonard-Duran

Nov. 26, 1980

New Orleans, La.

Roberto Duran quit Tuesday night. It is difficult to put the words down or to make sense of them. Difficult to believe that at 2:44 of the eighth round, under the harsh lights of the Superdome, Roberto Duran complained of a stomach cramp and yielded his welterweight title to Sugar Ray Leonard.

Leonard was not even sure the titlist had quit. They were on the ropes then and Duran had turned away with a sudden gesture of resignation. The referee, Octavio Meyran, was himself confused and did not prevent Leonard from assaulting Duran a last time. But Duran did not fight back and Leonard turned away, his eyes growing wide at the sudden realization that he had regained his championship. Duran's corner poured into the ring then.

Duran quit. The words echoed through the big arena and the crowd chanted quitter at Duran as he was led through the aisles into his dressing quarters. Duran a quitter, so inconceivable, so shocking that this street fighter met such a soft and harmless parting of his glory.

Duran was led through the tunnels beneath the dome. He wore a baseball cap with his name on it and a brilliant white jacket trimmed in red and blue. He spoke into the microphones.

"At the end of the fifth round," Duran was saying, "I felt cramps in my stomach that spread to my arms. I was getting weaker and weaker. It has never happened to me before. I couldn't pressure Leonard."

"Will you fight again?"

"No," Roberto Duran said. "I am through. I want retirement. OK?"

No, of course not. It is not OK and it suddenly began to smell in that room, not the odor of anything cataclysmic or sinister, but the hint of a kind of grief that Duran, the flash gone out of his brown eyes, could not find words for. It was as though he was wronged and that he was boxed into this ridiculously quick decision to walk away from it all. The Louisiana Athletic Commission even voted to withhold the man's money pending a medical examination.

"We have a duty to protect the public. The fight ended with a lot of questions," Commission Chairman Emile Bruneau said. Bruneau ordered that Duran be examined by a physician this morning. "You saw what happened out there," Bruneau told reporters. "We just want to know why it happened."

Before the eighth round the fight had vindicated all the souls who had come to view Leonard and Duran as the best fighters on earth, pound for pound. It began with a rendition of the Panamanian national anthem, during which Leonard shadow-boxed. And then Leonard, dressed in black trunks trimmed in gold, stood still while Ray Charles sang "America the Beautiful", and this was a rendition that brought the crowd to its feet and seemed to inspire Leonard.

And then they went at each other in savage fashion and with great respect for each other's talents. But Leonard was winning on points — later all three officials had him leading Duran — and it was as though Leonard was taking some joy in discovering that within him is a beast as mean and single-minded as Duran. He sidestepped continually. He was stalked and he slipped away. As early as the second round, Leonard was sticking Duran hard with left jabs. Leonard wore a smile, Duran a sneer.

The most incredible round of boxing, between any opponents, anywhere, might have been the seventh, when Leonard wagered the terrible risk of embarrassing Duran. Leonard mimicked and pursed his lips. He dropped his gloves and dared Duran to come at him. Leonard used a softball windup and suddenly Duran could take it no more and he charged Leonard in a flourish of arms and legs and fists and he looked as if he had scored.

But Leonard won the round 10-9 on the cards of all three officials, Mike Jacobs, Jean Deswert and James Brimmel. Leonard was bragging in the ring, proving that he had learned his lesson in Montreal, where Duran wrested the title from him back in June. He was showing off new skills. And in the eighth, Roberto Duran quit.

"I felt I surprised him," Leonard said afterward. He was surrounded by his manservants, by his family and friends. "He couldn't change his style of fighting and I could. I am a diverse boxer; I was versatile."

"But Duran quit," somebody shouted.

"That doesn't take away from the championship," Leonard said (to a yea from his Greek chorus). "I won it fair and square. He quit on his own free will, a personal decision. When he stopped and walked away, I thought it was a tactic. That's why I came back at him. And then I realized that I was champion of the world."

"Was the seventh round planned, or did it just happen?"

"It just happened," Leonard said. "I was in control and I was feeling good. Complete control. It just happened."

Leonard will not retire. He had wanted to after Duran beat him in June, but he will not retire now. He will continue to fight. It is the other man who quit. The fight, his career, something in Roberto Duran died last night. The "Campeon Panama" quit. Say it a thousand times. It will never sound right.

5 / Boston Marathon

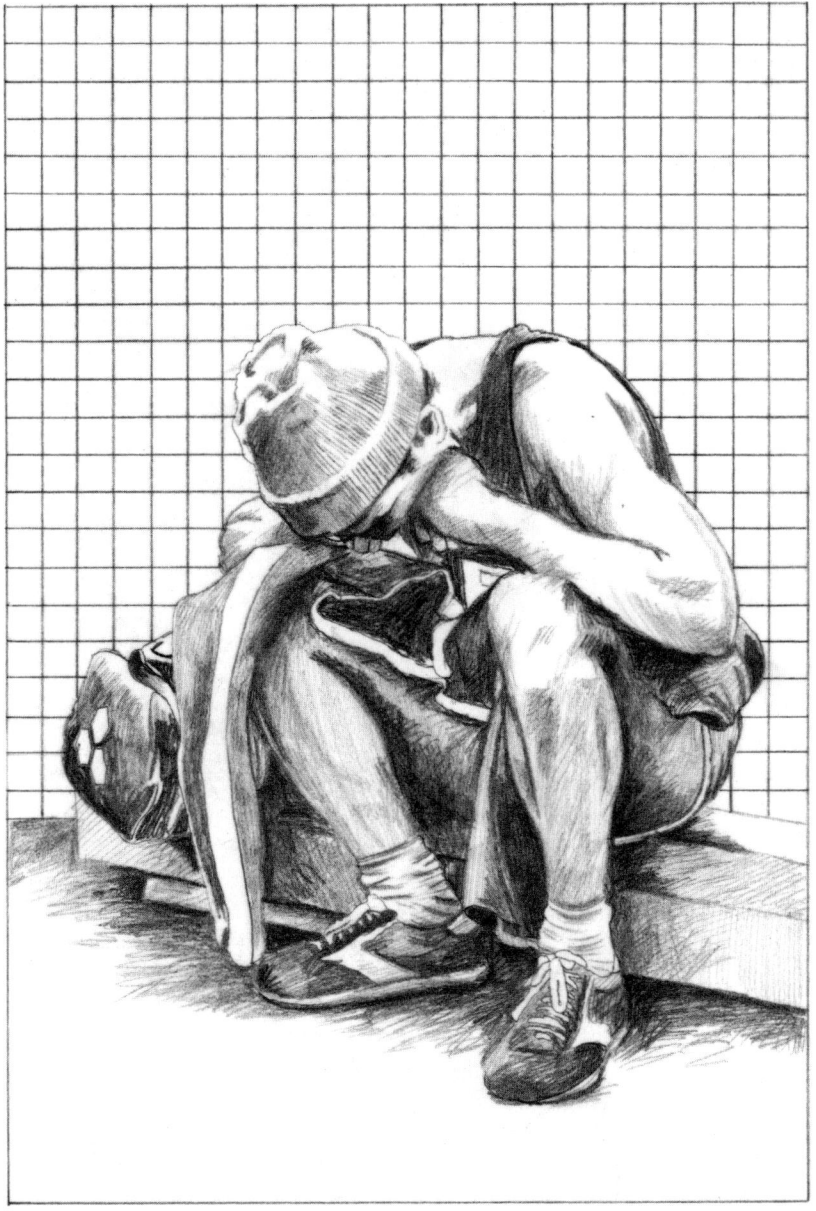

April 17, 1978

Boston, Mass.
Contestants in the world's largest celebration of human spirit and endurance have descended on Boston like a soft spring rain, silently.

The 82nd running of the Boston Marathon will begin at noon today when George V. Brown Jr., a former Brookline, Mass., selectman, fires a pistol over the village green in Hopkinton, 26 miles and 385 yards due west of the mayor's reviewing stand on Commonwealth Av., in downtown Boston.

A record army of 4,674 runners will move toward Boston to the delight and curiosity of perhaps a million observers stationed in Framingham and Nadick and Lower Newton Falls. Frank Shorter, the 1972 Olympic gold medalist in the marathon, will be making his first Boston appearance. If he wins, Shorter would become the first gold medalist to do so. Eight others have tried and failed.

Defending champion Jerome Drayton still has not decided if he has recovered sufficiently from a pulled hamstring muscle to wear Boston's No. 1 bib. Bill Rodgers, who set the American marathon record of 2:09.55 at Boston in 1975 and dropped out of last year's race at the crest of Heartbreak Hill near Boston College, has returned.

There are runners from every state in the union and nearly every country in the world, led by a 51-man Japanese contingent.

But try and listen to them. Try and listen to them Sunday as they crowded the lobby of the Prudential Center downtown to register and receive their number assignments.

Runners participate in the oldest of sports, but they have little to say about it. Running, most of them say, is simply an extension of one of man's most basic functions, walking. Short of those who have had visions, discovered God and found happiness on the footpaths, there is little to break down in a runner's life. It is, by necessity, a life of simplicity that becomes even more simple the longer and more proficiently one runs.

You do not hear runners analyzing style or form so much as you hear them passing time with polite and meaningless discourses on shoes and the benefits of nylon pants over cotton. It's as if basic conversation itself becomes a nonessential part of a runner's life, another one of life's intrusions that rob a runner of time with himself.

Listen to them, crowded into the lobby, studying the computerized printouts until they find their names:

"How's it going?"

"All right, you?"

"All right."

"Hey, Mac, you gonna run it?"

"Try."

"You?"

"Umm hmmm."

"Whenjagetin?"

"Yesterday."

"There you are, Jim, No. 476."

"Where do I go now? Now that I have my number."

"I don't know."

You remember a remark by Steve Hoag, Minnesota's premier distance racer until a back injury ended his competitive career two years ago.

"At the Boston Marathon," Hoag said, "or at any marathon, for that matter, you will hear a lot of talking and low-level chatter. But nobody listens. Before big marathons I've been told that I talked up a storm to certain people. I never remember even opening my mouth or who I might have talked to."

The runners couldn't wait yesterday. Suits and ties were bondage. Airplane travel had left some of them loggy and apprehensive. They needed to reestablish their routines. They needed to run. Lace up friendly shoes — where's my T-shirt, did I pack my favorite T-shirt? — pull on the shorts and run.

You become a runner, the best ones say. Bill Rodgers says that and Frank Shorter says that and the hundreds of running doctors say that. You become a runner to the point where a course begins to run you and you view the passing scene, according to Dr. George Sheehan, the running doctor, the way a passenger views the countryside from a train window.

You can feel guilty watching them. They ran through the Commons and the Public Gardens yesterday, they ran along the Charles and they ran through the city streets and they ran around Beacon Hill. Nothing serious, mind you. Tuning up was all. But you wonder if you're missing something. Hand in hand with the simplicity and the devotion of their lives comes a self-discovery. You become who you are. You wonder if you're missing out on that.

"I don't know why I run," said Dr. Larry Boles of North Oaks, whose 11 Boston Marathons heading into today's are more than any other Minnesotan's. "I like it. It feels good. But doctors don't know yet what real effect long-distance running has on the human body. If you're alive in 25 years, maybe you'll read the answer. We're all a human experiment is what we are. I know I don't run because I'm afraid of dying. I'm not worried about dying."

April 18, 1978

Boston, Mass.

The part of the Boston Marathon you may have seen on television Monday night was beautiful. Bill Rodgers came flying across the line to defeat Jeff Wells of Dallas by two seconds, the closest finish ever in the 82-year history of the world's most popular foot race.

Up the line on Lake St. and at Coolidge Corner and farther back toward the start at the village green in Hopkinton, bands played and old men perched atop stepladders with water hoses aimed at the runners. Even the helmeted riot police tried to smile. You saw the spectacle of 4,674 runners running for the fun of it. It made a nice picture, great film footage.

But you didn't see the real Boston Marathon. The Boston Marathon of record is contained in the precise times clocked by stopwatches. The real Boston Marathon, the one the television cameras never saw, began early in the morning when nearly 1,000 runners packed into the high school gymnasium in Hopkinton. Many were naked. They rubbed protective creams on their bodies. They taped the nipples of their breasts to prevent bleeding. Other runners were outside on the grounds and in the parking lot, and as the noon starting time drew near, they threw their baggage into the trucks that would transport it back to Boston.

The real Boston Marathon was not the early race between Rodgers, Frank Shorter and Esa Tikkanen of Finland. That group broke clean and free of the pack and ran with the wind at its backs. Those runners would be fresh at the end, two hours later.

For the real Boston Marathon Runner, the guy from the suburbs someplace, the afternoon was tortuous and sometimes frightening. A crowd of as many as a million people narrowed the course. Bicyclists, on the course illegally, often bumped runners into the crowd. Wheelchair contestants sped down hills and nearly were run over by police cars and the two buses that were allowed on the course to carry officials.

The best picture of the real Boston Marathon should have been taken in the underground parking garage near the finish line on Commonwealth Av. That garage resembled the burning-of-Atlanta scene in "Gone With the Wind". Runners collapsed on makeshift cots. Some had the skin worn off their feet.

Others were frozen into grotesque poses — one runner posed for nearly 30 minutes in the manner of a man about to break out of the blocks for a 100-yard dash. They tried to help each other up. They tried to help each other spoon the traditional Boston Marathon beef stew into each other's mouths.

"Was it worth it?" a man asked one of the contestants huddled on the floor in a fetal position. The runner began to weep.

Some men and women were not designed to run 26 miles and 385 yards and this year's Boston Marathon proved it. You would think after its long reign as the world's most treasured amateur race that the Boston Marathon would have exhausted its capacity to surprise and to provide drama. But This year's race was street theater, for good runners and bad.

Rodgers had stopped short of predicting his victory, which he achieved in 2:10.13, 18 seconds off his 1975 record. This year Rodgers had competition from Shorter, who was attempting to become the first Olympic gold medalist to win at Boston. Rodgers, Shorter and last year's defending champion, Jerome Drayton of Toronto, those runners were from a different world.

At the first checkpoint in Framingham, Rodgers was running abreast of Shorter and Drayton, Rodgers wore white gardening gloves against the 46-degree cold and overcast skies. At the second checkpoint in Natick, Rodgers and Shorter were joined in a pack that included Kevin Ryan of New Zealand, Tikkanen, but not Drayton. Drayton had dropped out of the race, still suffering from a hamstring muscle he had pulled in Toronto 10 days earlier.

At Wellesley, where schoolgirls lined the streets, Rodgers, Ryan and Tikkanen were alone in front. Shorter had faded badly. Rodgers made his move at Braeburn Hill, the first of three increasingly steeper hills that lead to the crest of Heartbreak Hill near Boston College. It was on those hills that a cyclist bumped Tikkanen into the crowd and John Thomas of Boston, the eventual fifth-place finisher, had to leap over a wheelchair contestant who had swerved to avoid Tikkanen.

Rodgers was alone and in familiar territory. The 30-year-old lives in Melrose, Mass., and yesterday's course took him by his own running-equipment store on Chestnut Hill Av. in Brookline. On Heartbreak Hill, Wells, a 23-year-old student at Dallas Theological Seminary, passed Ryan, Tikkanen and Jack Fultz of Franklin, Pa., the 1976 winner.

Over the final three or four miles, Rodgers was not even aware that Wells was his closest pursuer and closing. Rodgers had opened up a 500-yard lead on the hills, but because of some maneuvering by the official buses, Rodgers was never able to see who was running behind him. Wells, meanwhile, was cursing himself for feeling so strong. He had plenty left but couldn't tell where Rodgers was.

It wasn't until Rodgers turned onto Commonwealth Av. for the stretch to the finish that he saw Wells. Neither of them had seen a real Boston Marathon runner since way back in Hopkinton. Tikkanen was third in 2:11:15 and Fultz finished two seconds behind him. Shorter was the 23rd runner across in 2:18:15.

"What happened?" Rodgers asked. "I thought I had a big lead. The last guy I ever saw in second place was Tikkanen and then I saw Wells and I got afraid. I didn't want to lose, but this was the hardest marathon I ever ran. From 20 miles on, I was in pain and gutting it out."

"What about Shorter?" somebody yelled.

"I saw Frank breathing hard at the halfway point near Newton Lower Falls," Rodgers said. "I knew he was in trouble."

"And Tikkanen?"

"That Finn knows how to bide his time," Rodgers said. "I saw him get a drink at the 16-mile mark and he was smiling, like he was just waiting for his break. But when we came into the hills, I was fortunate to be strong. I train in those hills. But I never even knew about Wells. A cop on a motorcycle told me there was a guy behind me and closing fast. I was falling apart thinking about losing. I just gutted it out."

Wells had entered the garage and headed for the medical facilities looking for a place to rest. He was not injured, but the people around him were moaning, clutching their legs and talking about their failed dreams.

"I had too much left at the end," said Wells, who finished 12th here last year. "I should have been burning that energy up earlier on the course. I should have pushed harder. I'm grateful and I'm exhilarated, but I should have pushed harder."

Shorter was trying to drum up some companions for a beer. He is a good loser. "I just tightened up," Shorter said. "I haven't run a marathon since the fall of 1976, and, hey, you've got to train for these suckers. I was in over my head."

So were most of the real Boston Marathon contestants. Runners were still crossing the line a full five hours after the start. It had started raining hard by then and the wind increased and a spooky fog rolled over the Charles River, but they were out there and they would crawl in if they had to.

April 19, 1978

Boston, Mass.

Bill Rodgers was trapped in his own shoe store Tuesday morning by the very people whom he converted to running the previous day by winning the Boston Marathon.

Hundreds of novice runners wanted shoes and advice and Bill Rodgers T-shirts, but mostly they wanted an autograph from the man who runs like a dream, the man who runs better over long distances than any human alive.

The day broke fresh and sunny in the Boston area and runners were on the streets of Brookline, near the Bill Rodgers Running Center, a basement shop off Chestnut Hill Av., in Cleveland Circle.

Runners stopped and looked in the window. Cars stopped and cab drivers honked and at one point Rodgers stepped outside to accommodate a Japanese couple who wanted to photograph Rodgers against the backdrop of his store.

"I've been treated very well in your country," Rodgers told them. "Please, you pose with me. Is there anything I can do for you?"

"Hey Billy," a runner on the street called out. "You gonna run today?"

"Yeah, oh yeah I will," Bill Rodgers said. "I'll do a light three miles. Mostly I want to take a lot of hot baths and stretch my muscles. My legs are pretty sore."

"Did you have a beer or two last night, Bill?" another said.

"I had a couple," Rodgers said. "But I didn't get zapped. I usually don't celebrate a marathon victory until a few weeks later. But I'll celebrate sooner or later. It was an important win for me."

The scope of Rodgers's achievement cannot be appreciated until now, in the calmer moments following the most hectic and crowded Boston Marathon in 82 years. His winning time of 2:10:13 was just 18 seconds longer than his own American record established when he won his first laurel wreath at Boston in 1975.

Monday's victory also gave Rodgers a sweep of what can only be considered the grand slam of world marathons. Last October Rodgers won the New York Marathon in 2:11:28. In December he won the prestigious Fukuoka Marathon in Japan in 2:10:55. From May 1977 until Monday's Boston victory Rodgers won five marathons and 16 other races over distances ranging from 7 miles to 20 kilometers. It is doubtful that any man has ever tested his body so severely and so often in one turn of the yearly calendar.

Back inside his small shop Rodgers turned his attention to the second most important calling in his life. He is trying to convert his fame into something he can take to a bank. Rodgers is neither wealthy nor successful in the way that Frank Shorter has become. Shorter has his own national line of running gear, but Shorter also owns a gold medal for the 1972 Olympic marathon.

"I've had three faster marathons than Frank," Rodgers told a customer yesterday. "But the companies go to Frank. I don't have the medals. At least I don't have the right medals."

Rodgers is convinced he will break into the national scene with his own line of clothing. His wife, Ellen, has already designed a logo of her husband's silhouette in stride. Rodgers is handsome. Like most dedicated marathon runners his head seems disproportionately large for his spare body.

His clear blue eyes appear to bulge. His hands are cool and dry and full of bone and a close-up look at Bill Rodgers takes some getting used to. He isn't strong and he isn't big and he certainly isn't rugged. But he is tough, tougher probably than just about any athlete you can name. He steeled himself for Monday's 26 miles with one cup of black coffee.

Rodgers was born 30 years ago in Connecticut. His father, Charles, is a professor of engineering at Hartford State Technical College in Hartford. Bill's brother, Charley, works behind the desk in his brother's store. Rodgers attended Wesleyan and Boston College and he was a school teacher until he opened his store last November. His teaching duties intruded more and more ever since he ran his first marathon in 1973. He was virtually a nobody when he won the Boston Marathon in 1975.

"Will you walk for me?" A woman had dragged Rodgers out from behind the cash register and demanded that he walk. "My husband ran this damn marathon and he can't even walk this morning," the woman said. "Let's see you walk."

"I can walk just fine," Rodgers said and he walked in circles around his store with people pressing up close to him and clutching him, trying to take his secret from him with a touch.

"Can we see your shoes?" somebody said. Rodgers shrugged and said sure. He has a habit, when embarrassed by adulation, of sticking his tongue out and rolling his eyes. He did precisely that when Boston Mayor Kevin White crowned him with the victor's laurel wreath. He stuck his tongue out and rolled his eyes.

Rodgers reached down under the counter and produced his road shoes. "Had them built special for me," he said. "On the rack they'd cost cost $80 or $90. They're built up special along the outside."

He also displayed his trophy from the Boston Athletic Association, his laurel wreath and the No. 3 bib he wore in Monday's race. His shop is decorated with hundreds of memories of his marathons.

"What do you do when you're not running?" a man said.

"I read," Bill Rodgers said, "and I enjoy going to the movies. Horror movies mostly."

He was swept up again by the adoring crowd, touching and reaching and begging to shake his hand. Bill Rodgers rolled his eyes and stuck his tongue out. He could see himself reaching out and touching. Bill Rodgers could see himself becoming the most successful marathoner in the world. He could take that to the bank.

6/U.S. Women's Open

July 22, 1977

The first golf tournament ever witnessed through these eyes featured Jane Blalock at the 1973 St. Paul Open, where most of her touring partners treated her with about as much courtesy as a dog affords a stray cat. She attracted sizable and favorable galleries in those days, too, but the customers included spies dispatched by the executive board of the LPGA, in effect, her competitors, who were convinced Jane Blalock toured a golf course with chicanery on her mind.

Miss Blalock's admirers Thursday morning in the opening round of the U.S. Women's Open at Hazeltine National Golf Club were golf fans, or fanatics. Blalock, Laura Baugh and Hollis Stacy began their stroll while the dew still sparkled. Any one of them can swear that Blalock never gave herself an inch or said, "Oh look, a bear," while she toed her ball closer to the hole.

"I shot a good, hard even-par 72," Blalock said. "I'd have taken a 72 before I started the round. It was good. Usually I'm fighting from behind."

"You seemed to have hundreds of well-wishers," a man said.

"Maybe," she said. "Maybe they were looking at Laura. But I've always had the golf fan on my side, the people have always been behind me."

Blalock is one of the favorites to win her first Open, which is to say that she is one of the top 10 money winners on the tour and the women don't expect an interloper to crack that exclusive club in an Open championship. She didn't join the tour until 1969 but already she has 16 tour victories and stands sixth on the all-time money list with $373,929.35, and that doesn't include two victories this year and about $60,000 in fresh deposits.

When you think of Blalock you think of trademarks. She invariably performs in shorts and pigtails and she works harder than most to supply such stunning entertainment as back-to-back 6-under-par 67s to win last year's Dallas Civitan Open.

For the longest time Blalock's only trademark was the black spot. She was accused of improperly marking her ball in the 1972 Women's Bluegrass Invitational in Louisville, Ky., disqualified from that event during an impromptu meeting of the LPGA executive board and fined $500. She was allowed to play in the next tour event but in the following week a petition calling for her suspension was circulated and signed. She was hauled up before what she called a kangaroo court and suspended for the year.

She filed lawsuits, of course, and a judge granted a temporary restraining order against the suspension. In June 1973 it was ruled that her suspension was found to be in direct violation of Section 1 of the Sherman Antitrust Act because her own fellow competitors had tried to keep her out of the marketplace where she earns her keep.

Blalock devotes two chapters to the two worst years of her life in her book, "The Guts to Win". A review is not necessary here, but the book makes it plain that she won and lost at the same time.

"The book was my way of saying to a national audience that I never cheated and never tried to cheat in my life," she said. "No trial ever even brought that out. I'm afraid I've uncovered old wounds with this book but I'll never learn. I lost friends and made some new ones but I never lost the golf fan."

Blalock, 31, comes out of Portsmouth, N.H., and probably is the only woman on the tour who can credit the federal government for her career. After the air force took over the old and prestigious Portsmouth Country Club, the government built a new public course where the fee for a round was cheap. She and her two brothers took up the game but she was the first to win some hardware when she won the New Hampshire nine-hole championship as a 13-year-old.

"I picked up the game more quickly than people expected me to," she said, "but then I pitched on the boy's Little League team a lot better than people thought I would. Portsmouth only has about 30,000 people but it seems like they're all athletes.

"I went to Rollins College in Orlando, Fla., and became serious about the game but not quite good enough to make a living at it. I went back to Portsmouth and taught government studies in high school for a year but I got tired of living off my parents' money and I wanted to give golf a fair look. I packed up and moved to the Ocean Reef Club in North Key Largo, Fla. Bob Toski, the pro who helped Judy Rankin and Beth Stone, worked there and he let me work around the place and shag balls and he taught me on the side. I didn't win much, about $4,000 on my first year on the tour, but in 1970 I won the Lady Carling in Atlanta and took home a $3,000 check. I thought I was a millionaire."

Blalock could throw her clubs on a log fire tomorrow and never starve. Her more public investments include partnership with Billie Jean King in the Connecticut Falcons, a women's professional fastpitch softball team. Her father was an editor of the Portsmouth Herald but now he is a partner with his daughter in a family restaurant called the Old Ferry Landing on the Piscataqua River in Portsmouth.

Life is better now everywhere, on the tour, at home in Boca Raton, Fla., back in Portsmouth.

"Are there scars?" she was asked.

"Small ones," she said. "They heal in time. Every round gets easier and easier. I've finally discovered how to put the entire cheating incident out of my mind. I had to learn how to will myself into a trance to get over the rough spots. It worked. I tranced myself right out of trouble."

July 23, 1977

Jan Stephenson walks a golf course like a Scavullo model posing for Vogue; hair wind-tossed, lips pursed in private thought, eyes fluttering approval at solid shots. When she hits a bunker, and that isn't often, she lowers herself into the sand haltingly, as if navigating rocks in a stream. And when she bends over a putt (oh, joy!), she does more for a simple pair of slacks than her Parisian designer ever envisioned.

Please, you defenders of emancipation, don't write me letters. The Ladies Professional Golfers Association (LPGA) encourages these panting accounts. Stephenson, 25, Australian, built like a municipal statue, is probably the most arresting entertainer on the women's golf tour, and not just from the neck down.

The girl can play and they — they being a host of promoters, chauffeurs, LPGA intermediaries, private secretaries and her own true blue caddy, Dana Deroux — are going to make her a star. When? Today, right now, right this very minute.

When at last she emerged from the scorer's tent Friday at Hazeltine, she has screwed her face into a horrible contortion. A second-round 75 just won't do, she said, especially not after an opening-round par 72 and especially, well, especially here in the women's championship of the United States.

"Gentlemen," said Jim Sims, spreading his big hands, "let the lady through and give her room to breathe."

Stephenson may be the only woman in the history of golf who needs a Man Friday, a service Sims provides with a great deal of pride and authority. Not even Laura Baugh, the tour's first off-the-course million-dollar baby, needs a bouncer. Sims does things like point Stephenson toward cameras, for which she displays more affection than say, for a notebook or an autograph hunter.

"You know Laura Baugh made $1 million without ever winning a tournament," Sims said off to the side.

"No."

"Yes," Sims said. "But Laura isn't No. 1 any more, Jan is. When we're on the West Coast and there's a call from the Tonight Show, it's Jan who goes, not Laura. And Jan's just a baby yet."

It should be explained that when Sims speaks of this No. 1 position, he is not referring to scoring average or money winnings, both of which are claims of Judy Rankin, at least in 1976. Stephenson finished eighth on the money list last year with $64,827.64, and she had the seventh-best scoring average at 73.38 per round. She did win two events last year, her third year on the tour, and that's two more than Miss Baugh has won in five seasons.

"She's been practicing for this Open for six months," Sims said. "She practices harder than anybody on the tour. She's an emotional girl. She attaches significance to the fact that both she and the Open are 25 years old and that in the other Open here, the men's in 1970, an Englishman won."

"How did you two meet?" Sims was asked.

"Met her in Columbus, Ohio," Sims said. "I do some promotion work there. Her caddy, Dana, is from there. I believe she is an Ohio State football fan."

After her round, any round, anywhere, Stephenson practices for the next day. This is admirable, if not necessary for one whose goals are set so high. "Go on and follow her down to the practice tee," Sims said. "She won't mind."

"I practice harder than anybody," Stephenson said, "except maybe Sandra Palmer. I go through every club in my bag after a round."

"Everybody always mentions how beautiful you are," I said. "Who do you think is beautiful? Do you think Patty Berg is beautiful?"

"Yeah, I see what you mean," she said. "She is beautiful."

"But you're the cover girl," I said, remembering the Sport Magazine cover from a month or two back.

"That was awful," she said. "I had gorgeous pictures taken for that cover and they chose the wrong one as far as I'm concerned. It looked like a snapshot, and to think Scavullo took some beautiful photos of me. Well, if I win the Open I'll be on other covers."

"Does the LPGA encourage you to promote yourself as a sex symbol?"

"I certainly don't think they mind," she said. "I do a lot of work for the LPGA and they help me out in return. They set up the Sport Magazine cover, I didn't. Yeah, they encourage it. It's good for business. I don't mind a bit."

Sims escorted his boss as far as the practice tee and then watched her swing from a distance.

"I think I'm necessary for her," he said. "People can get too demanding. And let's face it, it's a sex thing. If Jack Nicklaus wants a beer before he sits down to talk to people, he'll go get a beer and nobody complains. If Jan did that, people would get pushy: 'Hey what's this girl think she's doing?' It's a sex problem. She doesn't have a husband around to protect her. A sex thing for sure. Why, I have actually had to put my hands on people and push them back."

Sims suddenly got a look on him that said he had spoken too much. He hurried off down to the green and squatted down behind the boss. She was oblivious to the people on distant hilltops and slopes staring at her, her swing and back at her again.

July 24, 1977

"Good bass fishing around here?" Don Carner asked as he waited for his wife to finish explaining her round of golf in the U.S. Women's Open at Hazeltine. "JoAnne is the best bass fisherman you ever saw. She likes to go up in the mountains with me and ride motorcycles, too. That kind of life is easy when you're married to an athlete."

"Not 10, 15 miles down the road from here," a man replied. "They're pulling big bass from Lake Minnetonka."

"Ah," Don Carner said, "but you see the problem. We're tied up all day. We'll go down and have a drink and then we'll go hit some balls and then night falls. We only take two weeks off a year."

"Yes, and then you get as itchy as I do," JoAnne Carner said, joining her husband.

"You played a fine round today," Don said. "You got out of that crouch we worked on."

"And talked on," JoAnne said. "We must have talked for three hours last night about how I was crouching in a putting position for all my shots."

She was called away again. After rounds of 74, 72 and 76, she stands in fourth place. She is in demand. Don said, "She's so adaptable. She takes advice easily and quickly. That's hard to do, but she does it."

"Why did JoAnne join the pro tour so late?" a man said. "She was 30 when she joined."

"No place else for her to go," Don said. He was holding one of those one-legged stools used by ice fishermen and golf fans. "If she wins this Open it will be her third. But do you realize that if she wins this Open she will have won nine United States Golf Association major titles and that will tie the record of Bobby Jones, my friend. She loved that amateur life. The match play, head-to-head competition. She must have won 50 tournaments. And she is the only golfer, man or woman, to win the National Junior, National Amateur and U.S. Open. Why, she was the first and only amateur ever to win a pro event and that was the Bundine in 1969. Won by two strokes. There was nothing left for her but the pros. Where could she go?"

"Could she play as well without you around?"

"We got married 14 years ago," Don said. "We made a deal that she wouldn't play in any tournament that I did not attend. Well, I've made them all. I have real estate holdings, billboards, an electronics company. Money doesn't keep us going. We want to stay married and this is the only way for us. This is our life."

JoAnne Carner should be witnessed in the flesh before her kind disappears from women's golf. Her long legs and strong arms are connected to a powerful chassis. She is made of guts. If she were a baseball player, she would be called The Boomer or the Bashful Basher from Power Alley. She does not pose. She is a lady who has golfed most of her 38 years and lived the last 14 of them in an Airstream trailer. With Don. On the highway. They are rootless.

"What do we need an apartment for?" Don said. "Someplace to store the trophies I suppose."

The Carners had seated themselves at a table in the Hazeltine clubhouse. It was one of their rules. She would sit with him and have a drink and cool down before working at the practice tee. The couple met at a national mixed tournament in Miami, but they didn't play well because they were having too much fun.

"You know what kills me?" JoAnne said. They had been sipping their drinks in silence. "It kills me how many pros can't hit a shot out of the rough."

"And the girls say the only reason you can do it is because you're so strong," Don said.

"And I tell them the best rough player I ever saw was Marlene Streit," JoAnne said, "the Canadian amateur. That girl can't stand more than 4-feet-10 and she wears a size four shoe. That's strong? It's not strength, its technique."

"Girls are turning pro too fast," Don said, "you know that. Girl wins herself a Detroit amateur or something and she thinks she's ready for the tour."

"Well it's technique," JoAnne said, "just letting the clubhead swing through the ball and do all the work."

"What's a good golf shot, a perfect shot, feel like?" she was asked.

She sipped her drink and smiled. She liked the way the words perfect and shot rolled off the tongue together.

"First," she said, "there's a click. Then there is a feeling of rhythm and the clubhead whips through the ball. A perfect snapping of the wrist. You can hear the click and just about feel it."

"Ben Hogan says that if you get five clicks a round you're one hell of a golfer," Don said.

"It's a feeling that keeps you in the game," JoAnne said. "That click is beautiful. I'm 38 and considered the longest hitter on the tour. They say you lose distance with age. But I'm not. I'll hit it farther when I'm 50."

"You'll be playing golf when you're 90," Don said, "and you know it." Don ordered another drink.

"I started playing when I was a kid at a little nine-hole course outside of Seattle," JoAnne said. "My dad's a carpenter. He and my mom don't know much about golf but my dad is a good pool player.

He can understand golf if I put it in terms of a billiard game."
"Want to hit some balls?" Don said.
"A few," she said, "and then go back to the hotel."
"Where's your trailer?" they were asked.
"Couldn't have gotten here in time with the trailer," Don said. "We were in Ohio last week."
"You don't want to be late for the U.S. Open," JoAnne said.
"That's for sure," Don said.

July 25, 1977

"I'm happy for you honey," Domingo Lopez said. "You played like a champion."
"Where's Mom, Daddy?" Nancy Lopez said.
"Honey, I left her back there around No. 12," Domingo said. "She about dropped dead from excitement. She got all excited. She's around here."
Domingo Lopez pulled his daughter to him and kissed her gently. He has made his life a gift for his daughter and Sunday afternoon at Hazeltine she paid him a little with a second-place finish in the U.S. Women's Open golf championship.
Nancy Lopez is only 20, but she was tied for the lead in the Open for six holes yesterday until she took a double bogey on the 12th hole. On the 375-yard par-4 12th Nancy Lopez hit a beautiful drive but her second shot, with a 6-iron, caught a tree on the right of the fairway and dropped straight down. Her third shot rolled past the hole to the fringe of the green and she three-putted.
Marina Lopez sat down on the grass then and wanted to cry. Domingo kept walking. He was at the edge of the 18th when his daughter's 2-over-par 74 was announced as good enough for second, two shots back of winner Hollis Stacy.
"Do you play golf?" a person in the gallery asked Lopez.
"I play a little," he said. "I'm getting older now. I'm 63."
Domingo Lopez runs an auto body shop in Roswell, N.M., and his spare time and money goes to Nancy, to make her a champion.
"A lot of athletes say they owe success to their parents," Nancy Lopez said. "When I say it, I mean it. My father never let me work a day in my life. I did work a month once, but I wanted enough money to buy my parents presents. They gave me golf clubs when I was 8 years old and when they saw how I enjoyed the game they both worked to let me play."
Domingo and Marina Lopez took their daughter to the Cahoon Park Municipal course in Roswell because they couldn't find a baby sitter. All her life they told her to play golf and act like a champion

and be the best in the world if that's what she wanted. They are common people. They could not buy their daughter any success.

This year's Open was Nancy's first as a professional. She declared herself a pro on June 19, but will travel to Perrysburgh, Ohio, this week, with her parents, to try to qualify for her LPGA touring card.

She had a remarkable amateur career, that Domingo witnessed whenever he had enough money put aside. He saw his daughter win the USGA Junior Girls title when she was 17. In 1975 Nancy Lopez finished second in the U.S. Open — the best an amateur had done since 1967. When she finally decided to attend Tulsa University, she won the national collegiate title in 1976. She finished runner-up in this year's college event. She told her parents that she wanted to turn professional and they promised all the help they could. Domingo took a two-week vacation to bring his daughter to Minnesota and then to Ohio.

Nancy Lopez believes that she is the only Mexican-American in big-time women's golf, a fact that did not go unnoticed by the International Management group headed by Mark McCormack. McCormack has signed Lopez to a three-year contract that will relieve Domingo Lopez of any financial responsibility for his daughter's success.

"I feel I'll go a long way," Nancy said. "A lot of Opens ahead of me. I don't think nervousness will ever be a problem for me. I have the same belief as Lee Trevino, that if you're meant to win, you'll win. I didn't feel nervous today. The heat got to me on the 14th hole and I felt dizzy but that was it. I played a great round."

Lopez began the day two shots back of Stacy and tied for the lead on the sixth hole when she sank a birdie putt from about a foot. Her putting stroke was solid all day — she made a birdie putt on the par 4 second hole from three feet. After the double bogey on 12 she parred until the 18th when she lipped out a par putt and took a bogey 5.

"I had a good amateur career," Lopez said. "But that's done. I'm starting over as a pro. I'm starting at the bottom and working my way back up, but I'll do it. I missed the cut in last year's Open by two strokes. Just calling myself a professional for this Open made a difference."

Domingo happily reports that his only other daughter is not a golfer. Delma Guevera, 32, lives in Los Angeles with her husband and three children.

"I just hope you don't get an ulcer," Marina Lopez told her husband.

"So I'm nervous," Domingo said. "Golf is a funny game."

7/Kentucky Derby

May 5, 1978

Louisville, Ky.
The old whitewashed grandstands and windowed cupolas of Churchill Downs were shrouded in mist and fog Thursday, two days before starter J.T. Wagoner clangs the gate bell for the 104th consecutive running of the Kentucky Derby, which is a horse race.

More than 100,000 one-day horse players will be at the track then and big money will pile at the betting windows, but now, in the gloom of late afternoon, only the hard-core students of the tip sheets and the Racing Form were about. You could hear them hooting and hollering as a horse called Her Crown sloshed down the backstretch of the muddy track to win the fifth.

Out back, in the tiled courtyards and in the rose gardens, television crews were laying cable and the proprietors of souvenir stands were tidying up for the big haul. The beautiful people who had arrived early were practicing their strut, but they won't play their cash until Saturday and then with an exuberance that seems disproportionate to a sporting event that lasts less than two minutes. Avarice is encouraged, has been since a horse called Aristides won the first Derby in 1875.

The 11 stars of this year's production are quartered in a compound of green-roofed red barns on the far side of the track. Here it was sleepy Thursday, here it was quiet and the screams of agony and joy of distant bettors were faint on the wind. Alydar, the home-bred hero of Lexington's Calumet Farm and current favorite at even odds, was killing time in his stall in Barn 42.

Alydar is a strikingly handsome chestnut colt and apparently no less significant to Kentuckians than a local politician who would go on to become president of the United States. Alydar is the 19th Derby entrant dispatched by Calumet Farm, which took credit for seven Derby winners from 1941-1958 and is now trying to regain prominence.

Alydar didn't appear concerned, but then it's hard to ask a horse if he's mentally prepared for a foot race. Besides, Alydar's trainer, John Veitch, had stepped out and the colt was too busy trying to have some fun with his groom, a man named Clyde.

"Clyde's asleep," said a guard stationed near Alydar, "but that horse has been bugging him for 30 minutes now."

Alydar was rattling his chain and stomping the ground. Clyde was curled up on a lawn chair under a tattered stable blanket that was covered with pieces of straw.

"Don't you be bothering that horse," the guard said to a visitor. "Clyde's eyes might be closed but he can wake up pretty fast. I've seen him do it. He wants this horse to spend a quiet afternoon."

Affirmed, Alydar's chief rival and winner of four of the six races they ran together as 2-year-olds, was alone and unguarded in the next barn. He was snacking on a ball of prime feed hung conveniently from his stall door. A visitor said hello but Affirmed shook his head, as if to say, "Not now. Come back Saturday and we'll talk."

Steve Cauthen will make his Derby debut on Affirmed, but like all the jockeys and trainers, Cauthen had the afternoon off, having completed his workday by the time most people in Louisville had opened the morning paper and discovered a sporting headline that promised drama.

Affirmed's owner, Louis Wolfson, had been cornered at the barn and asked for a prediction. "I don't know who'll win," Wolfson said, "but Alydar and Affirmed might be eight lengths ahead of the field." Affirmed is listed at 7-5.

Sensitive Prince (6-1 as of yesterday) had a huddle of people around him in the pathway outside his stall. He was getting new shoes and being very polite about it. The man holding his head was lightly and playfully socking him in the face. Sensitive Prince sneered. The man pounding the shoe nails said, "A good horse, as good a horse as I ever shoed."

"He only gets excited on the race track," another man said. They all nodded then. They all spoke the secret language of the stable. All over the barn areas men in sporty caps and soiled jeans were speaking this code, about all the Derby contestants, about Alydar, Raymond Earl, Affirmed, Esops Foibles, Special Honor, Hoist the Silver, Chief of Dixieland, Darby Creek Road, Dr. Valeri, Believe It and this perfect gentleman acquiring new shoes, Sensitive Prince.

Here in the barns yesterday it was peaceful and quiet enough for a man named Clyde to sleep at the foot of the star. Walking back to the ancient clubhouse and grandstand the voice of wagering grew louder and louder until finally you could see the bettors urging their horses on with wads of paper and clenched fists. And behind the grandstand, in the gardens and courtyards — yes! — there it is, the voice of the Derby building and building and building and getting ready to explode:

"*C'mon, C'mon, send home a set of six mint julep glasses, only nine bucks...*"

"Well, I don't care what you think," she said. "I'm betting on Esops Foibles."

"I know you don't care what I think," he said, "but you don't know anything."

"I've seen the horse and I think he's cute and I'm betting on him, so there."

"C'mon, send home a set of mint julep glasses. A key chain? A T-shirt? Bring the kids home a poster. C'mon."

"Listen, if you'd ever use your head at the race track you might win a few bucks. All you do is stand around the paddock and you're the big expert."

"You're damn right, honey. I'll be standing there Saturday. I *like* to look at horses. And I *like* to be looked at."

He lit a cigar. She followed him. Her yellow dress was splattered with specks of mud, but they didn't care. They were at the Kentucky Derby and they would do this town right. Oh, they would tear it up.

"C'mon, send home a box of these mint julep glasses. What are ya, cheap?"

May 6, 1978

Louisville, Ky.

R.L. (Bobby) Baird lit about his 10th Bull Durham in the span of an hour Friday morning and tried to remember how it was when he rode his last Kentucky Derby horse, Pintor Lea, in 1956.

"Try and remember, Bobby," said jockey Ray Broussard, who rode against Baird years ago in New Orleans. "You're so old you look like an antique. You'll be worth a lot of money if you become an antique."

Baird smiled and his face cracked into a hundred lines, like pottery. He twitched the corners of his mouth.

"I rode that horse for Calumet Farm," Baird said. "I was on the inside turning for home when my horse went lame and I rode him home on three legs. He took fifth and afterwards they had to help him into the trailer. He couldn't walk none."

Bobby Baird was at his peak then, before the booze got to him and his first wife got to him and before his world nearly caved in. Now Bobby Baird is 57, the oldest jockey ever to ride in the Kentucky Derby when he makes a Derby comeback today on a horse called Raymond Earl, a 30-1 shot who has drawn the inside rail in the 11-horse field.

"It's my fifth Derby," Baird said. "I rode Stranded in 1950 at my first one. It's an honor and I'm pleased, but maybe you should know that I've been a race rider since 1938 when I won my first race at Aqueduct. I've been around."

But yesterday morning there was no fuss made over Bobby Baird at Churchill Downs. There is too much tension now to celebrate the new life of an old man riding a longshot. Besides, there is youth about, and 18-year-old Steve Cauthen, who will ride Affirmed, is already wealthier and more photogenic than Bobby Baird can ever hope to be.

Yesterday morning was the final tune-up for the Derby superstars, Alydar, Affirmed, Sensitive Prince and Believe It. The four represent the soul of the 104th Kentucky Derby, the wealth and prestige and the future syndication profits that are at stake.

Affirmed was led to the track yesterday morning followed by a gang of cameramen, like a new ship being followed out to open water. His trainer, Laz Barrera, spoke Spanish to the horse. Alydar and Affirmed are undefeated as 3-year-olds and Affirmed is already the richest pre-Derby beast ever to appear here, with earnings so far of $700,127. Alydar has won more than $500,000.

Sensitive Prince posed coyly. He is a son of 1969 Derby winner Majestic Prince and the only undefeated horse in the field. He is coming off a shin injury. Believe It is coming off something better, a victory at the Wood Memorial, where four of the last five Derby winners have also won.

The trainers of the superstars are not worried about today's money. The $231,900 purse is negligible compared to the breeding fees for generations of unborn Derby horses. They are worried about strategy. Affirmed and Sensitive Prince are anxious horses; Alydar likes to chase and Believe It will have it either way. And maybe, *maybe*, the courage and skill of Bobby Baird will drive Raymond Earl into the quick lead and keep him there.

Raymond Earl hasn't seen a camera all week. He is a bay colt out of Loom and Ritura, Ritura a descendant of Ridan which finished third in the 1962 Derby. You can yawn about this because the experts say Raymond Earl doesn't stand a prayer. Even his trainer, Smiley Adams, who has trained three Derby starters, including last year's runner-up, Run Dusty Run, favors Alydar.

"I got a good horse," Adams said. "I'd rather have the outside, but what can I do? I got a jockey who has racing's greatest reputation for getting the lead and holding onto it. I got Bobby Baird to ride this horse and he's the best man for the job. I can dream, too."

Baird was embarrassed. He and his trainer were sitting in a shed at the far end of the barn area, away from the action. Around his tiny shoulders Baird pulled a ski jacket against the cold and cracked his smile again.

"You should be no worse than third by the ½-mile post," Smiley said.

"Funny things happen," Bobby Baird said. "Favorites don't always win the Derby."

Baird was born in Huntsville, Texas, and has spent 40 years at racetracks all over the country. He laughs at the publicity Gordie Howe gets for playing hockey at the age of 50. Baird is approaching his 3,700th winner and is the 10th leading rider lifetime in North America. He finished 13th on Stranded in 1950 at the Derby, seventh with Anyoldtime in 1951, 11th on Super Devil in 1954 and fifth on the lame Pintor Lea in 1956.

"I worked under Ben Jones at Calumet," Baird said, "back in the '40s and '50s when Ben trained horses like Citation and Whirlaway and Hill Gail. But this Derby now (Alydar is Calumet's entry) is my greatest honor. I rode Raymond at Keeneland a couple of weeks ago and we placed second and now I'm where every jockey dreams of being."

"People say you're straight as a string now," a visitor said, "and that before you had some rough times in your life."

Baird motioned for the door and stepped outside. "I got a beautiful wife now and two boys, 11 and 12," he said. "I love riding but I live for those boys now. See, I got two families really. My first wife and I had trouble. I'd come home after riding all day and she'd be gone and my four kids didn't know where she was. It got to me. I took a drink, a couple of drinks, but it's straightened away now and there's no sense printing more than necessary about it. Most people either forgot or didn't know about it to begin with."

"Robby," Smiley said, "run him now, a gallop, three-eighths of a mile."

"He'll be excited," Baird said and he held his hands above his shoulders and shook them. "He'll be shaking just like this. He loves it and he's fit."

Bobby Baird cracked his face into a hundred pieces one more time and rode off into the cold morning. He was not followed and not noticed and not given much of a chance, but he was not displeased.

May 7, 1978

Louisville, Ky.

The champ had changed from his flamingo and black-striped silks to a new brown suit and his boy's voice cracked as he told about his two-minute ride Saturday to win the 104th Kentucky Derby on a race horse called Affirmed.

Minutes earlier Steve Cauthen had guided the big chestnut colt into the treasured horseshoe of real estate at Churchill Downs where no horse had set foot since Seattle Slew won last year's Kentucky Derby. Steve Cauthen tipped his jockey's helmet then and a garland of roses was fitted to Affirmed and the cheers of 131,004 customers told Steve Cauthen he was Kentucky's No. 1 son.

Now, in the twilight of a gorgeous Derby afternoon that produced a seventh classical match between Affirmed and his homebred rival,

Alydar, Steve Cauthen the boy tried to explain the feelings and emotions of becoming a man in his Kentucky Derby debut.

Cauthen turned 18 Monday and he was the youngest jockey to win the Derby since Alonzo Clayton and Hames Perkins won Derbies in 1892 and 1895 as 15-year-olds and Bill Boland rode Middleground to victory in 1950 at 16.

"My horse was relaxed," Cauthen said. "He saddled up real good and he rode strong. Nothing bothers that horse. Out on the backstretch when Believe It and Alydar moved on him, his ears pricked and I had to whip him some to keep him about his business. I wasn't nervous. We didn't have problems."

The record between Affirmed and Alydar — for the first time in Derby history both horses had more than $1 million bet on each — now stands at Affirmed 5, Alydar 2. Cauthen's record is 4-1 on Affirmed against Alydar and he was trainer Laz Barrera's first and only choice to ride the horse yesterday. Barrera has long held that Cauthen is different from you and me, that he is a strong and mighty man wrapped in the frail body of a boy. Cauthen's mounts had won $6,151,750 in 1977 and he was named Sportsman of the Year about the time Barrera took him to California last year where the boy and horse could train together for the race that made the three of them immortal.

"Well, I had a good horse, heh," Barrera said, with Cauthen at his side. Barrera is a Cuban who trained Bold Forbes for his Derby victory in 1976 and he has been known to take great liberties with the English language. "All week long my horse, he look like he been at the beauty parlor, all shiny and nice. Such a calm horse. People said I shouldn't have trained him in California. California, China? What's the difference as long as you got a good horse?"

Cauthen stood patiently at his trainer's side and looked at the floor when Barrera began to speak about him.

"This kid was perfect," Barrera said. "You believe in reincarnation? Stevie Cauthen rides like he was here 100 years ago and now he's back again. He's unreal. Maybe a flying sausage came down here and dropped him off. He rode a perfect race."

"You didn't have trouble with the No. 2 post position?" somebody said. John Veitch, Alydar's trainer, had suggested earlier in the week that Affirmed might get trapped on the inside and never break free.

"I had No. 2 post with Bold Forbes," Barrera said, "and if God want me to have it again I'll take it. I'm sick of excuses. I got the better horse. We run five miles against Alydar and the results will be the same."

Barrera turned the attention back to Cauthen, who was snapping his gum and talking off to the side with his brothers, Kerry, 9, and Doug, 15. The Cauthens are from Walton, Ky., just up the turnpike toward Cincinnati and they will return to the family farm there for a few days to celebrate before Steve takes to the road again, in New York.

"I guess people want me to talk about stuff, and, I don't know," Cauthen said, "I'm just not the nervous type and I don't have a lot of fears. I love race riding. I thought about the Derby a little bit today and now that it's over, yeah, I guess you can say that it's the greatest thrill I ever had. It's neat, it's marvelous."

"God love you, son, God love you," said Louis Wolfson, the owner of the Florida-bred Affirmed. Wolfson had trouble with his voice. He is a man, but he was choked with emotion because winning a Kentucky Derby will tear a man up inside, not only because of the money, but because for one day he had reached the very summit of his life.

The restless crowd had geared itself for the Derby race since dawn, and when the band played "My Old Kentucky Home" people in the grandstand stood, as if at attention, and the teen-agers in the infield pressed up close to the fences and cheered at the name of Steve Cauthen.

It took only 2 minutes, 1.2 seconds for Cauthen to negotiate the mile and a quarter, holding Affirmed in reserve before taking command in the second turn. He said it might have seemed longer to him, he can't recall, the race was just a flash in his mind now, a blur. But he lost the lead at the mile mark and had to respond instantly to the challenge from Believe It, a challenge signaled by Affirmed pricking his ears.

Cauthen accelerated his horse then, held his lead on the home stretch by two lengths and finished strong over the onrushing Alydar by a length and a half. The cheers of a thousand different emotions filled the clear and warm afternoon air. The clients had bet a record $10,336,443 on the afternoon's entertainment, including another record $4,425,826 on the Derby alone. Cauthen responded to the crowd finally. He had ridden such an intelligent ride and he deserved this bow. He waved his helmet and stood upright on his horse.

There have been five faster Derbies, by a second or so. There have been larger Derby crowds, by thousands. There have been Derby fields twice the number of yesterday's 11 horses. But there has never been a rider like Steve Cauthen before, never, not in 104 Derbies. He is, as Barrera said, unreal, and yesterday his name was recorded in books that are treasured and cared for at Churchill Downs like ancient bibles.

"Are you aware of that?" Cauthen was asked. "Of how special you've become?"

"No," Steve Cauthen said. "I'm a race rider. That's all I am."

May 8, 1978

Louisville, Ky.

Laz Barrera hunched his shoulders against the cold rain and ran heavily through the wet grass and mud Sunday morning to Barn 41 at Churchill Downs. Barrera's expensive new shoes were flaked with dirt and his gray hair was slicked with water. Affirmed looked up and curled his lips over his teeth in a greeting of laughter.

"OK, big boy, OK, big boy," Barrera said. "How are you this morning, big boy? You looking fine. You hungry?"

Juan Alaniz, a Barrera stable employee, stood in the shadows nearby and ran his hand through a mixture of glistening oats.

"You can feed him now, Juan," Laz Barrera said. Barrera took another look at the big colt and leaned back against the stable wall and sighed. Laz Barrera is 53 years old and he had awakened early yesterday after a night of celebration to be near his horse in the morning.

It seemed like just minutes before that Affirmed came charging down the home stretch at Churchill Downs to win the 104th Kentucky Derby in 2:01.2, the sixth fastest Derby time on record. It seemed like just minutes before that the huge crowd stood and screamed for the Kentucky-bred Alydar, who had desperately closed to within a length and a half at the wire.

Now Alydar was in a stall one barn away and he had no visitors. He turned his head to the wall, as if he had disgraced his trainer, John Veitch, and his birthplace, Calumet Farm. There was breakfast in a pail for him, but he would not eat.

Laz Barrera, a Cuban horse trainer who had come to the United States in 1959, is the hero of horse racing now and his pupil, Affirmed, is the most celebrated horse in America as well as the fastest.

Barrera and Affirmed had raced together against Alydar six times going into the Derby and now after their seventh match of speed and skill and courage Affirmed is the indisputable champion with a record of 5-2. The Derby test was worth a winner's check of $186,900 and a blanket of roses. It also proved that Laz Barrera was able to overcome the winter rains in California that reduced Affirmed's training time from 60 days to 45 days.

"Affirmed ran the same race he races all the time," Barrera said. "Nobody wanted to believe I could train a Derby horse in California. I tried to tell people that California is in this country, it's not in Russia, you know. At this moment there is no other horse alive who can run a mile and a quarter in 2:01.2. We proved that. We proved we have the best horse."

"Alydar's people said their horse couldn't get ahold of the track in the early going," Barrera was told.

Barrera removed his glasses and wiped his forehead. "Any horse that can't get ahold of the track doesn't finish second," he said. He was trying to be patient. The Florida-bred Affirmed had been treated kindly during Derby week, but he was never accorded the attention and respect that went to Alydar. "The only thing Alydar couldn't get ahold of was Affirmed," Barrera said. He smiled. There, he had said it and he was pleased.

"Did Cauthen have to use his whip much?" Barrera was asked.

"Oh, a little bit," Barrera said. "Affirmed is such a happy horse, so full of life and happy, that when he gets in the lead he likes to fool around a little. Stevie had to use the stick on the stretch. Affirmed, he raised his head at that, like, 'What the hell you want from me, anyway?'"

There were other thoughts running through Laz Barrera's mind as the cold rain fell yesterday morning. He and his horse, and the boy wonder, Steve Cauthen, are now the only ones who can win the 1978 Triple Crown of horse racing. Barrera will ship Affirmed to his New York Stables today to prepare him for the Triple Crown's second leg, the Preakness at Pimlico in Baltimore May 20. The Belmont Stakes will follow. Only 10 colts have won the Triple Crown. Seattle Slew did it last year and Secretariat won it in 1973, but before Secretariat's victory there was a 25-year span back to Citation's Triple Crown in 1948.

"I'm going to start working him real slow in New York," Barrera said. "We'll go to Baltimore in a week and I'll complete his preparations there. So far, I can say he is the best horse I ever trained. Bold Forbes (Barrera trained that colt for the 1976 Derby win) was a great horse, but this horse, he is so happy. You can do anything you want with him. I'm the only one who can win it now. I'm the only one and I don't want to make any predictions. Predictions lead to excuses and I don't like to make excuses."

"The Preakness and the Belmont are longer races for Affirmed, can he handle that?" Barrera was asked.

"Yes," Barrera said. "Yesterday we could have kept on running and Alydar couldn't have caught us."

Laz Barrera said he would train more horses before his career is through. And he also said he would like to own a horse of his own someday that would be as good as Affirmed. But now, in the quiet hours after his Derby victory, he was in love with Affirmed. He stole glances at the horse as he talked and Affirmed nodded, as if listening. "So beautiful," Barrera said, "and so changed in one year. He had baby fat last year. Now he is all muscle."

Laz Barrera went back to work then. He had arrangements to make, for shipping his horse and for getting his employees to New York. All over Churchill Downs men were working yesterday. They were trying to restore the track to its beauty. They were trying to get the Downs ready for next year, when Affirmed will already be history.

8 / Joe goes fishing

May 25, 1977

I caught my first lovely bass of the season Saturday, which shouldn't have astonished me, as I was fishing for crappies. When I fish for bass, I usually haul in something like the popular dogfish, or bowfin, which has all the characteristics in the water of a concrete block, or two concrete blocks.

Before I knew so much about angling, I once tried to pass off a dogfish as a bass to a group of admirers on shore. Women and children were easily fooled, but then a wiseacre stepped from the crowd and said, "You should bury that fish, and I will provide the shovel."

If it's northern pike I'm after, that wicked game fish with a line of clean, sharp teeth, I attach a dainty strawberry-flavored plastic worm and go after sunfish. Sometimes that results in a bullhead, which I have difficulty removing from the hook because it is even uglier than the dogfish, although, to its credit, it doesn't bark. Is it the bullhead that spits on his captors?

The reverence for walleyes is beyond my comprehension, and I doubt I will ever land one of those even by accident. Great numbers of otherwise sane people stalk that delicacy by dangling a leech inches off the bottom of the lake. Leeches remind me of bloodsuckers, and the last time I was on the same lake with a bloodsucker, a doctor was required.

Of course I threw my bass back into the water. He (or she, how does one tell?) was out of season for one thing, and I didn't want to risk impoundment for an eight-ounce fish. Whether he or she was a largemouth or smallmouth is inconsequential, because when I say I hooked this fish by accident, I'm not being modest. He or she was sideswiped by the hook and ignominiously dragged to the boat on its back.

When properly hooked and retrieved, I understand, the bass should come through air and water like a finned Rudolf Nureyev. My bass was annoyed and wasted no time getting back to friends below. They were probably on their way to a movie, or a baseball game, or whatever it is bass do when they are "out of season".

There is a species of bass, called the rock bass, or redeye, or el rocko, that I have no trouble catching when I am fishing for crappies. Imagine a springer spaniel dog with a hangover, and you get an idea how beautiful the eyes of this creature are.

Whenever my companion caught a redeye, he tried to heave it ashore, where it would thrash until expiration. I protested, arguing that the redeye must fit somewhere into the ecological scheme of things, but he grunted and said, "No way." About the best way to describe the rock bass is to say that it is probably the only finned creature on the planet that could live comfortably in an oil slick.

Fishing is a complex "sport", and I certainly don't mean to tarnish its reputation by my misadventures. I do have a variety of excuses for my inadequacies, however. Perhaps I don't have the proper build, particularly through the forearm and wrists. Perhaps I'm not mentally prepared. My equipment is shabby. Like Vida Blue, I, too, was forced to discard my favorite cap.

Why, if you could see the vessel with which we pursue the elusive game fish of Bay Lake, Minn., you would surely laugh. It really isn't a boat, but more of a floating lodge. The genius who built the craft must have gone to a lumberyard and purchased the largest pieces of plywood he could have transported to his house in a big truck. He then attached the plywood to a pair of 23-foot cast iron pontoons that show scars and bullet puncture wounds from the Great War.

The contraption is corralled in chain link fencing, and there is enough room aboard for a dozen or so lawn chairs, the long, lounging kind. Imagine the trouble we have navigating this truculent beast through delicate lily pads and over rock shoals. In short, imagine the trouble we have placing this craft where the lunkers lie. Well, it can't be done, but we always try.

A curious exchange immediately follows the dropping of the anchor. You could drop a 1952 Oldsmobile over the bow, and it wouldn't hold us. Anyway, I drop the anchor, and my companion says, "Are we holding, are we holding?" I say, "No, no, no." He says, "Sure we are," and seconds later we are both knee-deep in water, trying to keep the old barge from destroying the nearest dock. Often there is a female sunbather on the about-to-be-destroyed dock, and she will scream and sprint for land.

On June 25-26, some experts will fish Bay Lake for bass and prize money. They have the right build, certainly the right attitude, and their equipment is slick, maneuverable and up-to-date. I will be the only contestant seeking crappies, for that is my surest way of catching bass, accident or not.

May 12, 1978

My friend Leo, whom I helped dig a cesspool once at his place up north when I was under the impression I was going on a fishing trip, is pulling a fast one on me this year. He has not invited me to his place up north at the stroke of midnight tonight for opening day, because, he said, he had to entertain some important business guests over the weekend.

"You will have to mooch off me some other time," Leo said.

I said to Leo, "And I bet these are the type of gentlemen who you won't fool by telling them to come up for a fishing trip and then hand them a shovel to dig a cesspool like you did with me one year."

"You are right," Leo said. "These are clients I'm talking about."

I would like to get ahold of these clients right now and warn them real good about Leo. Leo will find something for them to do, and I will bet cash money fishing isn't part of the package. On the five previous opening days of the fishing season I have spent with Leo, I have helped him repair his chimney, remove a hot water tank, put in the dock, chop wood and dig a cesspool.

Two years ago I actually got my fishing rod out of the car and was headed for the lake, when Leo stopped me.

"Where are you going?" Leo said.

"I'm going fishing, Leo," I said.

"Fine," Leo said. "Thanks a lot. I guess I'll just have to clear away this dead winter wood by myself."

Leo can pout with the best of them, although his wife, Harriet, who is also barred from this weekend trip, is the all-time pouting champion of the world. She starts pouting at Arden Hills, about two hours south of the place up north. Harriet has yet to hook a worm, to my knowledge, because on opening weekend, she spends 48 hours on the business end of a vacuum cleaner, saying things like, "I suppose it's nice that Leo gets away for his relaxation, but nobody ever thinks about me." Which is ridiculous for Harriet to say, because Leo is always doing something unrelaxing like rebuilding the engine on his yard tractor.

I have never personally witnessed Leo catch a fish, although to hear him talk over the winter, you would think he sat down and gave Ernest Hemingway the plot line for "The Old Man and the Sea". Leo attends all the sporting and outdoor shows in town, but when it comes time to buy equipment, he heads for K-Mart, where — and I have checked — they were usually running bargains on rakes, shovels and wheelbarrows.

Anyway, another friend of mine, who works for Leo, told me she heard him call the power company up north to make sure the electricity was hooked up. And then he called the rural gas man, because, he said, he wanted to have plenty of hot water for the shower. I would like to warn these clients that the only hot shower I ever got at Leo's place was in July, when it was 90 degrees out.

"You're not even dirty," Leo said then.

"Leo," I said, "we stood in a cesspool hole up to our eyeballs for six hours today."

"So go jump in the lake," he said.

"There's still ice in the shadows up here, Leo."

"Then get wet and go stand near the fire ... which reminds me to tell you to bring in some more wood the next time you go in."

It's nonstop with Leo. I mean, you don't work Saturday at his place and fish on Sunday. You work Saturday and come back for a double shift on Sunday. I snuck away once. I took Leo's boat out early on a Sunday morning and cruised down to the far shore to cast for something big in a weedbed. It was beautiful. The lake had a springtime smell, and it was perfectly quiet — at least, until Leo started up his power saw, which was his way of waking me up, only he didn't know I wasn't there. I was daydreaming when a strike nearly snapped the rod out of my hand. I fought that monster for 10 minutes. It swam around and around under the boat and circled back across the stern before I could get a net into the water. I was so excited I didn't even look at this fish. I dumped him in the boat and headed for Leo's.

"A 10-pounder," I screamed. "Leo, a 10-pounder. I was fishing, Leo. A bass. A largemouth bass. Ten pounds, Leo!"

Leo heard me finally and walked around from the back of the house and down to the shore. I held the fish aloft. Leo said just a minute and walked back up the hill to the garage. When he returned, he had a shovel.

"Here," he said, "bury it. It's a dogfish."

"A dogfish?" I said. I looked at the fish for the first time and practically got sick. It had an ugly mouth and skin the color of asphalt.

"Dogfish," Leo said. "And as long as you have the shovel now, bring it up to the cesspool hole where I will already have been working an hour."

I hope Leo's clients have a wonderful time. I heard that because of frost heave over the winter, his chimney separated itself from the cabin again. I can just hear Leo telling his business clients how to mix cement.

May 13, 1979

A friend of mine named Leo was kind enough to invite me up north to his cabin for the opening-day fishing ceremonies, which was very big of Leo, because I get along with fish in a very poor fashion. Leo's son, Floyd, was in attendance, along with Leo's brother, Len, and a host of Len's business associates, who wore plaid shirts and hats with hooks in them.

Introductions were made this way and that around the fire, but who could remember names in those anxious hours before midnight?

"Well, strangers," I said, "the biggest fish I ever hauled out of this lake was a 10-pounder."

"Northern?" one of the strangers said.

"Dogfish," I said.

I went to the window. "You boys trailered some nice rigs up here. Isn't that something? We got all the gas we need, but they were rationing minnows." I enjoyed a good laugh.

The strangers looked at Len, and Len looked to Leo. "Don't pay any attention to him," Leo said. Floyd rattled some change in his pocket, and it was like an alarm going off. The strangers each took a chair at the dining room table as Floyd shuffled a deck of cards.

I took a chair, and, for the first time since they arrived, the strangers smiled at me. "So I brought in this fish," I said, "had it dumped in the bow of the boat in a net. I was so excited when I caught it that I never even looked at it. When I got to shore, I started yelling, and people came from all over. Then I held it up. Remember what you told me, Leo?"

"Deal the cards, Floyd," Leo said.

"Leo told me to bury it," I said. "Dogfish is what Leo told me."

"I can't imagine why," one of the strangers said.

"Ugliest fish I ever saw," I said. "It had whiskers. I haven't fished too often since then, although I try never to miss the opener."

"Five-card draw," Floyd said. Cards flew around the table and money piled up in the pot. I asked for two cards.

"I wonder if they bark?" I said. "I raise a dollar."

"Call," Floyd said.

"Straight," I said. I raked in $7.75.

"A game called Kansas City," one of the strangers said. He glanced up at me. "Need three of a kind or better to win high and seven and under to win low."

"Could you please explain that again?" I said. The cards flew. "Quite a game. Look at the size of that pot."

One of the strangers bet a dollar. I stayed with him. He called. We each picked up a down card. "I'll be darned," I said. He put down three kings. "Four aces," I said. I pulled $12 off the center of the table.

"Seems to me I read that they barked," I said. "Not a bow-wow type of bark, more a muffled sound."

"Please," Leo said.

The deal went back to Floyd. He played a game called "in between". He put down two cards, say a king and a three, and you had to bet any amount that the next card would fall in between. He went around the horn. The pot was $40 when it reached me. Floyd dealt an ace and a six.

"I bet the pot," I said. He flipped a nine, and I won the $40.

"This is like every bad dream I ever had," one of the strangers said.

"Actually, when I first hooked it, I thought it was a bass," I said. "A largemouth. But it never did break water. It just kind of towed me around."

"It's your deal," Len said.

"Let's play guts with a spinner," I said. "I deal three, with two up and one down in the middle. Make that pot grow." I drew a flush, picked it up on the last card turned.

"Sorry, boys," I said. I collected $16 and some change.

The Twins were on the radio. The locals went into the bottom of the ninth tied at three. "I'll bet five bucks the Twins win it in the bottom of the ninth," I said.

"You're covered," Floyd said. By the time the Twins got two outs, I had won two more pots. Floyd suddenly became an expert on the Cleveland reliever, Sid Monge. Then Bobby Randall hit a run-scoring double, and I sent Floyd to bed. He was wiped out. The strangers had had enough.

"We'll see you tomorrow," the strangers said.

"Unfortunately," I said, "I'm driving back to town in the morning."

A stranger made a threatening lunge across the table. "I didn't bring a rod," I said.

"You can be my anchor," the stranger said.

June 10, 1979

Floyd, the son of my friend Leo who has a cabin up north for fishing, called me on the telephone and invited me to go walleye fishing on Mille Lacs Lake.

"The big lake that you pass on the way to Leo's?" I said.

"Yes," Floyd said. "We will go out there at night."

"You will do something bad to me," I said, "for when I robbed you in that card game on the night before opening day."

"I have completely forgotten about that," Floyd said through his teeth. "You better come. It will be you, me, Leo and my wife Esther."

I went is what I did. I have eaten Leo's walleye fillets (Leo calls them steaks) for years, and I have heard all the tales about what great sport it is to fish for walleye, so I went. I even stopped at a bait store between Mille Lacs and Leo's place and bought a fishing license, as Leo is personally convinced that he is being watched by a game warden.

Once I went to the shore in front of Leo's and threw in a bobber and worm for sunfish. Leo hurried down to the shore and yanked the line out of the water. He looked up and down the shore and checked the trees. No license, Leo said, no fish.

Floyd was already in attendance when I arrived at Leo's. He and Esther have a broken-down station wagon, but behind it, on a trailer, was a fishing boat designed for the 21st century. It had carpeting and high swivel seats and ditty boxes and front-and-aft-mounted depth finders and a little electric trolling motor on the front that looked like an eggbeater. He also had two poles in the boat with lightbulbs on the end, and I wondered if he planned to electrocute me for when I robbed him in that card game.

Leo came out of the cabin and looked at the sky when he saw me. I could hear Leo's wife, Harriet, running her vacuum cleaner through the place, up and down stairs, across the hard floor of the kitchen. Harriet never fishes.

"You got a license?" Leo said.

"Yes," I said, but I had to produce it before he believed me. Floyd came over and looked at the license and said, "It's real enough." Esther, who must have been excited to go fishing, was already sitting on one of the high swivel seats in Floyd's boat, and she was kind of flicking dust off it here and there like it was a new couch or something.

"So when do we go?" I said.

"After dark," Floyd said.

"One thing that confuses me," I said. Leo moaned. "Why don't you ever fish for walleye right here on your own lake?"

Leo acted like this was the dumbest question he ever heard. "Because everybody goes walleye fishing on Mille Lacs," he said.

"It's one of the four best walleye fishing lakes in the world," Floyd said. Esther reserved judgment.

"Come in and eat supper," Harriet called.

We ate. Harriet's kitchen is like a supermarket. She didn't eat. She started cleaning up plates right away. "Just seems silly," I said, "to double back to Mille Lacs when you have this nice lake in your front yard."

Leo smoked a cigar and watched it get dark, and finally we went. We slid the boat into dark water near Garrison and chugged out towards a group of flickering lights in the distance. There were a hundred boats from the 21st century out there. Floyd rigged my line, and I stuck on a minnow for bait. Esther used a minnow. Leo and Floyd used leeches.

Now, for anybody who hasn't fished for walleyes but thinks it's great sport, let me tell you what it is like. It is slow. You sit there with the line dropped right over the side of the boat and watch the bobber until your eyes get watery. Once in a while you haul in the minnow to see if he is all right and then drop him down again, and if you do this right, it can kill about 10 minutes.

"I wonder how fish see at night," Leo said. Two hours had gone by.

"Apparently they can't," I said.

"I'll put up my lights," Floyd said. I thought I was done for, for the card game. He stuck a pole up on each side of the boat, and each pole had a 60-watt bulb. This boat from the 21st century has electricity, and he plugged the lights in. It was like we were on stage out there on the black water. I wished for a book and was just about to nod off, when two things happened. Leo tossed a leech at Esther at the instant I got a strike. Esther screamed.

"Get the net," I shouted. Esther screamed again. I fought my fish. Esther stumbled around trying to get the leech off her back and crashed into me. We both tottered over the edge of the boat. "Get the net," I said. "Get the net." Floyd pulled his wife back into the boat with one hand and with the other scooped the net into the dark water and came up with my fish, which, as near as I could tell, resembled a strip of truck tire.

There was silence on our stage. "That fish," Leo said through his cigar smoke, "is an eel pout. Even worse than a dogfish."

"Half fish, half snake," Floyd said. "Get it out of here," Esther retched. I insisted on keeping it. Perhaps I would have it stuffed for Leo's cabin.

"Well, that settles it," Floyd said. "Haul in. We're leaving."

I own Floyd.

July 22, 1979

My friend Leo, the perfect Minnesotan, who has a cabin up north, and who has tried to make me into a fisherman, called me on the telephone.

"And how would you like to try for the big ones?" said Leo.

"I should stay around town, Leo," I said. "I should go to the ball park and do some work. Besides, I heard on the grapevine that you want some work done on your cabin, and you would just have me haul dirt or something."

"Thank you very much," Leo said. "Have I ever tricked you?"

"We dug a cesspool once, Leo," I said. "Everybody in the world was out catching the big ones, and we dug a cesspool. I should have been smarter that time, Leo. We went to Target for fishing gear, and you bought shovels."

"Thank you very much," Leo said. "Thank you very much. Suit yourself and thank you very much."

Leo made it sound as though he had a muskie waiting with my name on it. I went. I always do. And I about died when I got there, is what I did. Leo has a long drive through thick woods that winds down to his cabin. From the main road, I could hear the distant sound of work, and when I reached the lip of the final descent to Leo's place, I hit the brakes, but too late. I kicked up gravel, and Leo heard me. There, below me in the sweltering heat, were Leo and a couple of strangers tearing down the cabin's stone chimney. Leo was funny. He made a casting motion and pretended he hooked my car and dragged it down the hill.

"These are my friends, Bob and Gloria," Leo said.

I said hello.

"A new helper," Leo said.

"He don't look fit for work," Bob said. He had a 50-pound rock in his hand.

"He can haul loads," Leo said.

"I thought we were going after the big ones," I said.

Leo put me on the busy end of a wheelbarrow and told me to bring the rock to the front yard. There were people there. Leo's youngest son, Frankie, and Frankie's wife, Rose. Bob and Gloria's daughter was out there, too. Her name was Florence. The three of them were building a rock wall like slaves in a colony. I dumped the load and inquired as to the whereabouts of Leo's other son, Floyd, who is the only guy in the world who goes to Leo's cabin and actually gets a line wet.

"Oh," Frankie said, "I think he is sick."

"I think he's smart," I said. "Right now, I am thinking Floyd is a Rhodes Scholar. Right now, I am nominating Floyd for the Oscar."

On my way back, I stopped at the cabin. Leo's wife, Harriet, was inside. She was crying. "He came through the wall," Harriet said. "He came through the wall with his hammer. I'll have to cover everything in plastic."

I wanted to ask Leo why he wanted a new chimney. But Leo was going full speed with his tongue stuck between his teeth. Leo was working so hard at relaxing that he was using his working voice, one word at a time.

"Separated," Leo said, meaning the chimney. "From the house. Need new one."

Everybody was going full speed. Bob and Gloria were pounding rock, and Harriet was yelling. Leo wallowed around in the debris, loading good rock into the wheelbarrow. The three in the front jockeyed loose rock around on their wall. Water skiers were going by on the lake. Fishermen were out in the sun. A gentle breeze moved sailboats across the lake.

"Load," Leo called.

I brought the wheelbarrow around back. I went and got a beer and rested.

"He's from the city, isn't he?" Gloria said, pointing a hammer at me.

"He don't look fit for work," Bob said. He was on a ladder, and he stared at me for the longest time that I turned away, but when I would take a sip, I saw him still staring at me. He pointed at the beer. I got him one, and he drained it. He made a sound like a bear.

"Did Leo tell you folks to come up for the big ones?"

"Me and Leo go way back," Bob said, "to the navy. Leo saved my life once."

"How fortunate," I said.

"Load," Leo said.

It went on like that, except for a dinner break. And then, after dinner, it went on some more, and then everybody went to bed. I snuck out of the house, rigged my line and fished from the dock until I heard a window upstairs slide open and the voice of Bob come through the night.

"This ain't no resort," Bob said. "You got big loads to haul in the morning."

May 18, 1980

All the fishing buddies of my friend Leo, including me, were invited up to Leo's cabin on Bay Lake for the fishing opener. There was Leo's son, Floyd, Floyd's wife, Esther, and Leo's brother, Len. Len hauled along three of his pals from where he works, and I was especially delighted to see these chums, because I took a bag of poker money off them on the eve of last year's opener.

I had arrived at dusk Friday, and in the failing light I could make out the whole gang down on Leo's dock. They were filling buckets with water for minnows, and Floyd was holding up a leech for Esther to see.

"Hi, Leo," I said. They all looked up.

"Oh," Leo said, "you made it."

"Friends of brother Len," I said, "did you bring money?"

"It's that creep who stiffed us last year," one of Len's friends said, "the guy who pretended he didn't know how to play cards."

"The guy who was bragging about some dogfish he pulled out of this lake," another one of them said.

"He's all mine this year," the third one said.

"I had to invite him," Leo said. "He's relation."

We moved up to the cabin for dinner. Leo had a foundation built under the place during the off-season, and he was at this moment engaged in finishing work on the inside. He had a work table and a power saw set up in what used to be the kitchen. I went to talk to Leo, but he switched on the saw to cut trim pieces for a shower he was installing.

Len was stirring the booya. Len brought booya last year, too, but I figured sawdust wouldn't improve this year's batch, so I shied away.

"I'll make Polish sausage then," Len said.

Floyd had the TV on to Lawrence Welk, who was coming over very loud in order to compete with the power saw. Esther's dog was barking, and I do believe any fish in the vicinity decided right then to clear out the southern half of Bay Lake.

In between rips of the saw, Leo told of his plan to make a year-round home of the cabin. Len made him turn the machine off because dinner was on, a feast of sawdust-covered booya and Polish sausage. The occasion was ripe for ethnic jokes, but the friends of brother Len ate silently and glared at me. They couldn't eat fast enough. They were building to a showdown, and they wanted my cash. So did Floyd. I relieved him of a bundle last year.

I tried to wander away after dinner, down to the lake to contemplate the difficulties of serious angling. A hand clamped down on my shoulder. It was Len, and Len has a hand like a power winch. He jerked a thumb toward the cabin. I went.

"Game called Kansas City," one of Len's friends said. "Need three of a kind or better to win high and seven and under to win low."

The cards flew. I won $20. Just then, Leo came in from the back and switched on his saw. He was cutting through metal now, and the hair on Esther's head stood straight up. Len, who is very much Leo's brother, took a hammer to a wall in the bathroom. Floyd went to turn the TV louder. The friends of Len called in the cards.

"WE'LL TRY IT AGAIN," a friend of Len said.

Leo didn't take a hint. He had a pencil between his teeth, and his hair was messed, and sweat was flying off him, and he was feeling great. He took another rip through metal, and Esther's eyes went about clear around her head. Len banged the hammer against pipe in the bathroom. Floyd sulked, went off to sit with his dog, Rose. I won $15.

"WE'LL TRY IT AGAIN," the friend of Len said. This guy, Ralph, couldn't believe this evening. He took a camera from his pocket and stood up and took a picture. "I need proof," Ralph said.

Ralph dealt. Leo moved a piece of glass across his saw table, and Esther, shaken, gathered her money and left the table. Floyd put pillows around his ears. The friends of Len banged their fists down on the table, and the three of them leaned in toward me. I had just won $17.50.

"Look, you little punk," they said. "You got off easy tonight. We can't play cards with that saw going, so the game is over. But if you try and leave here tomorrow, we're coming after you."

I tiptoed downstairs at 6 a.m. Saturday morning. I reached for the door handle, and a flash went off in my eyes. It was Ralph with his camera.

"Ralph," I said, "a man has to set his bobber nice and early in these waters."

9/Athletes, past and present

Bob Allison

February 18, 1977

Bob Allison — big, tough, forthright, the kind of man who belongs in a high-backed leather chair — buzzed his intercom once and the secretary hurried in.

"I want you to find that newspaper clipping," he said, "the one about the ban-the-can legislation." He waited patiently for her while an hourglass on his desk ran its course.

Bob Allison has done hundreds of interviews in his life but he never was much of a conversationalist in the clubhouse. Now he is the general manager of the Twin City Marketing Division of Coca-Cola Midwest, Inc., and there isn't a man above him in the big office on Central Av.

Outside his suite are the retail price charts for his products, the meeting rooms for his salesmen and the plant, the plant that pumps out 4.5 million cases a year.

He can argue for hours eloquently and passionately for his industry. He would rather talk case output than base hits and he is too genuine about it to be harboring any secret ballplayer's remorse.

"I made a healthy split with the game," Allison said. "I still miss baseball, don't get me wrong. The hardest thing I ever did in this world was hit a baseball. A person cannot experience that without going to the plate in a tough situation. Just you and the pitcher. What will he do? Junkball? Off speed? He kicks his leg and whirls his arms and through all that you still hit the ball. At that point you get an unparalleled physical satisfaction."

"And this?" a visitor asked. "The sales charts and stock quotations ... "

"It's a perfect challenge," Allison said. "There is always some situation that has to be won."

Bob Allison was the first Twin. He and Jim Lemon were the only two Washington Senators who accompanied Calvin Griffith and other club executives to Minneapolis when the franchise shift was announced in October 1960. They were examined on television and in newspapers and Allison was just another ballplayer in another town that first day when a man approached him in the lobby of the Radisson Hotel.

"I'm Tom Moore," the man said. "I own Coca-Cola Bottling Company. I want to talk to you about a job."

Before he even knew what to do with it Allison had a second career that allowed him to examine life and its values more closely. He was the American League's Rookie of the Year in 1959, he was a home-run hitter making good money and he didn't need to be a corporate glad-hander but he took it because he had seen other ballplayers who were truly washed up when they washed up.

"All my life I knew the value of work," Allison said. "I played ball on sheer work and I knew there wasn't anything I couldn't do without trying hard at it."

Allison came off a farm outside Kansas City and his father worked for himself, driving trucks, building houses, farming. Allison went to the University of Kansas as a fullback but was lured from there with a free agent contract offer from the Senators. His career spanned 16 seasons and he finished with 211 home runs and a .255 lifetime average.

He patrolled left field with the urgency that passes for grace in a 225-pound man. He saved a no-hitter for Jack Kralick in 1962 when he snatched a home run away from Kansas City's Ed Charles, but it was his World Series catch in 1965 that forever marked him.

"I don't know if that was the greatest catch I ever made or not," Allison said. "There were a few. But that one got the most attention because the World Series tends to magnify these things."

In the fifth inning of the rainy second game, Jim Lefebvre of the Dodgers hit a rising line drive that began to turn left in flight. Allison was wearing football shoes in the outfield and he got a jump on the ball. The ball and Allison dived simultaneously and although he felt the ball hit his glove he wasn't sure he had it until he slid across the muddy warning track head first into the rolled-up field tarpaulin. He raised his glove and the crowd stood with him, screaming and dancing.

"That is a hell of a memory," Allison said, "the crowd noise was unbelievable, the roar, I'll never forget that roar." The hourglass had run down and the girl returned with the article he sought but he didn't care. He remembered the night he decided to retire in 1970. He was in Kansas City in his hotel room and it was 2 o'clock in the morning.

"Roomy," Allison said to Ron Perranoski, "I'm gettin' gout, this is the last season."

"You're 36," Perranoski said, "you've got time left and you aren't quitting. You know you aren't."

"Yes I am," Allison said. "This time I mean it. I've got a place to go."

Now he runs that place.

George Mikan

April 29, 1977

You could see the big man coming through the luncheon crowd from a block away, and it was almost comical the way the pedestrians shrunk around him. George Mikan was a notoriously tall basketball player, and now he is a notoriously tall businessman navigating the skyway system on banged-up knees.

He pulled into the travel agency that bears his name, shook hands with a young visitor and then lowered all 6-feet-10 of him behind a desk cluttered with vacation news from Hawaii and the Far East. Business is good, he told his guest. With his eyes and his manner he was saying that this, finally, is the last venture of a diversified career. He is committed.

The younger man, raised with the flamboyancy of Kareen and The Doctor, was there to ask Mikan how he withstood the pressure of being the most prolific scorer in the first half century of basketball. How he stood being so alone and unique in such an elemental world.

"I was always alone, for that matter," Mikan laughed. "When I was a kid and wore glasses, people wouldn't even let me try out for their teams. In the NBA I had only one gauge. Did I do my best? I don't know, but I think I did. I was ridiculed even in exhibition games if I missed a shot or couldn't get down-court fast enough. I was such an obvious target. I was beaten up on the court, razzed, hounded. The opposing players always said, 'Did you bring your clippings?' Like I said, I had my gauge."

Somebody once said that great tracts of Mikan's anatomy were composed of heart, and that is still worth a bet. He is quick to smile, still quick to share credit with old teammates — "Slater Martin and Jim Pollard could make passes that Julius Erving makes."

It is frightening to think what his accomplishments would be if what Mikan gave the world wasn't his best. He led the Lakers to six titles in seven seasons, scored 13,444 points in 590 games and saw the rules altered on two occasions in attempts to contain him. The lane went from 6 feet to 12 during his tenure simply to place him twice as far from the basket, and it also was ruled that a player could not block a shot after the break in its arc.

When the Lakers played in New York, the marquee at Madison Square Garden said, "Knicks vs. Mikan." In Minneapolis they read his newspaper columns and named a sandwich after him at the 620 Club. It was turkey, but in those days the word meant meat.

As he matured in the game he put up his great talents as collateral on diversification. He studied law as a Laker, and later, as a practicing lawyer, he came out of retirement once to help the old gang out. He was, at times concurrently, a lawyer, travel agent, investor, American Basketball Association commissioner, agent for his son Terry, and a failed politician, having missed out on the congressional seat from the old Third District by one-half of a percentage point in the mid-1950s.

"What was your ticket?" he was asked.

"Physical fitness," Mikan said. "I looked around at all the great schools we had, the great facilities in those schools and realized they were sitting idle all summer. I wanted to hire teachers on a 12-month basis and keep the places open for the kids."

Mikan spent the summers of his youth in Joliet, Ill., where he was born in 1924 and where his people ran Mikan's Restaurant and Coal Store. Mikan tended bar, cleaned fish, waited tables. For basketball he and his brothers Joe and Ed used a cheap beachball that they shot through the small hoop of a beer barrel nailed to the back of the restaurant.

Mikan never needed glasses until his brother's whittling knife slipped one day and penetrated his left eye. It marked him the way his height did. He was virtually a biological freak towering above the other kids, but that loneliness built the pride that was his trademark first at DePaul, then with the Chicago Gears and finally the Lakers.

"I dunked the basketball pretty good in my day, incidentally," Mikan said. "But they legislated that against me. Basketball was meaner then. You were liable to get tunneled up in the air. When I played, you took it as a personal affront if the other team scored. Now, these defensive players say, 'So what, he scored.' Lord knows what basketball will be like 10 years from now.

"I think the difference between Julius Erving and the player of 20 years ago is that he has the benefit of the game's evolution on his side. In my day there were individual players with special traits; Cousy with his ball-handling, me and my height, the speed of a Pollard. Doctor J is all that rolled into one. I watch the games on television now, very exciting at times, but it seems so sophisticated."

The younger man noticed an exquisite diamond ring on Mikan's hand and wondered if it was an NBA championship prize.

"My wife gave me this," Mikan said. "The things the NBA gave us were ridiculous. One of them had a diamond in it, they told us. I think it cost $18. We didn't get a pension either. We weren't equals with management the way the players are now."

Mikan had to get back to his business. From the hall in the skyway he was a shadow behind smoked glass. The city seems to have grown up around him, encaged him in steel and glass as if he were a civic treasure.

Stan Musial

June 26, 1977

Stan Musial boarded an airplane in St. Louis early Saturday morning and by the time it touched down in Minneapolis he was fast friends with everybody on the manifest.

He apparently told his traveling companions that he was going to play in the Duff's Celebrity golf tournament. So, when he stood in the concourse waiting for his golf bag labeled "Stan Musial" in big red block letters, people came up to him with words of love and encouragement.

"Stanley," said a priest, "hit it straight and keep an honest score."

"Oh, hiya, father," Musial said. "You bet I will. Say, what a great day. Ninety degrees, I heard. Say, that's a cool day in St. Louis."

"Stanley," said another priest, "watch your backswing."

"Hiya, father," said Musial. "Hey, I'm working on that."

"Stan the Man," a boy said, "will you sign this card?" The boy was propelled by his father. Musial was the father's hero, but the man appeared too frozen with delight to move.

"Hiya, where ya from, buddy?" Musial said. "Let me sign that for ya. Hey, you're all good fans, all of you."

The boy's father forced himself to walk forward. "Stan," he said, "you're the greatest. Good luck with your golf game."

"Hey, all right," Musial said. "Looks like we got a day for it. You people are beautiful. Good fans."

Stan (the Man) Musial will be 57 in November and he looks the very picture of health, contentment and charm. His long face is characterized by a sharp chin and prominent nose. He is tanned and lean and pointed out that he weighed only five more pounds than the 180 he played at for 22 years during which he was the very essence of the St. Louis Cardinals.

Every move he made said this man is an athlete, but he has the most slender pair of wrists I've ever seen on a batsman and his fingers are long, nearly pointed. I read that he once was a fairly accomplished amateur magician, adept with card and coin tricks. I stared at his delicate hands.

Musial once got five hits in a game at Ebbets Field in Brooklyn, each hit coming with a two-strike count. His Flatbush admirers named him "The Man". On May 2, 1954, against the Giants, he was the first major leaguer ever to hit five home runs in one day, during a doubleheader. Hands that performed magic.

Musial was met at the airport by Jim Gallagher, one of Joe Duffy's volunteer chauffers, and me, and after introductions, he said, "Hey, give me those names one more time, let's see if I got it right. All right. A beautiful morning. Let's move on."

"The Twins are doing very well," Musial said, "but they have six or so unsigned players. That's a shame. Maybe in a year or so this free agent thing will cool off. Hey, but they're drawing real well."

"Do you get much chance to see Rod Carew play?" I asked. Musial was one of the greatest hitters of his era, through the 1940s, into the 1950s and early 1960s, as Carew is the greatest of the current hitters. They seem to share similar, poor backgrounds as well. Musial came out of the coal mining town of Donora, Pa., Carew from the Harlem side of Manhattan. Both are left-handers. Both have unusual batting stances. Musial won his league's batting championship seven times. Carew is pursuing his sixth title.

"What a guy Carew is," Musial said. "He really slaps the ball around the field. Our stances are a little different and he's a wrist hitter like Henry Aaron. I got more of my body behind the ball."

Musial had a folded newspaper in his arms and he went into his famous crouch, the batting stance that a White Sox pitcher named Ted Lyons once described as something that looked like "... a kid peeking around the corner to see if the cops were coming." Musial dropped into the stance and involuntarily swiveled his hips in that little hula wiggle he performed.

"I'd get my whole body into the act," he said, swinging the newspaper. "You need a flexible swing, like Carew's. With a flexible swing you can bring the bat around level on any pitch and that's the secret, even on the sliders away.

"Another secret he knows is to keep the ball away from center field. I can't hit a golf ball down the middle of the fairway because I'm so used to hitting right or left with a baseball. Too many fast center fielders in the game; hit that ball to corners and openings. Why should I have hit a ball to Willie Mays? Good hitters, me and Carew, well, they know how to hit the ball where it's pitched."

People were gathering now at a respectful distance. Some recognized instantly that this man was the hero of their youth. Younger people tried desperately to recognize this handsome, engaging man who was giving a batting lesson in the airport.

"I wasn't a wrist hitter," he continued. "I don't know all Carew's secrets, but I timed each pitcher in the league until I knew them all. When the ball left a pitcher's hand I knew if it would be a strike. I loved to see a side-armed pitcher. I could see his delivery all the way and the ball came at me nice and flat."

People crowded a little closer now and Musial abruptly popped out of the stance but continued the discussion: "Hey, a good hitter will hit any pitch and the stance doesn't make any difference, just so the bat comes around level."

And then, in lower tones, while bouncing on his toes, he said, "The guys that discourage me are the .250 hitters who don't improve."

If I'm correctly interpreting his words and his inflection, Musial thinks it is slightly improper for a .250 hitter to command the kind of money that Stanley Frank Musial earned. Musial never begged. He was the first $100,000-a-year player in the National League and by age 29 he had invested his money into the hotels and restaurants and bowling alleys that now make him a wealthy man. He has friends all over the country, and in Missouri, where he is still king, he has been asked to run for Senate, for Congress, for mayor, anything. He refuses. He maintains a managerial capacity with the Cardinals but said, "I don't travel with the club as much as I used to. I don't have much in common with the young ballplayers. It's a different generation. I had my time."

During the ride downtown Musial talked about the city and wondered in amazement what the big building (the IDS) was.

"And great fishing here I bet," he said. "Beautiful place, just beautiful."

"Have you been happy all your life?" I asked him.

"If you can't be happy at the top of your profession then forget it," he said. "Yes, I'm happy and probably always have been. Always liked ballplayers, always liked the workin' guy, you know, the regular folks."

He flashed the ring he received from the Hall of Fame upon his induction in 1969.

"I had World Series rings," Stan Musial said. "But I wear only this one. It covers it all."

Bjorn Borg

July 8, 1977

Rochester, Minn.

Not five days after he won his second consecutive Wimbledon title, Bjorn Borg arrived in Rochester Thursday afternoon clean, crisp and polished in a fashionable tennis ensemble that bore his initials as well as his colors, red and cream.

He also was beardless, having found time in his schedule to razor the baby whiskers that he said brought him luck in stunning triumphs over Ilie Nastase, Vitas Gerulaitis and, finally, Jimmy Connors in Britain's centenary tennis festival.

They say that the young Swede ticks slowly to the tune of a strong heart that pumps life at the astonishing rate of only 35 beats per minute at rest. He looks it. Never has a calmer tennis player graced the old floor of the Mayo Civic Auditorium Arena and the bet here is that never has a 21-year-old so completely dominated his sport and mastered the demands of travel and time so easily.

His Cleveland team in the World Team Tennis league was in town to play against the Russians of the same league. The night before he was in Hartford, Conn. The night before that he thrilled a gallery in Buffalo, N.Y. Bjorn Borg apparently doesn't need the comforts of a permanent home.

He entered the arena armed with a dozen personalized racquets all strung as tight as crossbows. He began to gab.

"Sure are a lot of young players coming up, hey?" he said. "I signed with Cleveland in January. The World Team Tennis league drafted me as a 16-year-old but that was too young. Now is right for this. I play tennis nine months a year and it is right. I don't wear out. Already I'm looking forward to the U.S. Open."

"Look at him," said Mariana Simionescu, his betrothed. "Even when groupies are around, and they are around everywhere, he is patient, that is his job."

"Bjorn," called teammate Marty Reissen, the Cleveland player-coach.

"What?" Borg said.

"Practice, please."

Borg selected a racquet by banging its head on the head of another from the pile. He found one that made a ping and then proceeded to destroy the shot-making of a look-alike sparring partner named Bob Giltinan, an Australian with long blond locks. Borg used every practice stroke as a note to himself. His successful plays brought a tight smile to his lips. He studied the floor. On forehands, he guides the racquet back with a gentle push of his free hand, as if taking aim. On backhands he brings both hands back and uses both. His shots exploded off the concrete floor and he broke into a light mist of sweat after 30 hard minutes.

Simionescu, a Rumanian who is not yet 20, watched from the sidelines. The two met a year ago during the French Open and were engaged to be married. When somebody asked just when they would be married she said, "That is private. Who knows? We may end up like Jimmy Connors and Chris Evert. You never know. So why plan a marriage?"

No one had the answer to that and in the ensuing silence Simionescu volunteered that, yes, she played in Wimbledon and lost to the eventual women's winner, Virginia Wade, in the early going.

"One time I was No. 2 in my home," she said.

"Where is Bjorn's home?" she was asked.

"We have summer home in Sweden," she said, "and a permanent home in Monte Carlo. For tax reasons it is in Monte Carlo."

Bjorn and Mariana hugged briefly and traded privacies in the exchange of court time. She is also a member of the Cleveland Nets and went to practice as he finished.

"I'm still thinking about Wimbledon," Borg told people gathered around. He fidgeted with his wrist band. Now, words had to be pulled from him. Opponents say the same about his emotions. It is locked up inside a boy who had to grow so fast.

"Do you think," he was asked, "that you handle your success better than most 21-year-old Americans could handle it?"

"Yeah, I do think that," he said. "Maybe they are more spoiled, you know. I was never spoiled. If I acted foolish I couldn't play the kind of tennis I play at this stage. I hear you don't reach your peak in tennis until the age of 29. I've got eight years to go then before I am a great tennis player."

He was reminded that he already is the unofficial No. 1 player in the world. He was reminded that he advanced as far as the quarterfinals at Wimbledon when he was just 17. He was reminded that he was a teenage heartthrob before he could grow whiskers. He response was a shrug.

"Will you ever go back and finish high school?" another man asked.

"Oh yes, that is very important to me right now," Borg said.

"I see," the man said, starting to write the information in a notebook.

Borg put a hand on the man's shoulder. "Wait," he said, "I'm kidding. I would never go back to high school. Why should I?" He made a sound that must have been the Swedish version of "geez!"

"What will you do when you're 35 or 40?" the man said.

"What will you do at that age?" Borg said, growing impatient.

"What a stupid question," Giltinan said.

"This guy's got 20 million dollars and he should go back to school?"

"But what will he do?"

Borg had walked away.

"He'll do what we all dream about doing if we all had 20 million dollars," Giltinan said.

Butch Nash

October 30, 1977

George Nash grew up on Taylor St. in northeast Minneapolis during the Depression, three blocks from where he now lives on Buchanan St. His father, a conductor on the Soo Line, called him Butch because he was round-faced and tough. Clyde Nash died when Butch was 12, and his mother, Florence, went to work as a housekeeper.

Butch attended Lowry Elementary School and Edison High, and his own children did the same a generation later. Schoolboy athletics were more important during the Depression though, because a good game and a long run and all those friendships made you feel rich inside.

Butch was all-city in basketball at Edison and a fullback on the football team. For his ninth-grade civics class project, Butch planned a career as a football coach.

The University of Minnesota was a very big item with Butch. All through high school he went to the Gopher games on a cheap ticket in the bowl end of Memorial Stadium. He used to go over to the school on Friday nights before home games when traffic was stopped on University Av. and there was band music in the streets. A trumpet, a clarinet, a drum, he can still hear snatches of that at 61 years of age.

The Gophers were national champions under Bernie Bierman in 1934, the year Butch graduated from Edison. He wanted to attend Minnesota, but he didn't have any means and scholarships hadn't been invented. One day Butch was caddying at Midland Hills for Dave MacMillan, then the Gopher basketball coach.

"I sure wish there was a way for me to get to Minnesota," Butch said.

"Speak up," MacMillan said.

"I would like to attend Minnesota, but I don't have any money," Butch said.

"You're a quiet one, aren't you," MacMillan said. "I think we'll call you Noisy."

MacMillan got Nash a $25-a-month job with the Civilian Conservation Corps, and Nash played guard on MacMillan's championship 1937-38 team. He also played for Bierman's 1936 national champions and on the 1937 and 1938 Big Ten title teams. Butch Nash played on teams that won three straight Little Brown Jug games over Michigan. He called it the Big Brown Jug. There was a passion and significance attached to that crockery that young people today find hard to believe.

The state fans were crazy over those teams. You couldn't get a ticket, and people followed the games on radio — even hunters and fisherman up north, travelers, distant relatives. In 1938 when the team returned from Wisconsin, where it won the Big Ten title in its final game, there were 5,000 people at the railroad depot downtown and it was close to midnight.

Butch Nash graduated in 1939 and went to work. He was head football coach at Anoka and then at Winona, and his 1941 Winona team won the Big Nine league championship. The navy was taking people then, and Nash went away for five years. He married a girl from Michigan City, Ind. She liked football. When Nash returned to Winona in 1946, Paul Giel was making a name on the playgrounds, but Nash never coached him at Winona. Bernie Bierman had called, inviting Nash to join his staff in 1947.

It was still the way Butch remembered it. People had a feel and a concern for the place and its teams. Nash was B squad coach under

Bierman and the scholastic advisor for the team. He was the freshman coach until Wes Fesler came in 1951, and then Nash started turning out quality ends, including eight All-Americans so far.

It was a full-time job. From December through April each year, the staff showed Gopher highlight films around the state, often two showings a night and on Sunday afternoons. People couldn't get enough of the Gophers. Nash gave a speech with each film, but he was spare with his words.

He was a quiet and loyal employee. He was loyal to Bierman and to Fesler, and he was loyal to Murray Warmath when Warmath took over in 1954. In 1957 Nash could have become the head coach at North Dakota State, but he didn't feel right about it and turned down the job. He was waiting for his shot with the Gophers.

Something happened after the Gophers beat UCLA in the 1962 Rose Bowl. Changes were imperceptible at first, but Nash could feel the passion for the team was slipping. People were interested, but they didn't meet planes at the airport. Highlight films weren't in demand. You could drive a car down University Av. most Friday nights and not hear a note of music.

Butch Nash never changed the way he felt about Minnesota football, but he was getting older with a young man's hopes locked inside him. Maybe he was an anachronism and, if he was, maybe that wasn't so bad.

When Cal Stoll was named coach in 1972, Nash had the dubious honor of being the only assistant to survive the four coaching transitions since 1947. He was hurt and disappointed that he was never considered for the job, but Nash can only feel sorry for himself for about two seconds. And then he feels foolish. He is doing what he set out to do in ninth grade. He is rich inside.

Butch Nash was thinking about all this when he made a speech to the Gophers last weekend. It was his first speech to a full squad in 30 years, and mostly he told the team that he felt sorry for any breathing human being who never felt loyalty or tradition. He slipped back in time and took them with him. It worked.

"Win a Big Brown Jug," he told them.

Jim Hunter

August 26, 1979

Jim Hunter has his son, Todd, along with him on the current Yankee road trip that began in Kansas City last Monday and concludes in Texas on Wednesday. It's a long but relatively safe journey as opposed to swings through the double-bolt lock towns of Detroit, Cleveland and Chicago.

Todd Hunter is 10, chunky and round-faced like his father and even their pleasant drawl is so similar as to be distinguished only by a difference in octave. Jim Hunter came out of the country at 19 and now, in his last summer in a major league baseball uniform, he is showing his only son those baseball towns that might include glimpses of what country is left.

"When I first signed with the Yankees," Jim Hunter said, "a man wanted to give me an apartment rent-free right downtown, in Manhattan. He said it was worth $2,000 a month and I checked it over, saw that it was big enough for my family. But it was 20 floors up. I told the guy to forget it. I didn't care if it was $200,000 a month. I'd go crazy in a place like that."

Hunter made the comments early the other afternoon when he and his son were the only Yankees in the clubhouse at Metropolitan Stadium. Hunter can't stand hotels so he comes to the ball park early. His son has a uniform that he wears to play made-up games in the clubhouse and Hunter was wearing his long underwear against the chill of the day.

A man wanted to see him one last time, before Hunter retires this year at the age of 33 to his peanut and soybean farm in Hertford, N.C., before his flowing hair and flowing motions are gone for good.

Hunter might never start another game. The Yankee front office called him in before the start of this road trip and advised him that, considering the investment in Ken Clay and Jim Beattie, they would have to be looked at long and hard down the stretch. Didn't bother Hunter much except that he would love to help the Yankees down the stretch.

He has won 224 games, with Kansas City, Oakland and New York, and in 1976 he became only the fourth pitcher in this century to record 200 wins before his 31st birthday. Do not forget, either, his five World Series wins during three straight championship years in Oakland, or his perfect game in 1968 against the Twins, or his remarkable capacity for humility.

"The sun," Jim Hunter once said when things were not going well for him on the Yankees, "don't shine on the same dog's ass every day."

But this is the last year of Hunter's five-year contract with the Yankees —a contract that made him a household word, signed as it was, on New Year's Eve 1974, but never spoiled him — and, true to his word, he will not return. He has had enough. His son is 10, his daughter is 6 and there is another child due this fall, and James Hunter has had enough baseball. He will go home to farm. The accumulation of even more Hall of Fame statistics are as meaningless to him as the spent shells from his shotgun. Besides, a man came looking for the memories.

"My best memory was the first time I won my 20th game in a season," Hunter was saying. "It was 1971. Oakland got into Kansas City at 1 a.m. the night before I'm scheduled to pitch. I wanted to go hunting. Me and Paul Lindblad and Dick Green decided not even to go to bed, so we could go hunting at 4 in the morning. Sal Bando came up to me and said, 'you've got a chance to win 20, get some sleep.' Naw, didn't need it. We all went hunting and got back to the hotel about 3 in the afternoon. Took a shower and went to the park. Won my 20th."

"How did you get the name Catfish?"

The name is not familiar and Hunter has often said that back home in Hertford everybody calls him Jim.

"Before I even met Charlie Finley," Hunter said, "he called me on the phone and asked me if I had a nickname. I said no. He asked what my interests were. I told him hunting and fishing. He says, 'Well, you ran away from home when you was six years old. Your parents looked for you all day and when they found you you had just pulled in two catfish and were about to pull in the third.'"

It never happened, of course. Hunter was the youngest of eight children, and Abbott Hunter, who died last month, was too busy to look for lost children. He farmed other people's land mostly, and worked in a logging woods. He never wanted his children to become farmers or work in a logging woods where you could get your foot mashed or your hands jammed between trees. Until this year Abbott Hunter often visited his famous son in New York.

"And he wouldn't ever go to bed in New York," Jim Hunter said. "He was afraid to."

It was Hunter's farm — despite his father's message, Hunter and his brother, Ray, own a 110-acre working farm not a half mile from where they were raised — that ultimately caused him to seek release from Finley in 1974.

Before the public knew of Hunter's novel free agentry, he and Finley spoke over the phone. Finley asked what it would take to keep Hunter. Hunter told his boss that not only would he stay, but he would play for the previous year's salary, if only Finley would buy back the 400 acres Hunter was forced to sell to repay a loan from Finley that enabled Hunter to buy the farm. It would have cost Finley $400,000. He declined.

"So I moved," Hunter said. "Bought a place in New Jersey that had a yard. It's already sold. The first thing I'm going to do when I get home is take Ray fishing. He's been working all year without even one day off. When I was a kid I always hoped Hertford would grow into a big town. Now I hope they keep it small."

The Yankees will miss Hunter, just as surely as the fans will miss watching him when he is right. Roy White will miss Hunter's humor and character. Bucky Dent will miss the same. Graig Nettles, who fights for comedian honors himself, will miss his ride to the ballpark. Lou Piniella will miss "the dignity, the composure and the class".

"What is class?" Hunter was asked.

"Coming from the country and all," Hunter said, "I'd guess it's being too dumb to be scared of anything. To give 100 percent. Not 110 or 115 percent like some guys say. There ain't but 100 percent to give."

Sandy Stephens

October 28, 1979

An agent has been retained, the first agent he has ever had in his life. The feelers are out and the push is on because he is ready to tell his story now, and some of it is not pretty. The first 39 years of his life would make a great book, Sandy Stephens says, and even a better television movie, a kind of "Brian's Song" without death.

"Sandy was crossing barriers," the agent, Russ Rustad, is saying now. "The whole country was involved in social change and along comes a black quarterback at a major northern university whose coach is a white Southerner. And they love each other, the quarterback and his coach. Comedy and tragedy in this story."

"Comedy," Sandy Stephens says. "I got to get my recruiting in there. I mean I got 53 offers from all over the country. I was recruited heavily by Alabama, Mississippi, Tulane, these places that didn't have any blacks at all. Zero. Well, what they were doing, they were sent game films of me playing for Uniontown High and on these game films they can't tell I'm black. My mom was real light-skinned.

"So anyway, these Southern coaches are looking at me on the game films and they're saying, 'We got to have that kid.' Hell, an Italian looks darker than I do under a football helmet. Any letter I got from a Southern school I threw away."

Stephens chose Minnesota and its coach, Murray Warmath — and this could be part of the book, the way people like Carl Rowan interceded for the Gophers — and became, in those glorious autumns of 1960 and 1961, the premier college quarterback in the land. The Gophers visited two successive Rose Bowls in that span, beating UCLA 21-3 on Jan. 1, 1962, and drew 704,128 customers to Memorial Stadium, a two-year home total that hasn't been approached before or since.

Oh, it was wonderful, it was grand. Stephens was an All-American, the most valuable player for the Gophers and the MVP of the Big Ten. Stephens was so magnetic, such a household treasure, that he has virtually blotted out the names of his immediate predecessor and successor, Jim Reese and Duane Blaska, respectively.

"And tragedy," Rustad is saying. "The thrust of the book, the film, is what happened to Sandy after he left school."

"Never really got a chance to perform," Stephens is saying. "The New York Titans drafted me No. 1 and honest, they were going to call me Broadway Sandy. But the Titans wouldn't put any money in escrow for me. They were going broke. The Cleveland Browns drafted me and Ernie Davis right off the bat, I was drafted before Roman Gabriel and John Hadl. The Browns wanted no part of me as quarterback. I went to Canada."

It didn't last long. Sandy Stephens played for the Montreal Alouettes in 1962 and part of 1963 before he was waived to the Toronto Argonauts for $250. He finished the 1963 season at Toronto, was cut the following summer and then ... drifted, rolled about in the sea of the real world, two divorces, a dozen jobs, no place to call home.

He came dangerously close to fulfilling the cruelest sterotype, too, the college hero standing on a street corner with cheap wine in a paper sack. He has pulled himself up in time, always.

Sandy Stephens graduated Friday from a Control Data training program that will enable him to sell the firm's educational computers. He was talking about his new job the other afternoon in a saloon across the street from Control Data in Edina. He is still a chunky man, well-tailored and immensely proud, perhaps happy for the first time in years. The Control Data job is the best deal he has ever had in Minnesota.

"I came back to Minneapolis for good last May," Stephens said. "It's always been a real home. I moved my entire family from Pennsylvania to Minneapolis in 1965 and both my parents passed away in Minneapolis. I looked around and started with Control Data just a month ago. Now I'm ready to go out on the job, with my field manager at first, but then on my own."

He has been everywhere in the sea of the real world. In the mid 1960s he completed a degree in philosophy at Minnesota and worked as a real estate agent and a loan officer for a mortgage company in Minneapolis.

Most recently he had been in New York. For three years beginning in 1972 he counseled at narcotics addiction centers in Harlem and Brooklyn. By 1975 he was working with a firm that represented actors and athletes in contract negotiations and it got him to thinking about his own spoiled career. He was in a bar in Manhattan one night when he met a guy named Tony Brown.

"He had a television show in New York called Tony Brown's Journal," Sandy said. "He put together a profile of me and my career. It was nice. It made me want to get everything together and get back home, to Minneapolis. It was a hell of a four years when I was a Gopher, the greatest, memorable. I want to recapture something of that time, something sensible. I want to be a success in this community."

"Do you feel you are owed something?" Stephens was asked.

"Not a thing," he said. "I fulfilled all my dreams by playing quarterback at Minnesota. That's what people failed to understand. I thought that was it. Then I looked up at the end of college and there were the pros and a whole other dream presented itself. I felt I broke barriers at Minnesota. Other blacks were marching in the streets and I thought they were the bravest people in the world. I was doing my bit playing quarterback. But I was isolated here in Minnesota, didn't realize that."

Until he got out into the sea of the real world. Among other things Stephens discovered in the real world was that his popularity in the black population was overwhelming. A man came up to Stephens on a Kansas City street corner once and told him that he had named his son after him. Other people have stopped him and recited his high school statistics to him. It was incredible. And he wasn't prepared for it, not by the gilded environment created for him up here in Isolationville.

Stephens played well enough at Montreal, 1,542 yards gained on 109 completions in 1962. He was playing at 228 pounds, or three more pounds than his Rose Bowl weight. Montreal's new coach in 1963, Jim Trimble, ordered Stephens to get down to 220. Stephens got to 217 and Trimble wanted him at 210.

"I said no," Stephens said. "Where would it stop? I was always heavy. I weighed 205 in high school."

He was waived. Toronto offered no explanation for cutting Stephens before the 1964 season and no other teams attempted to claim him. Stephens was back in Minneapolis in September 1964 when he wrapped his car around a tree on the Nokomis Pkwy. He wasn't expected to live and when he did he wasn't expected to walk.

"It was after a Vikings game," Stephens said. "It was after a party with some of the Vikings and, yeah, I was going too fast. My lung was collapsed. I've still got a steel plate in my left arm. I was out of football completely in 1965. Earl Battey and I had a bar on Selby Av. in St. Paul, the Celebrity Lounge. I ran that pretty much through the spring of 1968."

Because Bill Kilmer had come back from a similar auto accident and because Sandy Stephens felt he had something to prove, he did not forget football. He worked out with his friends, Bobby Bell, Carl Eller, Jim Marshall, the guys Stephens credits for always being there when he was on the verge of the cruel stereotype. In 1966 Warmath took an interest and clocked Stephens at various distances on a running track and sent the times to the Kansas City Chiefs, where Bell was a player.

"In the summer of 1966 Bobby Bell and I drove to Kansas City together," Stephens said. "I had a tryout. I'd be standing around throwing 70-yard passes to guys like Otis Taylor. Hank Stram was impressed enough to sign me for the taxi squad. For the 1967 season

Stram told me to come to camp as a quarterback. I mean I'm fired up now. I came back at 220 and I was ready."

"What happened?"

"The Chiefs traded a backup quarterback, Pete Bearhard, to Houston," Stephens said, "and replaced him with a guy named Jacky Lee. Jacky Lee. Jacky Lee couldn't stand up, his knees were so bad. I got the message. I was cut in the spring of 1968 and that's it, no more football for me. I'll always know that I had the respect of players, in college and in the pros. I was close to all the guys on the Gopher team. I'm happy for Joe Salem, Smokey Joe. They used to call him the people's choice and they used to call me the crowd pleaser."

Stephens was by necessity controversial — a black quarterback in the pros. It was not only novel that he played quarterback, but it was shocking that he would not obey orders to lose more weight. But Stephens knew himself well. His character, he said, comes from Warmath. Murray Warmath was hung in effigy all over this town in 1959 when the Gophers were going 2-7 in Stephens' first season as a starter.

"Warmath took a lot of grief," Stephens said of that time, "but he never said a word, not a word to his players. But we knew. Me and Judge Dickson (Stephens's roommate and fellow Pennsylvanian) used to talk about it all the time and how we had to turn things around. I would have done anything for Warmath. He let me call my own plays. He had faith in me and we did turn it around. See, there was a point in my life where I learned never to give up. And I've lived by that."

His new team is computers. That's the way Sandy Stephens puts it and you believe him. He will give this his best shot. In his spare time the push is on for the book and the film and the whole long story to come out at last.

"The same kind of thing as 'Brian's Song'," he said. "But I don't die."

Bobby Clarke

May 11, 1980

The last word about it: If a hockey club is to win the Stanley Cup, that club must have on its roster a player capable of limitless effort and vision. The Veteran. He should be a veteran of the Cup wars, but young enough to remember that sacrifice is a learning process and requires tolerance.

The Veteran works harder than anybody else on the team, but he never points out how hard he does work. He doesn't have to. Younger players have no choice but to follow his lead because the wrath of a scorned coach does not compare with the wrath of a scorned veteran.

The Veteran has an ironic reputation. It will be said of him that he does not possess natural elegance and style, but more than makes up for his weaknesses with hustle. Look again. Desire does not preclude ability. He is the Veteran because he has learned to combine the two and achieve that rare and limitless effort.

The Veteran is first over the boards in good times and bad, in penalty-killing situations and power plays. Long ago he was told that luck often takes the long way home; you make your luck by never letting up. Nobody puts on the pressure like the Veteran.

The Veteran does not retain an agent to negotiate his contract. The Veteran walks into the owner's office and the owner says, "Where is your agent?"

"I don't need one," the Veteran says. "I know what I want and this is the figure."

"You got it," the owner says, "but you know you're worth more, much more."

"If you pay me more," the Veteran says, "there won't be enough for the other guys. There won't be enough to get the players to win the Cup."

Can such a conversation take place in professional sports? It has. You can believe it has.

The Veteran is always the first one to take a rookie under his wing. The Veteran is not above chicanery and hazing, but he is there to open up his own home to the rookie.

When a rookie comes up short and needs some money, he turns to the Veteran. The Veteran has made it clear that everything he has is to be shared.

The Veteran is always the first one to the hospital after a teammate suffers a serious injury. The Veteran doesn't just visit the player and tell him everything will work out for him. The Veteran arranges to sleep in the hospital so he might see the player through the tough times. Then, when the player wakes up, the Veteran is there to tell him everything will work out. And it will. The Veteran said so.

The involvement of the Veteran in his own community can be documented, but it is impossible to get the Veteran to admit as much. Because people have become hardened in many respects toward professional athletes, the Veteran retains a brusque manner. This can be penetrated in about 30 seconds. The Veteran is just protecting his interests.

The Veteran will go so far as to oversee the courtship of younger players on the team. This is not as far-fetched as it sounds. The Veteran is constantly alert for any influences that might disrupt the purpose of his club and, having succeeded with his own family, he will dispense domestic advice to those younger players who need it.

The Veteran doesn't wear a helmet. This is probably more the design of function than bravery. If the Veteran feels he plays better without a helmet, then his own safety becomes secondary to his cause.

The Veteran will buy his teammates a beer. More importantly, he will make sure his teammates drink their beer together.

More often than not, the Veteran is the first player on the ice, even for an optional workout.

The last word about it: If a hockey club is going to win the Stanley Cup, it needs a Veteran.

It needs a Bobby Clarke.

Mark Fidrych

August 22, 1980

Back when the analysts were having their way with him and he was putting nearly a million customers into American League ball parks, back in the ancient age of 1976, Mark Fidrych was the hottest act in show business.

On his income tax forms he was forced to record his profession as baseball pitcher with the Detroit Tigers, but this was a bald lie because Mark Fidrych had become a professional folk hero in one short, unforgettable, sweet summer.

He came out of Worcester, Mass., talking this beautiful accent of the New England street. He loved to drive his cah to the pahk when he could drool tobacco juice down his jersey front in order to parody the veteran ballplayers who regarded him with astonishment.

The kid loved ball. He was into it. He sculpted the mound and ran to and fro congratulating his teammates for flashy plays. Beyond these minor eccentricities was the shocking discovery that Mark Fidrych engaged in brief, but perfectly distinct soliloquies.

We all have memories of him from that glorious time, when he reached out and performed, really performed, and the ringlets of his bushy, bushy blond hair flew beneath his cap and he whispered love notes to the ball and he stood there on the mound in the haze of summer and we screamed for more.

Well, why do the good die young? And if they do not die, why do they suddenly and inexplicably develop mysterious injuries in the rotator cuff muscle? It is a measure of the current tour of blow-combed baseball players that not a one of them in four years has been able to displace Fidrych as the most delightful freak ever to wear doubleknit garments.

He is back up now, from Evansville in Triple A where he was 6-7 with a 3.92 ERA this summer. He will pitch for the Tigers tonight against the Twins. On Thursday he played pepper behind the batting cage. A day's growth of beard bristled golden in the late sun, framing a 26-year-old face that has seen pain and pleasure. We are talking about a face that knew how to smile with something on it.

"I don't goof around as much," Fidrych said yesterday. "I mean I think more before I goof around so I don't get hurt again. I've slowed down a little."

Fidrych is not exactly bad currency, but he is a bad bet. Will he ever regain the form that earned him a 19-9 record and Rookie of the Year honors in 1976? He doesn't know.

"I feel good that I'm playin'," Fidrych was saying now. "It's something I've done all my life and I love to play. But, hell, I haven't been playin' as much as I've been around, know what I mean?"

Oh yeah. And ain't that some sweet music, some sharp irony. Go over it real quick and it doesn't hurt as much. He wrecked a knee shagging balls in the outfield during spring training in 1977. He recovered. He had a 6-2 record by midsummer that year when he complained of stiffness in his shoulder. He never pitched another inning that year. He got off to a 2-0 start in 1978 when the stiffness mugged him again. He went off and on the disabled list, he got his shoulder manipulated by a big shot doctor in New York. He went down to the minors.

There is more. Fidrych made it back to the bigs last year and started his first game, here in Minnesota, on May 5. By May 23 he was gone again and this time entered the Sports Injury Rehabilitation and Research Clinic in San Diego.

"That wasn't so bad," Fidrych said, "they had people pushing you at the critical time, they understood the injury and they knew how to push you."

"What was the technical name of the injury?" Fidrych was asked.

"Tendinitis is about as technical as I figure," he said, "that rotator cuff jazz."

By the autumn of last year he was pitching in the Florida Instructional League, but in spring training he was dispatched to Evansville.

"No doctors were watchin' over me or nothin' like that," Fidrych was saying now. "I just came to the ball park and I pitched. I feel OK. And I never did have surgery."

Fidrych was called up August 8, greeted by Sparky Anderson, the new Tiger manager. Sparky Anderson loves baseball. He loves a ball player. He loved what he saw when the Bird pitched a few days back against Boston. The Bird lost that game but he had flashes of brilliance.

"Fidrych is a throwback to the old days," Anderson was saying before last night's game. "He came out of a middle class background, middle class at the very best, you understand. He has some values. He has something in him that tells him it is important to finish what he started. Those kind of guys always have a chance to rebound. I think the kid can look at himself in a mirror and the truth will not shame him."

That is nice stuff, powerful stuff and George Anderson means every word of it. George Anderson came out of Bridgeport, S.D., on the low end of looking up. He might have seen something in the kid that the rest of us overlooked in our swoons. The kid has some guts, he hasn't died yet. According to Anderson, a hero only goes out once, a coward thousands of times.

"Most ballplayers would laugh at that today," Anderson said.

Fidrych is certainly young enough to recapture it all, but the history of injury and disappointment is working against him. He is 0-2 since his recall and his high pitches are getting him in trouble just as they always have. Fidrych made his mark between the lines by making a batter dig his ball out of the depths of the strike zone. When Fidrych gets his ball up it flattens out, it gets tagged.

Keep the ball low, baby. Find your groove again and talk to that pill. Tug your cap. Flap your arms. Come all the way back and take your bows. Please.

10/The Minnesota Twins

Rod Carew

July 1, 1977

I had settled, even as the trumpet sounded the charge of this new baseball campaign, into the complacent assumption that Rodney Cline Carew could not fix us with any larger excitement than another season in which he would earn another championship silver bat for another lofty decimal around the .330 mark.

Then June arrived and on its first summery night, at approximately 10:30 p.m., in the bottom of the ninth against the Yankees, Carew slapped a deadly accurate single to left to score Jerry Terrell and Butch Wynegar and put a 4-3 victory on the scoreboard. Standing ovation No. 1 was recorded in memory as Carew sprinted, head down, arms and hands swinging robot style, into first base.

That ovation, like the smatterings of inadequate appreciation in the 10 seasons that preceded it, needed work. Carew was hitting .365 as of May 31. We were used to that. As his average flirted with .400 the ovations were automatic upon each of his arrivals at the plate and they improved with consistency and the boisterous ingredients of additional clients until they were like hallelujah choruses shouted to the heavens.

On Sunday last, before the largest congregation ever assembled for a regular-season game at the Met, Carew hopped from .396 to .403 and during the best of the month's Standing 0's (No. 38 or 43; the count is lost) he removed his cap. Later, after a home run, he emerged from the dugout for a howdy and a look-see.

Carew once said that hitting a baseball, and thinking about hitting a baseball, is the loneliest occupation in the world. He might appear a pathetic anachronism if his impeccable physical training, intense study of each new pitcher that comes along and hard singular purpose in life did not produce such glorious results.

Carew has no other burning intentions in life except, perhaps, to mount a golden glove next to the silver bats in his recreation room. He does not endorse politicians. He does not sing, woefully, of aftershaves or discuss, insincerely, the virtues of this popcorn popper over that. He did do an All-Star game commercial for major-league baseball during spring training and while a Reggie or a Rose or a Seaver could snap the same lines off in minutes, Carew took longer at it.

He is not unsuited to such tasks. He is a perfectionist.

For many years in Minnesota the word around the ballpark was that Carew was sullen, moody, childlike, immature, moody again and reserved apart from the normal bounds of clubhouse chicanery. Ted Williams, it says here, wasn't a standup comedian either, but how would you feel if the only thing you wanted, the only thing, was to consistently hit a baseball better than any other man?

Finally, in this month of standing ovations and tipped caps we have come to appreciate him on his terms for the only work he has ever wanted to do. That we are able to recognize him as the truest baseball star, and appreciate how delicately his accomplishments are balanced with the word "impossible", seems as great an excitement as one of his doubles off the wall.

The rest of the baseball country seems curiously out of focus with his magnitude, but then the rest of the baseball country may find it difficult to believe that here, in the hinterland, surrounded by gems of lesser brilliance, a purist remains.

The other day, as if news of Carew's prowess had rarely traveled east or west before, Sports Illustrated, Time, Newsweek, the Cincinnati Enquirer, People Magazine, the Washington Post and Los Angeles Times dispatched correspondents and photographers to package Carew for immediate consumption.

For Sports Illustrated, Carew and the photographer spent an hour in a makeshift studio amid gasoline cans and tractors in a machine shed under the stadium. Carew posed patiently. He waited calmly while lights were rearranged. A dab of sweat was removed from his chin. Click. Again. Click. Again. For an hour.

"For the magazine's cover?" I asked the photographer.

"If I'm still hitting .400," Carew answered.

And then another round of questions, each interrogator assuming that only he was quick enough to ask if all the pressure is getting to Carew yet.

"My life's in a shambles," Carew said when he was finally alone in the locker room. He allowed himself to laugh. "I've got to go incognito on the road," he said. "I've got to ask Gene (Mauch) if I can bring my blue jeans on the road. Put on those jeans and get away from the hotel. I can't let this stuff get to me."

"Why, you don't sound appropriately flattered," I said.

"I'm not," Carew said. "It's nice, it's fine. But the greatest thrill I've had lately is hearing these home crowds cheering. They know. They know and I know that the greatest thing is to be recognized by them. They know."

"Roger Maris had trouble handling the pressure the year he hit 61 homers," I said.

"I can believe that," Carew said. "I'd rather hit than walk. I'd rather play baseball than have my picture taken."

Major-league baseball does not keep month-by-month records of its most notable hitters, so here, for posterity, is Carew's box score for the month of June 1977.
- Hits: 54
- Plate appearances: 113
- Monthly average: .486
- Streaks: Hit safely in 26 of 28 games
- Ovations: Many.
- Peaceful days: None.
- Manager's comment: "I've never seen any one like him in my life."

Nov. 13, 1977

Rod Carew turned up the collar of his overcoat against the snow and wind the other morning when he walked through downtown to meet a man for breakfast in a hotel. The man wanted to visit Carew in his home, in the den with the silver bats, but workmen are adding rooms to Carew's house, and his biographer is in town, and the phone is ringing off the hook because of what Carew did on the baseball field last summer.

"I'm baby-sitting a lot now, too," Carew said, "and talking into a tape recorder about my life."

Carew, finally and irrefutably, became a national hero when he batted an astonishing .486 during the month of June. When he finished the year at .388 for his sixth batting title, he was the first man to reach that high-water mark since Ted Williams in 1957.

Carew has been in demand. But the most important interruption in the off-season should occur Wednesday, when Jack Lang, secretary of the Baseball Writers Association of America, calls Tom Mee, public relations director for the Twins, with the vote total for the American League's Most Valuable Player award.

Mee would have the honor of informing Carew of his selection. At least that's the way it worked when Zoilo Versalles became Minnesota's first MVP in 1965 and Harmon Killebrew became the second and last Minnesota MVP in 1969. Carew should be the third. If he isn't, baseball should either abolish the award or give eye examinations to each of the 28 American League baseball writers who decide such honors. Carew's average was remarkable, but his 239 hits were more than any player since Bill Terry established the major league record of 254 hits in 1930. Carew also drove in 100 runs for the first time in his career and scored more runs, 128, than any other player in the league. What more could he have done?

"Win," Carew said. "Maybe I'm at the wrong place at the wrong time for the award. Besides, I didn't gear myself to winning the MVP. My statistics were incidental to that. I did gear myself to winning the Gold Glove award, and I want that badly. I know I can hit and score runs."

The votes have been in since midnight of the last day of the regular season, so the man across the breakfast table speculated that Reggie Jackson's three home runs in the final World Series game came too late to help him in the voting. Despite their differences in life styles and winter fashions (Reggie prefers seal skin or some such), Jackson tends to regard Carew as he would someone who left the dance with his woman.

"I heard that some of the Yankees said I shouldn't get the MVP because I didn't play on a winning team," Carew said. "Reggie shouldn't get it. Reggie Jackson can't carry my jock on a baseball field."

"George Foster (the National League's MVP) didn't play on a pennant-winning team," the man said.

"Yes," Carew said, "but you've got to remember that he just played for two straight championship teams."

Perhaps Carew has a right to expect defeat. Again. In 1974, when Carew hit .364 for his fourth batting title, the MVP went to Jeff Burroughs, then with a Texas club that finished second, three games behind Oakland. Burroughs hit .301 that year with 25 homers and 188 runs batted in.

The next summer, when Carew hit .359 for his fifth crown, every major award on the planet went to Boston's rookie wonder boy, Fred Lynn, who had superlative stats — .331 average; 21 homers; 105 RBIs — but, more importantly perhaps, played for a pennant-winning team that left clients around the league breathless with excitement.

"If I was voting," Carew said, "I'd have to look at myself, Al Cowens, Mickey Rivers, Jim Rice and Ken Singleton."

The voters couldn't take it into consideration, but Rod Carew, had he chosen to become a free agent, could easily have established a major league record for most money paid to a ballplayer at an auction. But Carew signed a three-year contract before the start of the 1976 season, and his next contract most likely will keep him in Minnesota, even as the opportunity for a pennant grows weaker each passing day.

"I can't blame Hisle and Bostock and those guys for wanting more money," Carew said, "but one guy going to a new team won't turn it into a pennant winner. We didn't have Bill Campbell or Steve Braun this summer and we still created excitement. We weren't dead. If we could keep Hisle and Bostock, we'd still have the nucleus of a winning team, a pennant team."

"Yeah," the man said, "but even your manager might cop."

"Gene Mauch is a perfectionist," Carew said. "The guy is like Beethoven or Michelangelo, a perfectionist. I understand his point. If he feels he can't win, and he enjoys a win more than any manager I've played for, then he probably won't be back."

Carew seems unconcerned by the recent developments, including the impending MVP announcement. It must be a giddy feeling to be entering your athletic prime at the age of 32. Few other baseball players can make that claim, but Carew takes care of himself with such precision that he is convinced he will play long enough to win a pennant and enjoy a World Series.

"I've grown," Carew said. "When I was younger I played when I felt like it and didn't play when I didn't feel like it. I've gotten over that. You got enough?"

"Yes," the man said, "and I'll bet you win the MVP."

"I wouldn't bet," Carew said, and he laughed at himself heading back out into the cold.

Jan. 7, 1979

We have a genuine feet-up-on-the-desk hot stove dilemma on the local baseball front. Sad to say, but no less true, is the future departure of Rod Carew for richer baseball waters.

Maybe not this month. Maybe not this summer. But Carew is leaving the Twins as surely as Pete Rose left Cincinnati with a "for sale" sign around his neck.

It doesn't have to be, at least for the sake of argument. Despite the bickering between Calvin Griffith and Carew, and forgetting for the moment Calvin's gauche exterior, this is a drama without hero or villain.

Calvin's severest critic probably believes him when he says he can't afford the $3.5 million package that apparently would retain Carew's services for five years. But Carew already has turned down that same figure from San Francisco, which he will visit Monday, so reluctantly it seems, that he will leave his heart in Minnesota.

We know well of the penurious Griffith's behavior. But what are we to make of Carew's sentimental wavering? Carew is practically crying out for Griffith to take advantage of him.

"I'm not trying to be another Pete Rose," Carew said the other day. "I've been underpaid for so many years now that it no longer bothers me. I want to be paid well, but I've been willing to make concessions. I've been willing to take less money than people think."

There is only one way Carew can remain in Minnesota. He can sign a contract with the Twins that will not make him the highest-paid player in baseball. No one doubts that Carew deserves that distinction and no one doubts that Carew could fatten his bank account by playing elsewhere.

But Carew is unique among superstars. He does not need the glimmer of Broadway or the Golden Gate Bridge to sustain what is, by Carew's admission, one of the most comfortable and contented lifestyles ever enjoyed by a sporting man of his stature.

It's an uncomfortable proposal, this seemingly cavalier way of advising an athlete to settle for less when he knows he could get more. But if a proper number of developments clicked into place and attitudes became more clearly defined on both sides, Carew could turn his salary negotiations into a matter of the heart, a rare enough thing in itself these days, but not without precedent.

Even if Carew was convinced Calvin couldn't pay $3.5 million, a larger impasse would have to be overcome. At this point in his career, Carew wants and needs to play for a pennant winner. According to Carew's agent, Jerry Simon, it's likely that Carew doesn't play up to potential because he alone shoulders the burden of stardom with the Twins.

Nothing bears this out more clearly than a comparison of Carew's batting averages the last two seasons. In 1977, with Larry Hisle and Lyman Bostock in the line-up, Carew hit .388. Last summer, without those teammates, Carew dropped to .333. He still won another batting title, but he suffered more personal trauma, anxiety and pressure in the process.

Assuming Carew could accept Minnesota's offer of slightly more than $2 million for five years, he would have to make an even more miraculous request of himself. Carew would have to believe that the Twins will win a pennant soon.

Consider the salary question first. Calvin hasn't withdrawn his offer, he has done something worse. He has refused to tinker with it. Still, the question for Carew is whether an additional million dollars plus will compensate Carew for depositing himself in a new environment. It probably will, unless the new environment robs Carew of everything he holds special to him.

Numbers of executives in this town have rejected promotions in order to remain here. Perhaps millions of dollars weren't involved in the decision, but priorities line up very sharply when a man or woman has the luxury of choice.

Convincing himself the Twins could win a pennant would be the toughest part of Carew's decision. Calvin is not to be trusted with any predictions in that regard. But Gene Mauch is. When Mauch re-upped with the Twins last summer, there had to be something in it for him besides money. Mauch must be reasonably certain that he can pull Calvin's strings, even though everything in Calvin's record says otherwise.

Mauch's confidence helped to keep Mike Marshall a Twin, Marshall being a most recent example of a man who negotiated with his heart. He could have received more money from other teams, but those other teams didn't have Mauch, a man for whom Marshall would pitch on Saturn, or on a spaceship en route there.

Serious baseball fans also have a stake in Carew's decision. Calvin can almost become a hero by bartering Carew for a gang of eager young talent, a development that would have to be concluded before the end of next season. The pressure is on both parties. There is only one way Carew can remain a Twin. And if he does so, the money involved will go against the rules of nature. It will not talk.

Feb. 7, 1979

Trading Rod Carew to the California Angels for Paul Hartzell, Ken Landreaux, Brad Havens and Dave Engle was like trading Laurence Olivier for the Marx Brothers.

The sweetest hitter in baseball finally will get the cash he deserves, but there is a part of him that must be filled with embarrassment. Calvin Griffith should have gotten the moon and the rights to Venus for Carew.

About the best you can say to date for Hartzell is that he cuts a fine figure in baseball garments. Landreaux was a star in the dust leagues of Texas, but he didn't wear out major league pitching last season.

Havens, a pitcher, and Engle, a catcher-third baseman, are what baseball people call prospects. Suspects is more like it, but baseball people have huge imaginations when it comes to selling the clients a bill of goods, and we have just been sold one of those magnificent real-estate deals that turns out to be tumbleweed and sand.

Griffith settled for a second-rate deal rather than letting Carew play out his option this season. When the bartering with the Yankees was terminated, Griffith felt pressured into the California trade and he accepted, sheepishly you would think. As obstinate as Griffith is, he remembered that Larry Hisle, Lyman Bostock and Bill Campbell were among a dozen players the Twins lost in the free-agent auction over the last two years, and Griffith was determined to get something for his greatest star, even the Marx Brothers.

In many corners Griffith's decision is praised as a blessing of relief. But it says here the wrong motives forced the Carew trade, that Griffith, who has pretended to be an owner for so long, finally made a trade to see what being a real owner feels like. Until he traded Dan Ford to the Angels in December, Griffith hadn't made a trade since 1976, and now he has managed to lose the club's two best hitters to a team in his own division, where they will have sufficient opportunity to haunt him.

Trading Carew for the packages assembled by the Giants or Yankees would have been acceptable maneuvers, given the inevitability of Carew playing out his option. Carew felt he wasn't given enough time to contemplate a move to San Francisco, and Griffith dallied too long on the Yankee swap. Besides, Carew apparently had offended the Yankee owner, George Steinbrenner.

Griffith traded Carew to wash his hands of him and now he has a poorer ball club because of it. Even in the best of trades Carew is irreplaceable, and that's what hurts most about this deal. Carew was the one Twin who should have been satisfied year by year. He is one of only a handful of players who transcend the field. He came to represent the team as its only established star and spokesman.

Paying Carew what he deserved and building around him would have made more sense than dealing him for four essentially unknown players, two of whom (rookies Havens and Engle) don't even stand a good chance of making the team. Can Hartzell — a pitcher with six wins and 10 losses last season — replace Carew? Can Ken Landreaux, a .223 hitter, replace Carew? That's the trade Griffith made, and it doesn't work.

Gene Mauch will have to try Ron Jackson at first base. Landreaux will be given a crack at left field and Willie Norwood, who is something less than an all-star, will shag balls in center field. This trade was constructed so poorly that the Twins failed to strengthen themselves in either defense or hitting, and pitching was not a priority item.

As well as being the game's best hitter, Carew was developing rapidly into the league's flashiest first baseman.

Carew was right in forcing the decision. If the Twins hadn't traded him he would have played out his option, but that did not preclude the possibility of Carew continuing to negotiate with the Twins for a proper salary.

But it's too late. The ticket windows are open in California. They're open at the Met, too.

April 18, 1979

Rod Carew was in the enemy clubhouse Tuesday afternoon preparing his cheek for baseball. He selected a major league chunk of Red Man, basket weaved it with several sticks of chewing gum, hoisted the mess and then worked at it until every last strand of dangling tobacco had disappeared into the right cavity of his jaw. It was a league-leading performance, and while others may miss Carew's hitting or his slick fielding, this ancient and messy ritual of the chaw has been removed to California as well.

"No quotes," Carew said. "My lips are sealed."

Thus fortified and barely able to speak for the lump in his trap, Rod Carew entered the Metropolitan Stadium field for the first time in the gray doubleknits of the road team.

Only a sprinkling of fans, treated to marching music and a team of wandering jugglers, had gathered in the morning sunlight. They called out to Rod Carew. He busied himself with pregame chores, trying to outmaneuver the gang of reporters who finally corralled him near the batting cage. It suddenly struck the assembled that almost everything had already been asked of Rod Carew, over the long winter, into the spring and upon his arrival in Minnesota Monday.

"Will you hit .400 this year?" somebody asked him.

Carew chose not to believe he had heard such a question.

The parking lots around the ballpark were crowded with activity even before noon yesterday. Tailgaters and back-yard baseball stars were out in force. Out behind the batter's eye, in a picnic ground beyond center field, the Save the Met organization offered beer to passers-by.

When he wasn't saving the Met recently, the group's leader, Julian Empson, lobbied Calvin Griffith to retire Rod Carew's No. 29 on opening day.

"Calvin said there wasn't enough time," Empson said. "Maybe he'll do it later in the year. When he needs a crowd. But we did get the Senate to pass a resolution naming this Rod Carew Day in Minnesota."

It was impossible to determine, from casual listening and casual asking, whether Carew alone was responsible for yesterday's gate. After all, the Twins broke to a 7-2 start on the road, the sunshine was brilliant, the sky blue.

And yet... When Carew was introduced, 37,270 celebrants rose in a standing ovation that finally moved Carew to doff his cap to all corners of the park and then use a microphone at home plate to thank the fans for his 12 years in Minnesota.

Two Angels, Brian Downing and Carney Lansford, had better averages than Carew's .368 entering the game and Minnesota's Roy Smalley was batting .400, but the pure joy of witnessing him in the flesh once again earned Carew standing ovations throughout the afternoon.

It wasn't until the eighth inning, facing Pete Redfern, that Carew got his first hit of the game, a single to left. Disinterest had become fashionable by then, what with the Angels leading 6-0. Dave Goltz had handled his former teammate admirably in three appearances until Goltz cracked in the fifth.

But one of Carew's new joys, not discounting his millions of dollars, is batting in front of hitters like Don Baylor and Joe Rudi. Carew may be the star of the Angels but he doesn't necessarily have to stir the drink.

His teammates reminded Carew's visitors afterward that he only had one hit. This was a looser Carew now, switching from his pregame reticences to postgame frivolity that comes with winning. The burden of his first return home had gone smoothly and now in the Angels clubhouse, dressed in a red union suit, he allowed himself words.

"I don't want to get any letters or notes from people," Carew said, "but we kicked their butts. We sent a lot of people home unhappy. If pitchers keep worrying about me it just makes it easier for our other guys."

"Was this an emotional day for you?" Carew was asked.

"I had butterflies," Carew said, "but I wasn't emotional about it. It was over for me here at the All Pro sports banquet last winter."

A man persisted. "But you must have wondered how the crowd would react to you?"

"They can boo me or they can cheer me," Carew said. "I can't worry about that. They booed me for four days in Seattle. There's always a few people who think you jump to the greener pastures. The people here knew I gave them 12 years of good baseball."

Carew, removed of his tremendous chaw, said he had to go. He had to feed his dogs, who haven't yet made the trip from Minnesota to California.

"I wish the Twins luck," he said. "I just hope they don't finish ahead of us."

The home club quarters were quieter. Dave Goltz had no explanation for his success with Carew. The manager, Gene Mauch, just smiled when it was suggested that by Carew's standards he had suffered an off day at the plate.

"Over a period of years," Mauch said, "I guess you could say one for four is a bad day for Rodney."

Aug. 17, 1980

Rod Carew, the erstwhile favorite son and perennial American League batting titlist, woke up one day a couple of weeks ago and discovered that even when he did not speak, his check from the California Angels was still delivered on time. This was an amazing discovery.

Carew buttoned his lip one night at the ballpark, didn't make a peep, and still was able to hit the ball in his consistent fashion. Furthermore, his name appeared in the box score the next morning.

This was too good to be true. The formation of words puts a great strain on the larynx and Carew might have remained mute the rest of his days except that verbal communication is practically a law in

California at places like the filling station and the haberdasher.

Imagine the difficulty in acquiring a nice hat, for example, if the clerk insists that you look perfect in a straw boater.

Carew had to make a choice. He would have to talk away from the job, but once he got to the ballpark he could make like Harpo Marx and leave them guessing. Them would be the representatives of newspapers, many of whom were placed on earth to misquote Carew and those of his strata who have decided to plead the Fifth Amendment.

The Fifth has generally been favored by thieves and other malcontents so it probably makes sense that baseball players have become constitutional experts on the matter of silence.

When Carew arrived in town for this weekend's entertainment against the Twins, he was greeted at his clubhouse by a noted Carew apologist of long standing. I can't help it. There is a long distance between singular achievements in any sport so I am attracted to any performer who has won seven batting titles and might be working on an eighth this season.

"So you're not talking to the press at all?" I said.

"Saves me a lot of trouble," Carew said. "It's just simpler this way."

"And this is it forever? I mean, you won't talk to the press even when you make the Hall of Fame?"

"Not even when I get to Cooperstown," Carew said.

"Sid Hartman must have your number."

"Not even Sid," Rodney said. "Only my mother and my sister-in-law have my new number."

It had become apparent to me that Carew was able to speak and that words were formed without difficulty. I pressed on, mentioning that as of that moment only George Brett, at .391, and Cecil Cooper, at .344, were ahead of him in the batting race. Carew, at .338, was ahead of Buddy Bell (.332), Willie Wilson (.332) and Fred Lynn (.317), and none of these fellows ever had won a batting title and could not — would not — be considered serious challengers for the silver bat.

"What am I worried about?" Carew said. "I've got seven of them. I don't get juiced up about it. I play my game and I've been consistent. My worrying days are over."

At this point I was invited to Carew's locker and a delightful conversation ensued, mostly about the playground he had built for his children at his new home, a fantastic paint job he got for his car and his curiosities about various local characters he had known.

Like most athletes who do so, Carew did not enjoy having to adopt a policy of silence. At least he said he did not. About 10 days ago when he bopped a home run off Al Williams to beat the Twins in the 15th inning, Carew would have enjoyed the discussion. He could not believe that he had been thrown a fat curve on Williams' first pitch and when the second came in just as fat, he launched it.

Overtime was over. But policy is policy and Carew will not talk; the realities of his new wealth, in combination with a press corps slightly more vigorous than what he was accustomed to, made it seem impossible for him to discuss baseball between the lines. And earlier this season he insisted that remarks he had made about the fans in California and around the league had been taken out of context. So he made a policy.

Carew was pulling on his uniform all the while he talked about not talking. For the last three weeks he has been playing with a hip pointer on the left side and his left thigh is black and blue. He played through the injury, running like a man who had been shot, which might surprise those observers who have occasionally accused Carew of malingering.

"I just grit my teeth," Carew said. He knows. He knows how to drop the timely self-deprecating remark.

No judgment will be made here on the psychological twists that have moved him to seek safety through silence. His own words were probably never that necessary to appreciate what he does best. And at the age of 34 he still is the best hitter in all of baseball.

Spring training

March 5, 1980

Orlando, Fla.

You hate to find out these guys are so nice, these journeyman ballplayers who will not let go. Pete Mackanin had his hand in with the Rangers and the Expos and the Phillies and with a half dozen minor league clubs, but Pete Mackanin has always taken the fall.

Maybe Pete Mackanin will get his chance with the Twins now. He is a bargain and the Twins are a bargain ball club. The Twins traded a bargain pitcher named Paul Thormodsgard to the Phillies last December for Mackanin, a utility infielder coming off arm surgery.

Aside from finding a pitcher to replace Dave Goltz, the Twins badly need a player who can hit with power from the right side and maybe Pete Mackanin is the guy. He hit 12 home runs in 1975 with Montreal, or 10 more than Jose Morales hit last year when Morales was Minnesota's principal designated hitter from the right side.

"Designated hitter?" Pete Mackanin said Tuesday at Tinker Field. "That's fine. I can play all four infield positions too. I could be used when a guy is going into a slump, not just a physical slump, either, but mental slumps. Put me in there."

There was the implication here that the Twins are looking as well for a man who can occasionally spell Roy Smalley at shortstop. Smalley played all 162 games last year and it wore him down. Maybe Pete Mackanin is the man for this job, although a journeyman named Guy Sularz, a bargain acquisition from the San Francisco organization, has the same designs.

Early trials indicate that Mackanin can hit and Sularz can field. It's a good thing each of them can't do both because the Twins would probably unload Smalley, who is not a bargain.

"I don't think the club wants me to play 162 games," Smalley said yesterday, "but now that I've done it I don't want to sit out any games. I like playing better than sitting, but realistically I could use a few days off here and there."

Realistically, a few days here and there is what Pete Mackanin needs to regain his worth. He played hard in Gene Mauch's intersquad game yesterday. Sunshine had returned to Florida and Pete Mackanin played so hard in the heat that streaks of dirt-flecked sweat lined his face. Gene Mauch calls these exercises situation baseball. For a guy like Pete Mackanin, this was survival baseball, even though he has brought with him from Philadelphia the final year of a guaranteed contract.

"How is your arm?" Pete Mackanin was asked. He is 28 and last year he lost a whole season trying to hang on with one hand.

"It's all right," Mackanin said. "The pain that's there, at least it's pain I can understand. That other pain I had, I didn't even know how to describe it."

Last spring, in camp with Philadelphia, Mackanin developed soreness in his right elbow. One day he played two innings at third base and the next day his arm was so swollen he couldn't lift it to brush his teeth. He made the Phillies and he traveled the early part of the year with them, but the trouble in the arm wouldn't let go. In Chicago, in late April, a doctor drained blood from the elbow and gave Mackanin a shot of cortisone. It didn't help. In May he was operated on and the doctor removed two bone spurs.

"Said it was an arthritic condition," Mackanin was saying now. "I didn't get back in uniform until Sept. 1. I had nine at bats last year. Last year was the year the Phillies could have used me. Manny Trillo broke his wrist last year and Larry Bowa broke his thumb. I could have played every day last year."

Pete Mackanin sounds like the name of an everyday player. He thought so, too, when he was drafted out of Brother Rice High School in Chicago in 1969 by the Rangers, who were still the Senators at that point. Mackanin and Smalley both apprenticed for a time under Toby Harrah at Texas but Mackanin was traded to the Expos in 1975.

Gene Mauch used him as a starting second baseman in 130 games.

The next year Karl Keuhl used him at second in 114 games but by 1977, the grip starting to slip, Mackanin was down to 55 games.

"I played in Denver in 1978," Mackanin said, "and I had a great year. I had to have a great year to get back to the big leagues. Then Montreal puts me on waivers and the Phillies, of all teams, the Phillies, claimed me. I wanted to go to a team that needed me. The Phillies had a lineup I wasn't going to crack."

Before his arm went bad, and before the Phillies traded him, Pete Mackanin bought a home outside Philadelphia for his wife and son. A journeyman ballplayer needs one place for all the bills to come to, one place to call home. Pete Mackanin bought the home and he enrolled at Villanova to finish the college education he had begun years before at the University of Illinois, Chicago campus. And then Pete Mackanin got traded.

"So I played ball in Venezuela for two months this winter," Mackanin said. "I couldn't take the chance of coming here with my arm not in shape. It was great in Venezuela. My wife and I wanted to be in the home we just bought and our kid got sick for three weeks. Beautiful. But it worked. My arm feels good. I could play in a game right now."

Because he has had friends who tried and did not make it in the big leagues, Pete Mackanin wants to stick. Because he has seen players in their 30s, players like Champ Summers, finally make it, Pete Mackanin wants to stick. Because he is a ballplayer and he has journeyed all over this country trying to prove it, Pete Mackanin wants to stick.

"And if I fall again," Pete Mackanin said, "I'm not quitting. I'll start over again. Somebody can use me."

March 6, 1980

Orlando, Fla.

It has become the ritual of Gene Mauch's baseball camp for Mauch to view the springtime frolic from a folding chair behind a screen behind home plate. Four hours were spent in this position Tuesday, another four Wednesday and there is no reason not to expect the same today.

"Situation baseball," Gene Mauch said yesterday, before strolling to his chair. "I love it."

Perhaps Calvin Griffith wishes Mauch would use a batting cage, as these devices tend to keep more baseballs on the property and baseballs cost do-re-mi. But there is a method to Mauch's marathon games of contrived situations. More than most managers, Mauch comes to camp each spring trying to replace an escaped star from the previous season. Because Dave Goltz has defected to the Los Angeles Dodgers, Mauch is studying 19 pitchers, 9 or 10 of whom will stay with the club, and one of whom will theoretically replace Goltz and his 14 victories.

"We won't necessarily replace Goltz," Mauch said yesterday. "We will find someone to step in as a middle-inning reliever. If we find that guy, then Pete Redfern, if he can do it, moves into the starting rotation. Redfern, Darrell Jackson and Goltz won 25 games last year. I want Redfern and Jackson to win 25 this year between them."

Mauch retreated to his chair. He sat in the sun and thought out his plan. If eight of Goltz's 14 wins last year were earned against Toronto, Oakland and Seattle, then it is not far-fetched for Redfern and Jackson to make up slack against these same undernourished clubs. Geoff Zahn and Jerry Koosman and Mike Marshall are locked into their jobs; they don't count in the figuring. Assuming that Paul Hartzell, Roger Erickson and Gary Serum make the club, then Mauch needs a reliever.

"I have a chance of being right," Mauch said yesterday. "I happen to like Doug Corbett. I like him as a relief pitcher. I like a guy with a sinker ball."

Doug Corbett, purchased from Cincinnati's AAA club at Indianapolis last December, has pitched well enough in Mauch's situation games to leave an impression. Unlike a lot of pitchers in their first major league camp, Corbett is not afraid to let a batter get around on a pitch because chances are it will spin into the dirt. Corbett's sinker is a natural pitch off his fast ball; the ball comes in fat and in the strike zone and then takes a dive. Beautiful. A pitch like this is like money in the bank.

"I like sinker ball pitchers that trust their stuff," Mauch said. "If Corbett gets hit, he gets hit, but he still trusts his stuff. We'll see."

Corbett, 27, is another bargain that Calvin Griffith got by shopping downstairs. For five years Corbett worked for Kansas City and then Cincinnati without once getting invited to a major league training camp. Cincinnati left him unprotected in 1978 and Corbett went unclaimed.

Last year at Indianapolis he appeared in 69 games and had a 2.95 earned run average, third best in the American Association. He also secured permission from the Reds to play ball in Puerto Rico this winter, for Cal Ermer's team. When Cincinnati left Corbett unprotected again, Ermer recommended that the Twins buy him.

"Cincinnati had me on the shelf," Corbett said yesterday. "I was stuck in the old Catch-22. They didn't bring me up because I didn't have experience, and I couldn't get major league experience to get brought up."

"Mauch seems to think you might fit into his plans," a man said.

"I'm going to force myself into his plans," Corbett said. "I think because I have that label of release on me, I've had to prove myself twice at every level. Now I'll have to prove myself twice at this level."

Corbett was born and raised in Sarasota, Fla., and attended the University of Florida, where he got a degree in physical education. When he left college Corbett allowed himself two years to make a major league roster. There are a lot of guys who do this, a lot of guys who do this before they develop a curve ball or a change-up. Corbett was one of these guys and he learned. Two years became four and then five.

"It got to the point," Corbett was saying now, "where I wouldn't quit until it was proven to me I couldn't pitch in the big leagues. Well I'm here, and this is the most relaxed atmosphere I've ever been in."

Maybe Corbett is Mauch's find. Maybe not. Mauch likes everybody he sees this time of year, which is why he sits behind a portable backstop four hours a day and thinks.

"I like Bob Veselic, too," Mauch said yesterday. "He has a good curve. I like a guy with a good hook. I like a guy who trusts his stuff."

March 7, 1980

Orlando, Fla.

Something is wrong in spring training. The sun is warm and Tinker Field smells of new paint and there are clients in the seats hooting and cat-calling. But something is wrong with the way things feel.

Even the ballplayers have noticed it and it is not uncommon for ballplayers to go through a workout with about as much spirit as soldiers on a death march.

Feet are dragging. Dust tastes bitter in the mouth. The players are quiet and nothing of very much substance passes for humor.

You would think a ballplayer should be enjoying the time of his life now, when he is young and well-paid. But the ballplayers who choose to make idle conversation are job applicants, nervous and tightly wound. The veterans sound like investment lawyers, arguing the pros and cons of baseball's stalled labor negotiations.

The Twins need a character to come in and do card tricks. They need somebody to stand on the mound and make an elephant appear.

"Roger," said a man to Roger Erickson, "let's sit in the dugout and shoot the bull."

"I kinda thought I'd stay away from that this year," Erickson said. "I think I'd just as soon not talk to anybody."

This can't be. Roger Erickson has the potential to be one of the game's great characters. He looks like he stepped out of a bubblegum card, with his toothy grin and tufts of black hair flying out from under his cap. This was the player who was called Kid Marvel because he was not embarrassed to admit that his deep reading consisted of comic books. This was the kid called Pudge, after his family's nickname for him was dragged out of him. This was the kid whom Calvin Griffith put in the newspaper ads because this kid was going to be a star.

"Let's at least talk about why you don't want to talk," the man said to Erickson. The way Erickson sees it, there was trouble last year and he was injured more deeply than most people thought possible. After all, he was a character, the kid who won 14 games in 1978, his rookie year, and he had become public domain.

But Erickson was pitching in pain last season and when he got off to an 0-7 start he tied the record for ineptitude by a Twins pitcher at the start of a season. And when he couldn't come around with the big club, when his altered pitching delivery did not release the pain in his right elbow, he was shipped to Toledo. Roger Erickson dawdled on the way down. He did not report directly to Toledo.

"He didn't have a bad attitude last year," Gene Mauch said Thursday. "Or if he did have a little problem with his attitude, it didn't develop until after he had a physical problem. There's not a better kid than Erickson. He figures strongly in my plans."

"Maybe he was a one-year wonder, like Jim Hughes," a man said.

"No parallel at all," Mauch said. "A guy like Hughes was a trickster. He was doing it with mirrors. Erickson is all hard work. He doesn't have a strike-out going for him. He throws the ball to be hit and that makes it tough to be a nine-inning pitcher. But he's all work."

Erickson was operated on last October by Dr. Harvey O'Phelan, who scraped the bone area around the ulnar nerve in Erickson's pitching elbow. The problem had developed over the last month and half of Erickson's rookie year. The twinge was there at the start of last season. Constant wear and perhaps overwork by the right arm — Erickson pitched 266 innings in 1978, when he was 21 years old — had created an inflammation of the tendons in the arm and aggravation of the ulnar nerve, the funny bone of the arm.

"He pitched as well as he ever has on Wednesday," Mauch was saying. "Ball was down, ball was alive. Roger will be OK."

But last year Erickson had to change his motion. He was tinkering with a curve ball, as well. Nothing was going right, and when he was sent down to the minors he drove the long way. When he got to Toledo he did not enjoy being on the mound. And then he pulled a muscle in his back and was on the disabled list for three weeks.

Erickson came back up to the Twins at the end of last season and won three games, but he was killing time before the surgery. Over the winter, Erickson couldn't even touch a baseball. He hung around home, rode around with his brother, who had a liquor delivery route.

It says here that Erickson has taken a vow of silence because he began to question the celebrity status that was so willingly given to him. Being an honest man, he also couldn't understand how some of the things he said and did appeared in completely different light on the newspaper pages.

It also says here that this vow of silence will not last. It doesn't have a chance. When Roger Erickson reclaims his health and his slider, he will also reclaim his peace of mind.

He is only 23, and if he is not naturally outgoing, he is at least a curious and innocent soul and it would be a shame if we couldn't share his mysteries with him. There aren't many ballplayers left with a sense of wonder. Erickson won't be quoted on the matter, but he has a sense of wonder and spirit that is desperately needed in this camp. Roger Erickson should loosen up.

March 11, 1980

Orlando, Fla.

Because he and he alone is the master of his own portly being, Mike Marshall has not joined the Minnesota Twins for the communal perspiration of spring training. But Marshall was in uniform Monday, apparently reasoning that if he was to cast his vote in union matters, he was to have been costumed in the uniform of the rank and file.

Marshall and the Twins voted unanimously yesterday to go out on strike on or about April 1 in the event that baseball owners do not come to reason and scrap the proposals currently on the bargaining table. Marvin Miller, director of the Major League Players Association, was present as well but he probably had to slide his words in edgewise what with Marshall on the same platform.

"I have now visited five camps," Miller said after his meeting with the players. "The vote to strike is 196-1."

"The one," Marshall said, "is a Kansas City player who wouldn't vote strike for religious reasons. I don't know his religion."

Witnesses couldn't imagine what business consumed the unionists for two hours yesterday. They held their meeting in the left field bleachers, closed to the public. Baseball management, in this case Gene Mauch and his coaches, watched and waited and scuffed at the dirt from the right field corner. Most of Mauch's comments would have gagged a horse or a censor but some of what he said was important.

"The gains made by ballplayers in the last few years," Mauch said, "would have been made without Miller. I will never be convinced that better working conditions for players couldn't have been made in a more gentlemanly manner. Mr. Miller creates the need for his services and then feeds on it."

Even those remarks are cut with buckets of water. Baseball is the game Mauch loves, and baseball is taking a beating with these publicly aired labor disputes that, in Mauch's estimation, "will be with us every four years until the day we die".

There is a risk of insult in reviewing the issues because more men than not in this country can no longer subsist on annual salaries of $30,000. When you talk labor problems in baseball, you are talking labor problems among men who make an average of $135,000 a year and do not exactly work in the conditions of an open pit mine.

Ray Grebey, during a swing through the Minnesota camp Sunday, said that collective bargaining is a tough game and that both sides should be keeping their mouths shut. No one can deny that Grebey is a partisan observer, but he feels that the baseball labor situation is not in the panic status that Miller would have the public believe it is.

"We have proposed," Grebey said Sunday, "that the baseball free agent system stay in effect exactly the way it is with only slight modification. For a team signing a top-ranking player selected by eight or more teams we have proposed that the team losing that player get the chance to sign a player not on the team's protected list of 15 men."

"What," a man wondered, "would prevent the owners from arranging to have each free agent selected by more than eight teams?"

"That question burns me up," Grebey said. "There is integrity among the owners and if that is a problem that really bothers the players we have proposed to take a different approach. I doubt that we will negotiate compensation away."

Marshall, the Minnesota player representative and the American League's player representative in bargaining sessions between Miller and Grebey, is convinced that management is trying to recapture the gains made by players in the 1976 go-round.

"If we were Teamsters," Marshall said yesterday, "and management came in and said they wanted back the rights we had previously won, they'd get their cars blown up. Management has insulted us. And they've underestimated our strength and unity."

Strong stuff. Marshall is not afraid to speak out. When he says that players will never yield to a salary structure, another proposal offered by management, or any form of compensation for lost free agents, you better believe it. Marshall may be overbearing, but his will is like a steel trap. You cannot cross the man.

"When will you be concerned about fan reaction to baseball's labor problems?" Marshall was asked.

"The fan should realize that we know more about our business than he does," Marshall said. "By all we can account for, salaries represent 27 percent of baseball's revenue. In labor-intensive industry salaries typically represent 50 to 60 percent of revenue."

Remarkably, Marshall will insist that any strike by baseball players will not be over money. It is Marshall's belief that a player will earn his worth in a free and open marketplace. It is the potential shrinking or tightening by the owners of that marketplace that disturbs Marshall. And to Marshall's credit, he has been telling players to temper the kind of stupid remarks that imply that the world owes a ballplayer a living. What Marshall wants is a situation where a player can command his value relative to his profession.

Before Miller left Tinker Field yesterday he said that contrary to management's belief, baseball's old contract will not theoretically remain in effect until a new agreement is signed. Miller said that should management declare an impasse in the current negotiations, management could then take back everything and it would be as though no agreement had ever been reached at anytime between players and owners.

Before he went to a downtown hotel in Orlando to sit in on Miller's meeting with Grebey yesterday, Marshall got in some throwing. He will work out with the club again today. He will return for keeps on March 22, at which time, given his bent for uniquely designed exercises, he will be more fit than most to hoist a picket sign.

March 12, 1980

Orlando, Fla.

I want a ball club. More than anything I want the Twins and I will keep them in Minnesota until the next glacier rolls.

My team plays outdoors, on real grass, at Metropolitan Stadium. Nobody woos me downtown. Nobody insults my intelligence with a domed stadium.

My team gets a new public address system. My team will take batting practice to music, maybe a little Pink Floyd or the Eagles or the Beach Boys. Definitely the Beach Boys. For one summer, this summer, I would play only music from 1965, the hits of 1965, the last year the Twins won a full pennant.

I want my grounds crew in uniform. Something snappy. And I want these guys to entertain. My grounds crew guys can clown around out there, like the guy with the broom at Tiger Stadium in Detroit. My grounds crew will have the best field in baseball and they will deserve to clown around.

Back to music for a minute. Music is important in a ballpark. There is no reason for this. It's my team and I want music. There will be no organ music in my ballpark, no organist. I want rock 'n' roll music between innings, volume that will fade as the next batter comes to the plate.

I want the insignia of every visiting team chalked into the on-deck circle, the way they used to do it. The stencils for this purpose are still in the basement of Metropolitan Stadium. Why aren't they used? Did the price of white chalk go up? I use them. When Detroit comes to town, you will see that distinctive Tiger face painted on the field.

Gene Mauch is my manager.

I want Bill Lee.

I will try to bring in Linda Ronstadt at least 25 times a year to sing the national anthem.

For day games during the week, I let everybody in for $2 a ticket. I figure it's better to have a full house at two bucks a seat than 2,324 people who pay full price.

I want Dave Winfield in my outfield. I can't pay him $20 million, so I make him a part owner of my club.

There will be no disco music by the way. No disco. No disco nights.

I don't like the Yankees. My club will be urged to cream the Yankees. There isn't a Yankee I desire for my ball club, except maybe Ron Guidry. We'll see.

I want characters on my club.

I want Jerry Koosman to be 25 again. I want my guys to hang around in the clubhouse after a game and drink beer with Koosman. I want my guys to come early and stay late.

All my players give autographs. If Mike Marshall won't sign an autograph, he can take a hike.

I don't want Nolan Ryan. I want James Rodney Richard.

I don't want any short people dressed up like chickens or dodo birds or Mickey Mouse. No mascots. What could possibly represent a Twin?

My pitchers walk in from the bull pen.

I'm installing new lights and in the meantime I'm replacing the burnt out bulbs. I think there are 62 burnt out bulbs in the light towers. That is inexcusable and I will do something about it.

I like my scoreboard. If you want a television screen for a scoreboard, you shouldn't come to the ballpark. My scoreboard will always be painted green.

I will try to get my team its own jet airplane. The pilot will be named Buzz.

If Gene Mauch isn't available, I want Earl Weaver to run the show. I will not call the dugout during games.

My team will come to play.

I want George Brett.

I won't stand for any contract problems, I'll treat my players well and they will be expected to never publicly discuss any labor or management problems.

I will attend every game. If I feel like joining the announcers in the radio booth, I will. Herb Carneal is my radio man.

For my television announcers, I want Steve Martin and Richard Pryor. You better listen to the radio.

My team will always win the playoffs and they will always win the World Series. All our World Series games played at home will be during daylight hours.

Bowie Kuhn will never be invited to my ballpark. Neither will Marvin Miller or Ray Grebey. Jimmy Carter will never be allowed to phone my clubhouse and his mother will not be asked to throw out the first ball.

It's spring now and my ball club is in first place. We are always in first place.

Gene Mauch

June 4, 1980

The stories that followed him over 20 years of bad roads and bad ball clubs were wild and mysterious, full of the man's quaint, antiquated baseball charm. The stories that followed him to this place. The man has suffered a great many of baseball's ills and he was often cold and behind in the bottom of the ninth but he always, no matter how bad things got, he always slammed the door on indignity.

You know this guy. You know Gene Mauch. He could trip through sludge and come out with a gleam on his shoes. He could always do the same with ball clubs, make them respectable and workmanlike and teach them the lesson of pride.

This fierce and utterly unquestioned self-discipline, this burning desire for perfection, is what he has tried to impart to his ballplayers and he has succeeded more often than not. He has fought for ballplayers. He has schemed for them. He has torn up clubhouses around them as they stood there in their shock. Once, long ago when he was managing the Millers in this same ballpark, he kept his club on the field after a Memorial Day doubleheader and worked them until the moon came up.

Mauch used to rant. He could rave. He could lay ruin to a postgame buffet. And he has stuffed a few creeps into a locker in his time.

But now there is something wrong with his door. Indignity is barging in, loud and unwanted and ugly. The Twins are playing like the lunatics, the hilarious asylum team in Philip Roth's "The Great American Novel".

The other evening Mike Marshall fielded a ball in front of home plate, wheeled and threw to second to start a double play that never came off. The bases were loaded at the time. Twins runners are getting gunned down at third. Cutoff men are missed. Routine ground balls are beaten into exhaustion around the infield.

This isn't funny stuff. This is indignity and Mauch is watching it bust through the door. Maybe indignity is too strong a word and maybe Mauch doesn't even want to hear such a thing, but you can be sure that in his 20 years of big league managing the current Twins are the first team he has not been able to brand with his own stamp.

The current Twins are not Gene Mauch's Twins. He hasn't ranted at them and he hasn't torn up a clubhouse around them, at least not yet. They don't have his mood and they don't have his passion for the game and this was the same mood and passion that kept the Twins in contention last year. Time flies. Last year everybody in America pulled for the Twins because they were knocking off giants for the longest time.

Yesterday afternoon, under a hot sun, Gene Mauch walked back and forth across his outfield and there was steam coming off his neck. The only other figure in the park was Don Zimmer, the manager of the Red Sox, who was in full uniform sitting on his bench and staring out at Mauch. Earlier, in his clubhouse, Zimmer was asked if Mauch might be losing his intensity for the game.

"No," said Zimmer, who has been Mauch's friend for 30 years. Zimmer has an unfortunate reputation as a dunderhead, but he is a perceptive man, perceptive enough to recognize a veiled question when he hears one. Baseball has suffered this year, with labor negotiations, with a mini spring-training strike and the threat of a long, more damaging regular-season strike. Some men in baseball had bombs dropped on them.

"You turn your head now to a lot of things a manager would never turn his head to," Zimmer said. "I used to play for Chuck Dressen. If he fined a player $150, you walked in and paid the $150. Now, I fine a player, I've got to fill out three forms, one for the player, one for the owner, one for the whatchmacallit, the abitration or whatever.

"There's been a lot of changes in human beings in my 33 years in the game. You swing with the times. I hope people in this town realize what an amazing job Mauch has done with this club. He's in a bad streak now, his whole club is."

The bad streak was killing the man out there walking in the sun. According to Mauch, he has never had a bad ball club. The prospect that his current batch of players does not care deeply for the game scars him far more than the irrefutable evidence that they are playing like lunatics. Ineptness he can stand. Indignity kicking at his door is a different thing and he will not tolerate it. Something will happen with this club in the next few days. Use your imagination and dream up whatever it is that you want to happen, but something will happen.

Mauch most probably will not win a pennant with the 1980 Twins. But Mauch will no longer allow the Twins to embarrass either him or themselves. One way or another, there will be a door slammed on indignity.

August 8, 1980

It would serve on his players certain poetic justice if Gene Mauch were to up and quit Calvin Griffith's ballclub.

Rumors have speculated as much and there is precedent, dating back to his Philadelphia days, for Mauch to extricate himself from impossible situations. In 1968 Mauch and Dick Allen, were featured in a "him or me" showdown and Mauch took a hike because Mauch can rarely tolerate breaches of his authority.

His current ballclub celebrates no player with the stature of Allen, who fell out with Mauch over a question of the slugger's sincerity, among other matters of moodiness and effort.

But about 20 of the Twins are moody enough and stupid enough and uncaring enough to drive a manager to cover.

It's bad enough that they can't play ball, and here they are on the current road trip allowing themselves the luxury of indifference. Gene Mauch won't quit on them, at least not this year, but they have quit on him. The current road trip has demonstrated that ballplayers who drop fly balls, get picked off and run through signs are generally ballplayers who are keeping both eyes on the clock that marks their time in Minnesota garments.

Mauch, a renowned fundamentalist, is easily blamed for these public failings. He is also a logical target for those souls on the periphery of management who insist that the club has been stocked with the finest available talent — even Calvin ain't that blind.

But Mauch cannot catch a ball for Kenny Landreaux and he cannot punch out a hit for Butch Wynegar. He has taught these players well and he cannot be held responsible now if they have decided to impersonate all varieties of dogs. Landreaux seems to favor the role of a tired hound who cannot bring himself out from under the porch because it is August and it is hot. Wynegar possesses the characteristics of a sheep dog, big and friendly but not eternally bright.

It was not intended here to single out Landreaux and Wynegar for full blame; it takes nine men playing stupidly to stoke a good losing streak. It's just that Landreaux is absolutely unpredictable and that it seems impossible to tune in a game when Wynegar is not at the plate waving feebly at a ball that could have driven in a run.

Dan Ford had to run backward from third to home to get himself dispatched from Calvin's employ. Perhaps it is Landreaux's plan to mood himself out of town and that of Butch to inept his way to greener pastures. Only John Castino has distinguished himself with any pride in his entertainment. The rest of them perform under the foolish notion that this ordeal here on the tundra will soon be over and they can then peddle themselves off to real ballclubs for real money.

Imagine if the outside world operated that way, if doctors in small towns purposely goofed up in order to move on to a big city hospital, or if struggling attorneys promoted themselves to the firm of F. Lee Bailey by falling asleep in front of the judge.

By background, then, it is not difficult to see why rumors of Gene Mauch's quitting are so popular these days. As mentioned elsewhere on these pages a few days earlier, the rumor started in Boston where, presumably, a reporter could have received some information from Mauch's close friend, Don Zimmer. Reached in Anaheim, Calif., Thursday morning, Mauch cleared his voice of sleep and addressed the subject again.

"We just can't catch a break, is all," Mauch said. "The club will come out of this. Wynegar is snakebit and Landreaux is snakebit. I've seen worse. Maybe three times I've seen worse. I'm not quitting."

"But would you admit it if you were going to quit?"

"I would."

He isn't quitting. He will continue to dream up sayings like snakebit to cover for his players. He will continue to believe that his club will turn around and that they will stop getting chinked and blooped to death. Gene Mauch, thorough in all things, even prepares excuses for his players, realizing that they are inept in that department as well.

September 3, 1980

The only something solid I have of his departure — I wanted instead an autographed ball or a handshake or a look in the eye — is a rain-smeared log entry recorded at 6:58 a.m., Monday, Aug. 25, 1980.

We were out of sight of land on Lake Superior, but picking up FM radio station WIMI in Ironwood, Mich., when the newsman said that Gene Mauch had quit his job as manager of the Minnesota Twins. My curse echoed through the mist to the distant shores, to ore boats and freighters. To three states and Canada this wail traveled. It brought them running from the cabin.

"What!"

"Gene Mauch resigned." I motioned to the radio.

From the tone of my cry they thought I had severed an arm or spotted a submarine, or worse, that the mast had fallen. These companions were solicitous in their way and didn't speak for the longest time, nor did I. My immediate wish was to be on the scene, although maybe it was better this way; there is nothing quite so tranquil as water rushing past a hull.

The morning sun began to burn off the fog, and with the lifting came a wind. The motor was silenced, the sails raised and a course set for the Upper Peninsula of Michigan. There is time enough on a boat to think, about navigation (this was no dainty cruise around the Apostle Islands), about the trouble behind every cloud, about the depths of this mystical lake. About Mauch. About how I am supposed to react to a man like him, or to his departure.

Theoretically a journalist is to remain distant from his subjects in order to perform the role of ombudsman for the fan. It is not hard to remain distant from players, as only a very few athletes do not regard newsmen with suspicion or spite or fright. It is not hard to keep distance from those coaches or managers who anticipate the open souls among us and create their distance through condescension or arrogance.

They are only protecting themselves is the conclusion I reached on water. Bud Grant is an example of the latter. He is probably a wonderful man but I have a feeling I will never know that. And it is not difficult to keep distant from the front offices and the politicians who have tramped through sport, at least not for a younger generation of writer. We have nothing vested in their ledgers.

It is important, without a mark on land, to stare at a compass. An occasional glance will not do, but I cannot be certain that my Mauchian reverie detached us from original course and put us into port hours later at Ontonagan, Mich., nearly 50 miles south of our destination.

But I was thinking about the distance between Mauch and myself. There wasn't any, never was from day one. There are those who think it is Mauch's technique to slip reporters small confidences, to own them so that they might always speak on his behalf.

I do not care if that is true (we might have veered off course right there). If I was manipulated by him to always carry his message, I was compensated with an education that I could not have acquired from any man, an education that I will value and remember forever. The man was whole, he opened his heart and spoke of his desires and he was a complete man and he did not hide behind the convenient walls that are available to any celebrity in his position.

"Maybe you should call him," one Soucheray or another said out at sea. "When we reach land you could call him."

The quick, obligatory eulogies would have been written. A call was unnecessary and there was nothing I could contribute from a yacht basin in Ontonagan except sadness. Even though I felt certain Mauch would have finished the year here I was not surprised that he resigned. A certain mourning period, after all, had to be established before he could accept another job and he might as well get a start on that because he wasn't returning next season. But honesty was working its way through his bones and he was being honest with himself by taking a hike.

One of the greatest attributes the man had was his dream for the working class ballplayer, the marginally paid ballplayer who dives after ground balls. It would have given Mauch more pleasure to win his first pennant with a group like the Twins than any other club afloat because it would have been a once-in-a-lifetime opportunity — to have the entire country pushing behind an underdog club before they became wealthy and famous and dispersed for good. The Twins could not understand his dream, or did not believe in it, and they failed each other miserably in the end.

"What made you feel so strongly about him?" one Soucheray or another asked out at sea.

"There was no phony in him," I said.

March 1, 1981

Palm Springs, Calif.

During the first moments of the transition, he had become a stranger even to himself, as though he had become frightened by some sound in the dark. He was all alone and trying to be discreet.

Gene Mauch stood there on the perimeter of the municipal stadium adjacent to Palm Springs High School and he watched the California Angels engage themselves in the gentle rhythms of spring training and he was not in uniform.

Gene Mauch was not in uniform for the first time since 1943. The sun was burning a hole in him. He put a hand to his collar.

The San Jacinto Mountains rose up behind him and around him, so close as to reach out and be touched. Long shadows in the mountain range caught his eye and craggy peaks, too, where the sun glistened off the snow-covered points in the distance. We will never know — he was never good at telling his darkest secrets — we will never know if his soul was like a hall of mirrors in this first, frightening moment that his life changed from active to ... less active.

"My God," he will say later in the evening, "I was Jim Fregosi's first manager. He was 17 and I had him in an early camp for the Red Sox at Ocala, Fla., in 1960. I thought he was so bad I wanted to fire the scout who signed him. After 10 days I wanted to give the scout a raise. I thought so many things in the first moments. I looked out at those players and I knew that they thought they were good, guys who can win. I thought about me, is what I did, and I had never done that before. I had always thought about baseball."

"There isn't much of a distinction," said a voice who has tried to understand Mauch.

"No, no," he said, "there really hasn't been."

Tuesday was his first day on the new job. He had hooked up over the winter with the Angels as "vice president in charge of anything I can do to help". That was changed to director of player development, a more palatable euphemism for the press and diplomatic smokescreen for his actual purpose; Gene Mauch was hired to ensure against another breakdown. The Angels sank from first place in the American League West in 1979 to sixth place last year at 65-95, the worst record in the club's history.

Gene Autry, the owner of the Angels who has authorized the purchase of and the trading for the best talent in baseball, authorized himself to lure Mauch out of retirement.

Mauch turned down four managing jobs this winter with San Diego, St. Louis, San Francisco and an American League club he will not name. But Mauch buckled when Autry called, even though the Angels are the kind of team Mauch never managed, a team with a millionaire at every position, the kind of team that might never need his brand of underdog psychology. Autry painted a bright picture, virtually assuring Mauch that he will succeed Buzzie Bavasi as the club's executive vice president and general manager.

"I had made up my mind to take a year off," Mauch was saying now over dinner in Autry's Palm Springs hotel, "figuring that I should take a year off in the middle of my life rather than at the end of it. I didn't see anything irrational about that. The Cowboy — Autry — the Cowboy kept calling me and calling me and he has considerable charm. There are times now that I wish he never called."

Because of the stories and the rumors it seemed only logical that Mauch was hired to replace Fregosi as manager. But Mauch's duties were carefully outlined to him, his order of succession and the inevitable rank he will command out of uniform, so that the first thing he did as "vice president in charge of anything I can do to help" was have a 30-minute talk with Fregosi.

"I told him he was the manager," Mauch was saying now, "and that I was not there to take his job and that I hoped he would win manager of the year five years in a row. Jimmy felt nine feet tall when we finished that talk. I'm not unfair and I'm not stupid. Jimmy wants help and he'll get it. He'll get everything I ever learned."

Gene Mauch is not being groomed for anything. Horses are groomed. Dummies are groomed. Gene Autry hired Gene Mauch for his presence, for the implied threats in his stern countenance, for his expertise. And then, at the appropriate time, after an appropriate transformation, most likely before the end of the year, he will succeed Bavasi and he will be running the kind of show that Calvin Griffith could only dream of.

"You will never manage again?" said the voice who has tried to understand him.

"The Angels have hired a lot of people," Mauch said, "to see that there is never another breakdown. To see that we win."

"That is not an answer," said the voice.

"That's my answer," said Mauch. "I never consciously set out to give up managing. It just happened."

The Angels have no uniform for Mauch. He works out of his home and he shows up at the field in his golf slacks and a poplin jacket and his observations are channeled, to this coach or that one. At first the sun did burn a hole in him and his innards cried out and he felt a quick stab of withdrawal and pain.

But it passed. He hasn't lost a fight yet and he is not about to lose one to himself.

11/Calvin Griffith

November 10, 1976

The people who monitor Calvin Griffith for a living, and those who do it just for fun, don't know whether to kick him while he's down or help drag him back to his feet.

Baseball, as Griffith grew up with it, changed radically in 48 hours last Thursday and Friday in New York's Plaza Hotel, where baseball's owners met to conduct the legal raids of baseball's free agents and then the dispersal of lesser talent in the American League expansion draft.

Griffith lost on both accounts. The reentry draft, the official designation given to the auction of baseball's freed slaves, saw Twins pitcher Billy (Soup) Campbell become Mr. William Campbell, millionaire employee of the Boston Red Sox.

Thousands of players have switched uniforms at significant points in their careers, but this was the first time it was done at the player's discretion and it was the first time the players pocketed the transitional funds instead of the owners.

Campbell thus earned an asterisk in the history books. Although Catfish Hunter and Andy Messersmith beat him to free agentry, Campbell was baseball's first million-dollar baby in the revolutionary open market created by the abolition of the reserve clause.

"This is the weirdest thing that ever happened to baseball," Griffith growled when he returned from the bidding, shocked and distraught. "These guys aren't worth a million dollars. No player is. You try and keep an even keel, you try and build your club for the future and then this comes along."

What came along was a new four-year agreement worked out last summer by Marvin Miller, representing players, and John Gaherin, representing owners, that had as its most dramatic clause a method for players to achieve free agentry. The owners cursed and moaned, but they ratified the agreement and won some concessions of their own, like a maximum roster of 25 players.

Aside from this initial crop of available bodies, players who signed contracts before the new agreement may become free agents by playing out the renewal year in their current contracts. Under future contracts a player with six years major-league service may become a free agent by notifying his club in writing after the season that he wants to go on the auction block.

As prescribed in a gentlemen's agreement between Larue Harcourt, Campbell's agent, and Griffith, Campbell promised Griffith the chance to meet or exceed his finest offer. Griffith called it the right of first refusal and he was indeed the first one to refuse Campbell.

"We've got an offer of a million plus from Boston," Harcourt told Griffith. "We need $700,000 up front, plus . . ."

"Stop right there," Griffith said. "We don't have the $700,000 up front. You don't have to come back."

Campbell returned from the bidding with a new checkbook and, with all the humility an instant 28-year-old millionaire could muster, pronounced, "I'm not worth it." Campbell had asked Griffith for an $8,000 raise last spring and was refused. It would have brought his annual stipend to $30,000. He shivers to think about his turn in fortune.

"During the year my agent and I saw that Rollie Fingers and Vida Blue were offered a million," Campbell said, "so we thought, 'Why not us?' "

"Did you ever think Calvin could match your offer?" a visitor asked.

"I'll probably never know," Campbell said. "I think Calvin has the money, but I could be wrong. We've seen how tough he can be in negotiations. The owners are admitting they let baseball get screwed up. I talked with the St. Louis people as well as Boston and they admitted they didn't like the new setup, but they also said they'd work with it. Not Calvin. If you want to be with a winner you have to leave that team."

Old-timers may view Griffith as a brave and courageous soul for his stance, but you can't win games any more on luck or tough talk. In the new regime it takes money. "Well, I don't have the money," Griffith said. As further proof, he let Bill Singer go to Toronto in the American League expansion draft because he didn't want to pay Singer's $100,000 salary.

"Baseball people better come to their senses," Griffith said. "A lot of these teams are owned by corporations and those corporations are going to raise hell with the teams for spending so much money. I heard rumors in New York that four or five clubs will go out of business because of the spending situation. I'm staying in. We might be called something else in the future, but we'll still be in business and I think the public is on my side."

Because he is the corporation, Griffith will raise hell all by himself. That won't win many games either.

December 14, 1977

Stubborn, thrifty to a fault and forever nostalgic for the pre-union days, Calvin Griffith recently attended the baseball convention in Hawaii so he could stand around and pretend he was an owner. He locked his purse and didn't make a trade, but he didn't have to. Calvin restocked his team before the winter meetings with enough questionable talent to forecast the return of minor league baseball to Minnesota after an absence of 17 years.

Exactly four months from today local customers will get their first live look at someone called Bombo Rivera. Mr. Rivera is the outfielder Calvin obtained from Denver in the American Association to replace either Lyman Bostock or Larry Hisle, or both, for Bombo Rivera is reported to have a big talent.

Also making their debut at that time, assuming they make the club, will be Mac Scarce and Dennis Lewallyn, pitchers.

Scarce, whose own name is even more appropriate than Bombo's for anyone wearing a Twins uniform, suffered a sore arm all last season. He says he feels better now, which is about as small a package as consolation comes in these days.

Lewallyn split time last summer between the Dodgers and Albuquerque, compiling a combined 16-13 record with a 5.24 earned run average, not quite good enough to linger as the last man on the Dodgers' staff. Calvin paid $30,000 for Lewallyn, so he no doubt expects him to win 20 games.

Calvin can't stand the heat of baseball's new and open marketplace but he refuses to leave the kitchen. It was in Hawaii, where his own lodge brothers wouldn't deal with him, that Calvin must have realized what a poor condition his condition is in. He tried to trade for Jerry Koosman but dillydallied until the Mets traded Jon Matlack to Texas, making Koosman's departure from New York unlikely, if not suicidal for the Mets.

But Calvin never has been one to do today what he can put off until it's too late (see Bostock, Lyman, and Hisle, Larry) and he soon discovered that there isn't a team afloat that covets any of his talent because there isn't any talent. At least there isn't any available.

Quick, name the five major league caliber ballplayers on the Twins, not counting the dear and recently departed such as Bill Campbell and Bert Blyleven and the aforementioned outfield duo. The good, rich teams got better and richer in Hawaii through interleague trading and cash transactions. But Calvin had no one to trade even if he were so inclined.

In the American League West, where the Twins will laughingly reside, the White Sox, Royals, Rangers and Angels all improved, doing what they could to add talent or compensate for departed free agents. Chicago obtained Bobby Bonds and Ron Blomberg to compensate for the departure of free agents Richie Zisk and Oscar Gamble.

The Angels could sacrifice Bonds for pitching help because they signed Zisk and traded for Matlack and Oliver and the Royals traded Mark Littel to St. Louis for Al Hrabosky. Hrabosky, the Mad Hungarian, is a splendid reliever as well as an impressive gate attraction when he is up to his spellbinding and wicked form. Those are the kinds of big moves the Twins should have been making.

But the most disturbing thought of all is not that the Twins didn't make any moves, it's that very recently the Twins were in a position of such respectable power in the American League that they didn't have to make any moves.

Imagine Calvin's fortune today if the Twins had kept Campbell in the bullpen and Blyleven in the starting rotation this past summer. At the start of the 1976 season Calvin could have signed Campbell for the same figure for which he just purchased Lewallyn. Blyleven, Bostock and Hisle all could have been kept happy by a less offensive owner. Keeping those players would have required that the owners come equipped with foresight. Calvin is walking blind into the future, but if he could see, if might be he and not George Steinbrenner who could afford to pick up a Rawly Eastwick or a Rich Gossage or an Andy Messersmith.

The miserable truth is that summer's hope now rests on the shoulders of a Bombo, a Scarce, a Lewallyn and whomever else Calvin can drag down to spring training for minimum or less. This is no way to run a ball club. The manager so much as said so when he threatened to hide or play golf all summer until he could hook up with the Angels.

There are three things Calvin must do to keep the respect of the six or seven hundred thousand fans he will be lucky to attract in 1978. He should lower ticket prices to a level comparable to what they charge at the Triple A level. He should forever hold his peace on his desire for a new ball park (the Met is a grand major league facility; it unquestionably will be the best minor league yard on the planet). And he should quit pretending that the Twins have a chance. The Twins don't have a chance. The owner won't give them one.

March 2, 1978

Orlando, Fla.

"What do you need my opinion for?" Calvin Griffith said Wednesday morning. "You just write what you feel like anyway."

The Twins president was standing across the room in his winter office at Tinker Field staring at me. I hadn't seen him since December, when I was critical of his inaction at baseball's winter meetings.

"The manager values your opinion," I said, "so do I. I wrote something nasty. You're forgetting all the nice things I said."

"People remember the bad stuff," Griffith said.

"I'm sorry you feel that way, Calvin," I said, "I'd like to talk to you."

In an awkward silence that followed I studied a roster and Calvin shifted from foot to foot in the door frame of his office.

"I'll be in the stands in a few minutes," he said. "You meet me out there."

Outside the sun was shining, the wind had died and Gene Mauch had officially begun the formidable task of paring his roster to the 25 professionals who will accompany him north in a month's time. One month. The ball club is green. But you have heard all that before. You know the names of the faithful departed as well as the names of your own children.

I said Griffith didn't give this club a chance to win and I still believe that. I believe he should have signed Larry Hisle and Lyman Bostock and I believe he should have traded for a left-handed pitcher. He can still make a trade, but Calvin will come at you with all his baseball knowledge and perception and love for the game and tell you that a trade isn't necessary.

He took a seat behind and just to the left of home plate and called my name. He shaped a smile as I sat down and took out a notebook.

"You don't know anything," he said. "You don't know the truth. Telling the truth. Telling the truth to you as a reporter is instant headache. I couldn't have made any trades. What I was offered for some of my ballplayers was embarrassing."

"Will you keep trying to trade?" The interleague trading period concludes March 15. It started two weeks ago.

"I doubt it," Griffith said. "The only thing we're looking for is left-handed help and good left-handers are like gold. Any left-hander we can trade for is only as good as any right-hander we already have."

"So you'll hope to get lucky?"

"We're a little hard up," Griffith said. "We brought guys like Tommy Hall and Mac Scarce to camp but maybe we'll hit the jackpot. We did last year with Geoff Zahn. Maybe this Hudson kid (Rex Hudson, a right-hander who last appeared with Albuquerque) can replace Ron Schueler. Hudson's got a good curve."

"Have you completely ruled out a trade?"

"This trading period is all wrong," Griffith said. "It should go from March 1 to April 1. We don't know what we need right now."

Griffith leaned forward to study his team. The stands were dotted with customers, many of whom have been regulars at Tinker Field for 18 years. They know Calvin, or at least think they do, and he had a greeting for all of them. "We're going to surprise a few people this year," Griffith said to a few fans.

"You've got the right man to manage the club," I said.

"Now that is the truth," Griffith said. "Like I told Gene, I said,

'Gene you be the nice guy, I'll be the — — — — —.' I've taught some of these player-agents a lesson or two. They say I've got a track record, tough, but what good are you without a track record?"

"Maybe history will justify that you didn't sign your free agents," I said, not really believing myself.

"I didn't lose money," Griffith said. "I'm money ahead of even the teams that drew more fans. The Phillies drew 2.7 million and were so embarrassed about losing money that they said they made a few hundred thousand. Deferred payments are the killer. You're paying dollars down the line that might be worth only 15 cents by today's standards but a dollar is a dollar. Where am I going to get that dollar in the future, because if I expect to get it out of the turnstiles I'd have to raise prices too high. I want to survive and we'll see what history has to say about it."

"What about the old baseball belief that you must give the fans a winner every three years? If there aren't any fans you won't survive."

Griffith has loosened his tie. He shaped another careful smile.

"You give the fans an entertaining ball club," he said. "A ball club needs to entertain just like the theater. Provide some thrills, like a good song or a good joke. People need to talk about your ball club and they will if you entertain them."

It was getting near noon and Griffith mentioned that he'd like to be on the golf course. He said the golf course is the only place where he really enjoys the sun. He played with his brother-in-law, Joe Cronin, the other day and they talked baseball while they enjoyed the sun.

"We arrived at the conclusion that I hope the ballplayers realize," Griffith said. "There's only so much milk in the cow."

I stood and offered my hand and Griffith took it. "I've got some things off my chest," Griffith said. "We're friends again."

"Yes," I said, "of course."

"And remember," Griffith said, "good pitching is good pitching, doesn't make any difference which side you're throwing from. We'll put something together. We'll surprise a few people."

Griffith stood up then, a king in his freshly painted ball park. He moved down to the field level and Mauch wandered over.

"It's a nice day," Griffith said.

"It's a nice day," the manager said.

October 22, 1978

Baseball has concluded its annual exercises in customary fashion. Pete Rose and Rod Carew hit, the Phillies collapsed, the Yankees repeated as champions of North America, attendance was up across the board in both leagues and an old man flew into what most people thought was a rage.

The medieval babblings of a character named Calvin Griffith darkened an otherwise brilliant campaign of stunning entertainments, surprises, streaks and sudden-death play-offs. Griffith had to ruin the party by shooting off his mouth. He railed against blacks, advocated inexpensive sex and condemned the big money paid to good players.

What he really did, and what may have been overlooked by astonished editorialists and civil servants, was to reveal that he still has his roots in the gothic parlors of his long-dead lodge brothers. To this day Griffith is neither contrite nor saddened by his remarks, which were heard round the world. But he is paranoid. He actually believes that somebody's out to run him under for what he said, as though what he said was perfectly suitable for intelligent listeners in 1978. So what's all the fuss about anywho?

The topic is mentioned here to point out (1) that Griffith's views aren't necessarily representative of baseball owners in general and (2) that Griffith, along with the press, has done a pretty nifty job of convincing people that he owns an important voice in society.

Take number two first. Griffith's miserable outfit didn't pump as much money into the local economy as, say, a good quick-order hamburger joint. The proprietor of a hamburger joint might be given to Griffith's backward views and might even speak the same in the circle of his companions. But we don't know that and we don't hear it because hamburger joint owners don't make the newspapers, at least until they own a baseball club.

We put stock in sports for a variety of reasons, not the least of which is the vicarious thrill of watching another man do what we can only dream about. Sports is a release and a charm, but it isn't real in terms of affecting the important issues of the day. Griffith didn't decide an election, cast a ballot for the pope, float a school bond or discover a cure for cancer. He put a ball club on the field, and not a very good one at that. The problem comes when a baseball owner, or any team owner, feels he contributes something so extraordinary to society that his views on any subject become important and therefore quotable.

None of this is to excuse Griffith's remarks. They were unforgivable. But his remarks should be tempered with the knowledge that he doesn't carry a lick of weight in our decision making processes. Griffith's views won't affect social policy, politics, the economy or the will of reasonable thinking people. He just happens to own a ball club and he's probably no more or no less evil than the neighborhood theater owner or baker or hardware merchant. That he probably isn't as bright as the butcher, the baker and the candlestick maker isn't to be debated here.

Take number one second. Griffith has been lapped by his fellow owners. He is the only individual left in a baseball world of conglomerates and tax accountants and investment counselors. As new ownerships assumed control of established teams (a ship builder owns the Yankees, for example) the new owners came equipped with knowledge of the real world, the business world, the political world, the social and economic world. Knowledge of the real world doesn't guarantee a pennant, but the new regimes are light years ahead of Griffith in public relations.

Griffith only knows baseball and his scope of the pastime is limited to the events of the roaring '20s, when he was a batboy for the Senators. Griffith has existed so long in his fantasy world that he suffers the delusions of privilege that *were* paramount to ownership in the '20s. Now he is lost.

His words are either ignored or pelt him on the ricochet, but they are meaningless nonetheless.

So why doesn't he relinquish control?

Because he would stop breathing.

July 20, 1979

Nobody in this world can maneuver himself between a rock and a hard place better than Calvin Griffith, who is entertaining second thoughts about occupying the new domed convention facility in downtown Minneapolis.

Calvin wanted a domed convention facility to play baseball in and he said as much on many occasions. Now Calvin might not want to play baseball in a domed convention facility and for more reasons than his inability to secure a more lucrative concessions arrangement with the stadium commission.

"I can't say too much, people tell me to keep quiet," Calvin said Thursday. "But I don't really know if I'm close to signing the lease. I don't really know if the dome is the kind of facility the people in this state can be proud of."

We have come to know and either love or hate Calvin for his candor, but his last statement could be read in a variety of ways. There is some suspicion that the planned dome is neither as glamorous nor as futuristic as Calvin once envisioned.

He doubts, for example, that $55 million can provide such comforts as elevators and escalators and whatnot. We already know it cannot provide air conditioning. There is also some suspicion that Calvin, being the old salt that he is, really prefers his baseball under natural light and on turf that can be mowed. And despite what he has been told to believe, Calvin isn't entirely sure that his ball club increases its value by playing in a new home.

Calvin, of course, can't win either way. If he signs a lease to play dome ball he will lose fans. That cannot be proven and no study has ever suggested as much, but it is written here in guarantee that baseball under a roof is a ruinous and embarrassing enterprise, as anyone who witnessed the All-Star game from Seattle's Kingdome will gladly testify. The dull, underlying feeling during that game, or any played there, was the feeling of disorientation, that somehow, like a bruised ecosystem, a thing that we once knew as rhythmic and whole was decaying a little around the edges.

A man is spitting into the wind with these sentiments and has been for a long time. You can only remind people so often that summer nights are not to be spent indoors in Minnesota. Those summer nights are too valuable, never to be retrieved in February and March as they would be in Houston or New Orleans.

"Well, maybe," Calvin said, "they could paint a moon and some stars on the roof. Aw, hell, I don't know . . ."

He really doesn't know. Calvin holds the key to a domed stadium and he really doesn't know what to do. Aside from the additional rent he would have to pay in a dome and the apparent loss of concession revenue, Calvin doesn't really know if he wants his club to play indoors. Calvin attended the All-Star game. In what must have been a tremendous effort for him, he declined comment on the game itself.

The proponents of a domed stadium are wise men with civic vision, which unfortunately has absolutely nothing to do with baseball, the *game*. To say that a large building can accommodate baseball is like saying that a day of sailing can be enjoyed in a swamp. You get the feeling Calvin wants to say that, or at the very least, believes it somewhere deep in the folds of his heart. Football, incidentally, in no way figures into Calvin's dilemma. Football is a perfect indoor game. You can't ruin any attraction that features as its highlight 93 identical collisions among 22 men.

If Calvin doesn't sign the lease and chooses to somehow remain at Metropolitan Stadium he might ensure himself not only the loyalty of old fans but hordes of new fans as well. By killing the dome — and saving baseball — he would be acting in the best interests of the average citizen who never did have the voice of referendum in this matter.

But by not signing Calvin loses whatever friends he has in the business community — the guys who put money on the line to acquire land for the stadium site. Millionaires are not exactly the backbone of Calvin's attendance, but they could ruin him, one supposes, just as surely as baseball will be ruined under the roof.

June 25, 1980

Unlike the majority of whip-crackers in his lodge, Calvin Griffith does not enter the clubhouse where his ballplayers dress, shower and read fan mail. All right, dress and shower. This is a policy of Calvin's dating back to the time when his uncle, Clark Griffith, set Calvin on his knee and decreed that a clubhouse was a ballplayer's palace.

"Besides," Clark Griffith told his nephew, "you could go in there and make a simple, light-hearted remark and offend some guy or the other and all hell could break loose."

Clark Griffith was clairvoyant, which is neither here nor there. So rigorously has Calvin exercised restraint that the last time he poked his head between the lockers was in 1967, when he announced to the assembled that Cal Ermer would be succeeding Sam Mele as manager. Calvin, of course, has a country way about him that manages to offend the populace, not to mention his employees, and he doesn't have to go through the clubhouse to boil up controversy.

"The ballplayers today are so individual," Calvin said the other evening, "that I'm almost afraid to say anything. It could turn into a grievance against me if I open my mouth the wrong way so I just stay away. I'm not really the boss, anyway. Gene Mauch is."

But silence is often misconstrued by temperamental souls and the modern ballplayer needs at least a dollop of new psychology to keep himself afloat. Ken Landreaux, for example, has been quoted from coast to coast insisting that Calvin Griffith does not exist and that he might very well be, for all Landreaux knows, a myth, albeit a myth of large proportion. There was a time not so long ago, at the conclusion of his remarkable 31-game hitting streak, when Landreaux would have appreciated Calvin's hand extended in the manner of a friendly shake.

A fistful of dollars in the form of a bonus would have been more appropriate, but Calvin has been given to seizure in that moment that requires his right hand to reach for the pocketbook. All in all, Landreaux accomplished the hitting streak without one word from Calvin, save notice that the outfielder was being fined for the improper display of his uniform hose.

"I don't worry about that stuff," Landreaux said the other evening. He was unconvincing.

Kenny Landreaux is moody, recalcitrant and occasionally suffers from flights of fancy. But he is just as obviously and undeniably a gifted entertainer and a perfect example of a ballplayer who needs his back patted and his hand pumped. These gestures tend to keep his mind focused on the playing field, where he has the makings of a genuine superstar.

"Don't need to be a superstar in this town," Landreaux said. "The fans make you a superstar, the media makes you a superstar. I don't worry about that stuff."

Sure you don't, Kenny. On the evening in question, Landreaux's name was removed from Mauch's initial lineup card. Officially, Landreaux was said to be suffering from an allergy that blurs his vision. This may be so. But there seems to be some question whether Landreaux is allergic to something in the air or to what he perceives as injustice. The Twins later acknowledged that he had missed pregame practice, too.

Compounding Landreaux's suspicions and miseries was Bowie Kuhn's recent verdict that the player with the longest hitting streak cannot be eligible for the $1,000-a-game prize offered by the manufacturers of Aqua Velva, an elixir so potent that on television commercials it brings women out of the stands to cling on the batting cage.

Bowie said that the Aqua Velva winner may donate his prize to the charity of his choice. There is little doubt that Landreaux considers himself a charitable case, but the commissioner has come out against performance-type bonuses lest they inflict even the shadow of doubt on the game. Might a player who needs a hit to extend his streak refuse a manager's order to advance a runner in a critical situation? That type of thing.

Pete Rose was allowed to keep the money he earned for last year's 23-game streak, but according to Vince Naus of the commissioner's office Rose took the money (which he gave to his coaches) as an extension of a personal services contract with Aqua Velva. Landreaux has no such agreement with the toilet water people so he can't get around Kuhn's verdict in that fashion.

So far then, Landreaux has established a 31-game hitting streak — the longest in the American League since 1949 — and has received for his effort a fine, word that he may not keep the $31,000 should he win the Aqua Velva award, and no word from Calvin. Add to that some discomfort with his peepers, real or imagined, and you have a ballplayer in need of his owner's handshake.

"The way I look at it," Calvin said, "is that we're paying ballplayers to set records. Records are made to be broken. It should be the pride of a ballplayer to earn all the accolades he can so that he becomes a drawing power and in turn makes more money for himself. The hitting streak was Landreaux's honor."

"Will you give him a bonus?"

"No."

"Do you think, if he wins, that he should be able to keep the Aqua Velva money?"

"Yes," Calvin said. "And I hope it works out that he does get to keep it."

That's something. It doesn't necessarily update Calvin in the departments of warmth and new psychology, but it's something.

12/The Dome

March 22, 1977

Tom Stocking got up before the sunrise Monday, thought about what he had to do and went to the typewriter to rewrite the first page of his argument. He put the finished text in a black plastic briefcase and boarded the Como-Striker Bus No. 5 that took him from his apartment in southeast Minneapolis to the foot of the State Office Building in St. Paul.

Downstairs in Auditorium 83 he took a seat and watched the members of the House Local and Urban Affairs Committee settle down around a big horseshoe of mahogany desks. Yesterday was the day the committee set aside for taking public testimony on the various stadium bills before the legislature. The committee's chairman, Tom Berg, was busy elsewhere with matters of gun control, but Victor Schulz, DFL-Goodhue, filled in and hurried the meeting along.

The legislators talked among themselves throughout most of the testimony and some of them laughed behind their hands when one elderly lady identified as a Miss Marks told the committee that she didn't want a new stadium anywhere because it would require the energy that she and others like her need to heat their homes. Miss Marks could have been talking to the wall.

Finally, Schulz called Stocking's name. Stocking placed four typewritten sheets of paper on the podium and tried to keep his fingers from trembling because he had never faced the government like this before. As soon as Stocking opened his mouth the audience quieted and the legislators leaned forward in their seats.

"I think it is unfortunate," Stocking began, "that the average sports fan has been considered primarily as a source of increased revenue from ticket and parking charges, and that little real concern has been shown for the interests and values of the sports fan in this state...It is not in the best interests of the average fan to construct a new stadium...because the much maligned Met Stadium is one of the best baseball facilities in the country. Fans sit close to the action, even in general admission seats, and watch the game in a manner that is most enjoyable, outdoors and on real grass."

How perfectly accurate! Of course a new stadium might be in the best interests of business, but here was Stocking telling people who should have known that no stadium should be as viable an alternative to this question as any new stadium. Here was a man who rode a bus for 30 minutes to remind people about the pleasures of the games themselves, the aesthetics of the games.

Stocking had it all down on his paper and he had their attention. He is a 28-year-old political science student at the University of Minnesota who recently completed his Ph.D. dissertation on "Political Objectives of American Foreign Trade Policy: 1948-1973."

He has been a school teacher, a church worker, a fan of all Minnesota's professional sports. He became interested in the stadium controversy when he volunteered to work for one of the committee members, Rep. Ann Wynia, DFL-St. Paul, whom he met through her husband, a political science instructor at Minnesota. Stocking worked on his statement for two weeks, and thought the best way to approach the committee was to come at them as a fan, not somebody with his hand out.

"I agree that the sightlines that make the Met ideal for baseball," Stocking continued, "are not ideal for football. But this is the stadium the Viking franchise knew it would play in when the team was organized, and for which the Vikings financed the construction of the left-field grandstand in the mid-1960s.

"Why were the Vikings willing to construct seats in Met Stadium in the 1960s and then ready to flee the facility in the 1970s? A new stadium most likely will result in higher ticket prices for all sports. The vast majority of Minnesotans who follow the Vikings do so on television. A new stadium with expanded seating would likely result in fewer sellouts, meaning that Vikings fans in the Twin Cities would miss home games because of a blackout on television."

Stocking paused for breath. "While it would be unfortunate to lose the Vikings I think it is important to keep a perspective on sports and what they contribute to our life here. I would suggest you do not succumb to the pressures of the sports business whose interest is to make more money from the fans. The Met is only 20 years old, it can last another 20 years."

Nobody applauded but everybody was thinking, thinking what it would be like to follow the flight of a baseball under a roof in a seat more expensive and distant from home plate than one now available. Thinking about life without tailgating or snowmobile suits, life without the legends we've built. They went right to the other speakers, and Stocking stayed in the room to hear them all out.

"I'm glad I said what I said," Stocking whispered. "I wasn't nervous, I just wanted to make an impact from the fan's standpoint. Everybody is losing sight of the games to be played. The Met is the greatest ballpark in the country next to Fenway in Boston. They shouldn't tear the Met down, they should make it a landmark. We can afford that."

Then Stocking went out to catch a bus home.

January 18, 1978

Dear Members of the Stadium Commission:

As you may have gathered from past correspondence, I have been highly critical of even the mention of a domed facility for our local sporting clubs. My biases were based solely on perception, however, as I had never been inside a domed stadium until recently when it was my privilege to join 76,000 other people for the Super Bowl. I am referring to the Louisiana Superdome, the eighth or ninth wonder of the world, depending on who's counting.

I can assure you it was an experience I wish every Minnesotan could have enjoyed, although they can probably duplicate it by going to an office building and viewing the action on the street from the 27th floor. But why quibble?

Never have I felt so totally at ease, so totally cut off from the world as I did at that football game. I couldn't even hear the sound of body-to-body contact between the participants. Can you imagine how easy it was for two people to have a pleasant chat? Why, you almost forget why you came.

The structure's ventilation system is apparently so strong that it sucks a good deal of the game noise right off the floor along with the cigar smoke. Mind you, I'm only guessing that's why I couldn't hear the game, but I doubt it was because of my seat location. I didn't appear to be any farther from the field than the customers 20 or 30 acres across the way. I think it's one of the few stadiums I've been in about which you can truly say "there isn't a bad seat in the house." I read somewhere that they were orthopedically designed.

I was formerly opposed to a domed stadium because I thought that weather — any kind of weather — not only necessitated a great deal of strategy by the teams but that it often provided a feeling of camaraderie and even excitement for the fans. Nonsense.

Dallas field goal kicker Effren Herrera missed three field goals and believe me, there wasn't so much as a whisper of wind in that building. And Herrera couldn't blame those misses on the sun or the moon because electrical lighting has replaced them both. He couldn't blame them on the turf because that uniformly green carpet is laid over hard and level concrete. And it would surprise me to learn that Mr. Herrera had the jitters because from where he stood he was at least 75-100 yards from the nearest fan, who was enjoying a chat with his neighbor anyway.

What I particularly liked about the Superdome, once my eyes adjusted from the brilliant afternoon sun, was the incredible sense of security I felt inside. I mean, New Orleans could have been attacked by Communists or something and you wouldn't even have known it until the game was over. There are no windows in the Superdome and the doors are constructed of tinted glass so that once inside you are no longer a part of the world but hiding from it.

I haven't even touched on the advantages of a domed stadium for baseball. Sentimentalists will argue that a ballpark is a thing of character and what makes baseball so beautiful is the virtually limitless boundaries it enjoys. Nonsense again.

I lingered after the football game and watched the dome crew take up great sheets of the carpet in steamroller-like contraptions. Almost in minutes they can have that building ready for baseball with all the same characteristics and features that make it so attractive for football.

I know from experience in Minnesota that few things are more annoying than watching a baseball game at the Met when half the field is in sunshine and the other half in shade. And I would suspect the games would be more evenly contested if the pitcher never again had the advantage of throwing from sunlight into shadow.

These fortunate and proud people of New Orleans don't have a baseball team, but when they get one they won't even have to bring a jacket to the ballpark, or a sweater, or sun glasses. And they certainly won't perspire much and who among us in Minnesota hasn't experienced the inconvenience of a sweaty night at the Met when the wind blows in hard and hot from the south?

I don't know how I formed my misconceptions but I'm here to apologize for them. Nevertheless, your task remains difficult. Some misguided sports fans in this region have the perverse notion that our kind are a little bit hardier than most and that our sports teams have acquired a certain amount of legend because they play their games outdoors in a variety of seasons.

Send those people to New Orleans is what I say. It's about time people in Minnesota took a look at the future and realized that if the games are to be made as uniform as possible then so should the buildings that house them.

January 27, 1978

Psssst. Come here, I've got a confession to make. Remember last week when I wrote that I loved the Louisiana Superdome? I was kidding. It was a joke. Really, it was.

I hate domed ball parks. I HATE BALL PARKS WITH ROOFS. OK? GOT THAT? I DO NOT ENDORSE, PRAISE, FAVOR, DESIRE OR LUST AFTER A DOMED STADIUM FOR THE TWIN CITIES. FOR MORAL, ECONOMIC, PHILOSOPHICAL AND AESTHETICAL REASONS I AM OPPOSED TO THE CONSTRUCTION OF A DOMED STADIUM.

Pardon me for writing in big letters like that, but I'm terribly rattled about the events of the last week. I had groomed a careful image as a domed-stadium opponent and now I'm afraid it has been tarnished.

On Jan. 18, in a mock letter to the local stadium commission, I wrote what some people — too many people — regarded as a glowing tribute to the Louisiana Superdome. I mentioned how the dome cut you off from humanity, how unnecessarily plush it was and how it was so lavishly insulated and ventilated that you couldn't even hear the football players crashing into each other.

I didn't think those were nice things to say about a place that was supposed to be a ball yard, but a lot of people did.

I went on to say that there wasn't a bad seat in the house, but I thought you'd get the hint when I said it was because the seats were orthopedically designed.

And I wasn't kidding when I said any Minnesotan could duplicate a Superdome experience by going to the 27th floor of an office building and watching the people on the street. In the upper reaches of the Superdome that's about how far you are from the field, 27 floors, get it?

I thought I sprinkled enough clues throughout the piece for people to realize that the Superdome is nothing but a big chunk of blight that is bleeding those poor people dry. That thing will be nearly impossible to pay for, and even if you could pay for it, it wouldn't be worth it.

It's too big, too unmanageable and too hauntingly impersonal. Worse yet, a game in the Superdome just isn't any fun unless your idea of a good time is to sit in a big dark building all afternoon and wonder what the world is up to.

So anyway, the newspaper prints the column and I'm thinking that it was a nifty piece of satire. Lady Mary Wortley Montagu, who was very big in the poetry business between 1689 and 1762, once said, "Satire should, like a polished razor keen/Wound with a touch that's scarcely felt or seen."

Baloney. If you want people to get your message, you better hit them over the head with it.

The next day the phone was ringing. People wanted to know if I had flipped my lid or what. Others wanted to point out the tremendous costs of running a domed stadium and why didn't I mention that?

Mostly the people who called were confused. "Just what does that creep mean?" is what these confused people wanted to know. Incidentally, I'm not aware of a single caller who wanted to thank me for saying something nice about a domed stadium.

You know what I think that means? I think the people who favor a domed stadium are too embarrassed to admit it.

Then the letters and post cards came in, from as far away as Sioux Falls, S.D., and from as near as this newspaper building, where some of the executive types had bets with each other on just what I meant.

Here's a post card from a guy in Sioux Falls who wrote, "I'm very glad you had a nice time in the Superdome, but please tell us if they are in the black or red. What's the place like moneywise?" Moneywise, the place is a mess. The politicians made big promises, said the Superdome wouldn't cost more than $35 million. Ha! Final construction costs were about $175 million and interest might push the price to $300 million.

But I don't want to get into that. I want to stick to setting things straight. The part that apparently tripped up most people was the last paragraph. I said it was about time people in Minnesota realized what the future holds — uniform games and uniform buildings to house them and how we should hurry up and conform.

What Lady Montagu and I really meant by that was "Yuuuuch!" The local teams, particularly the Vikings, have developed a character and legend by playing their games outdoors in what is basically a very enjoyable and healthy change of seasons. Why would anyone want to pay $100 million to rob us of the charm and uniqueness that doesn't exist anywhere else in this country?

Still, I wasn't going to write this clarification until I opened the newspaper Thursday morning and saw a letter to the editor from Jim N. Karcher of Burnsville, who wrote in opposition to last week's column.

That the paper would print such a letter indicates that the people I work for were as confused as Jim Karcher. I'm on your side Mr. Karcher. It was a joke. Really, it was. It was satire, and I promise never to do it again.

August 20, 1978

Max Winter has aged gracefully to 74 now and his life has been colored by the feel and power of money. He is a silver-haired patriarch, but his roots are in the streets of north Minneapolis where his father, Jacob, sold apples from a pushcart and where Max hawked newspapers and performed delivery boy chores when the city was little more than a grain depot on the river bend.

Max, who had sailed to America from Austria below decks on the liner George Washington, hustled with the immigrant's dream of wealth and respect and he acquired all of it because Max Winter was the guy who would take the extra step, always.

From where Max Winter sits, practically alone at the top of this city now, the landscape is incomplete. Max Winter wants a shrine. He worked hard to acquire the Vikings in 1961. Max Winter wants a shrine of a stadium for the football team that made him famous.

What else are we to make of his remarks a few days ago when he confirmed his wooing by the Los Angeles Coliseum Commission? This is a group of men searching for a team to replace the Rams when they move to Anaheim in 1980. Max Winter's real message, the message from his gut, screamed between the lines of his public comment.

"We already have an open stadium, why build another one?" Winter said in reference to at least one commissioner's desire for an open-air stadium. "I think for the amount of money the legislature has allotted for a stadium ($55 million maximum) they could put a cover on the thing. I am not in favor of the austere stadium the commission is talking about now."

Our society is living in a danger zone of inflation and energy costs, but a new football park must be embellished with grandeur. Rome went in the tank once for this kind of thinking. It comes down to a roof for Max Winter and the football team that made him famous. A roof to cover the playing field.

"Deep down I don't want to move," Max Winter said. "I want my money in this town, my family is here and I don't have that many years left. I'd love to stay here."

But the threat is there, weakly disguised. Winter does not make foolhardy comments. He apparently is convinced that the Minnesota Vikings ("And the Twins," Winter said. "I'm not in this alone.") need a dome for their clients who apparently suffer miserably in spite of the spirited legend that has built around the team's following.

If it comes down to a roof, then it comes down to aesthetics. And if it comes down to aesthetics, here's betting that most Minnesotans would prefer a sensible and handsome open-air stadium, where they can cheer outside and keep alive the legend that distinguishes this community from those who watch their games in ignoble concrete cylinders and under artificial light.

Max is not to be underestimated. He was raised in the company of hustlers, of Sid Gillman and Morris Chalfen and Bill Boyer and other graduates of North High who went on to be big men in the world of power and money. Max Winter will act in his own best interests because that is his law. He would move to Los Angeles under the right circumstances. His lodge brothers would undoubtedly step in at that juncture.

The NFL rules prohibit one team from moving within a 75-mile radius of another. The Rams would be only 30 miles away, but their president, Carroll Rosenbloom, has given Max his blessing for a continuous romance with the Coliseum Commission.

The NFL would have to waive the 75-mile rule. NFL rules also require a unanimous 28 votes to shift an established team, and it seems unlikely that the NFL would condone a move to Los Angeles by the Vikings. The league opens itself then to lawsuits from Minnesota interests who would be arbitrarily denied their team. How could the NFL condone five teams in California while some states have none?

The problems around a move by the Vikings would be complex

but no more complex than a just way to settle the stadium issue here. The millions of dollars that will inevitably be spent on some stadium plan should satisfy a lot of people and the local stadium commission should not quake at the words of one man.

We don't have to assume a quaking posture because of what Max Winter says. Max Winter is a beautiful man in the ways of vision and drive. But none of us, in this time and age, are worthy of shrines. They're too expensive to operate.

October 1, 1978

A roof on a ball park is the last doorslamming insult to the sports fan and player already burdened with contrivance, gimmickry and technology. But a domed stadium in downtown Minneapolis is one of apparently two new stadium choices available to us after cost estimates predicted such a facility could come in, barely, under the $55 million wire.

The other alternative is an open-air, multiple-use stadium in Bloomington that also would gobble up all but loose change of its allotted $42 million. Anyone who believes either stadium could be built so daringly close to budget would stand in line to buy the Brooklyn Bridge. Don Poss, executive director of the Metropolitan Sports Facilities Commission, advises fanatics to remain calm nevertheless.

"The people doing our estimating (Construction Management Group)," Poss said by phone the other day, "are the same people who may very well submit a bonded and guaranteed bid to build the project. If the project came in over cost, they'd lose the money."

An important third alternative went unreported when the commission was presented cost estimates Wednesday. An open-air football and soccer stadium built in conjunction with remodeling Metropolitan Stadium for baseball has not been overlooked, according to Poss.

"A lot of people are rooting for that alternative," Poss said. "The commission hasn't drawn any conclusions against it yet."

Round one in the stadium debate is now completed and all participants are winded, except the money men. Money talks. The guys with money are perfectly willing to let the commission continue with its task, so long as it remains a charade for what's really going down. The guys with dollar signs in their eyes are charging ahead with plans to privately finance the Industry Square site at the tune of $11.5 million.

Harvey Mackay, a leading money guy and president of the Greater Minneapolis Chamber of Commerce, had enough breath left after round one to make a proclamation. "The business community will not accept an uncovered facility," Mackay said.

So there. Begone with the rest of us. And begone with the games. Somewhere between the ball park and the bank the sporting priorities in this country have been twisted beyond recognition. Sporting events have become excuses for a guy to make a buck in his restaurant, sell another suit off the rack and keep the traffic moving through downtown.

The games and the establishments in which they are conducted, have become inconsequential in a grand scheme of uniformity. Commerce ain't wrong, but it sure gets ugly when it attaches itself to something that should remain distinct from the flow of our lives.

The fan has put up with enough. Seal the pure fan under a roof and he won't hang around too long. Games were meant to be played outdoors. In football particularly, the weather is the saving grace of a game already gone dry and predictable because of television. Take nature out of football and you're left with a long nap.

Baseball is a beautiful game because of the inherent boundlessness of its perimeters. A roof begets artificial turf and artificial turf begets injuries, the strikingly unfair base hit, all uniformly so.

No less a football authority than George Allen, in a guest column in the Los Angeles Times, recently argued for the preservation of his sport.

"Football was meant to be played outdoors, on grass," Allen wrote. "The weather is part of the game. A football game in the snow or downpour is an exciting contest because of the alteration in strategy and tactics such conditions require. The real fan isn't bothered by the weather, and he appreciates that the game won't be postponed regardless of the barometer."

In the same column Allen wrote, "Half of the games in the NFL are now played on artifical turf. From the standpoint of player safety, this is the worst thing ever to happen in football. With synthetic turf, all you've got, in effect, is a concrete slab with a carpet over it."

Some sort of stadium will be built in this community. Here's rooting for the third alternative above, less expensive than the other two more-publicized alternatives. Save Metropolitan Stadium for baseball. If they must build, build a football-soccer stadium on the adjacent grounds. The games remain pure. The grass remains real. And the fan remains an individual, with something distinct in the flow of his life.

June 13, 1979

The need for a domed stadium was never more evident than on Tuesday evening, when along about 8 o'clock a blinding sunset would have deprived Metropolitan Stadium viewers in the outfield bleachers of a clear picture of home plate.

In the old days, people out there would have made sunshades of their hands and outfielders most certainly would have needed dark glasses against such an inconvenience, this display of hot orange light.

It was terrible, what with a temperature in the 70s combining to make baseball viewing on this summer evening reminiscent of that day — it seems so long ago — when a nice breeze and a beer were the only comforts against outside baseball.

Thank goodness for the new dome is what I say. Here inside the new building, still smelling of concrete, fluorescent lights gave a uniform sheen to the neat plastic sod. And without wind and shadows, there was no mistaking the crack of bat on ball or no excuses either for an outfielder misjudging a fly ball, unless the ball bounced off the roof.

But that didn't happen last night in the new dome in the game between the Twins and the Yankees. Everything went really smoothly and many of the customers agreed that even 80 degrees cools down so much faster inside a building. Last night was one of those nights when heat would have lingered at the Met until the moon came up.

I wonder, too, if we all aren't a little bit happier now that the entire entertainment scene of downtown Minneapolis is available to us baseball fans. Before, most people went home from the ball park after a game. Now, with the lights of the big town blinking and tempting, many of us can stroll around the streets and perhaps buy a new suit or take in a late dinner at one of the many fine restaurants within walking distance.

With the Twins batting in the sixth against the Yankees last night, I wandered through the concrete hallways, ramps, and runways and talked with fans. Here was a happy family, the Bud Ray family of south Minneapolis. Bud, his wife, Sally, and three children, Todd, Brian and Mary, had seats along the third base line.

"How did you get to the building tonight, Mr. Ray?" I asked.

"Why, we took the new rapid transit system, of which the domed stadium is such a natural hub," Mr. Ray said.

"And are you enjoying the game?"

"Very much," Mr. Ray said. "It could be raining out right now and we wouldn't even know it. With a domed stadium you can always count on a ball game. You can imagine the comfort felt by outstate fans who will no longer turn back at the first gathering of clouds."

"Your kids certainly seem to be having fun," I said. "Todd, Mary, Brian, what do you think?"

"I can't wait until the game is over," Mary said, "because Mommy and Daddy promised they'd take us for a stroll on the brightly lit downtown streets."

"Perhaps I will buy a new suit," Bud Ray said.

"I'd like to talk him into trying a late dinner at one of the many fine restaurants within walking distance," Sally Ray said.

"I haven't heard a peep out of you boys," I said.

"It's hot in here," Brian and Todd said.

"Nonsense, boys," their father said. "Just think, you could be outside right now."

"And taking chances with that darn Mr. Weatherman," their mother said.

"Yeah, but. . ."

"Quiet, boys," Mr. Ray said. "Something is happening on the field."

Roy Smalley was lying in a twisted position near second base, holding his knee and crying out for a trainer.

A stretcher was required. As Smalley was being carried off the field, the giant and expensive new replay scoreboard showed Smalley sliding. One of his spikes appeared to catch a loop in the plastic turf and his knee turned at a right angle away from his leg.

"That's the fourth Twins regular to leave a game this year," Mr. Ray said. "I'll tell you. I watched a lot of games at the old Met and I'll tell you. They just play a rougher brand of baseball now. Nobody can say this game is for sissies. It's just a better game all around."

I thanked the Rays and zeroed in on an elderly couple enjoying the game from behind the first-base dugout. Harvey and Rose Wood said the new dome was a blessing in disguise for them. Rose Wood fanned herself with a program while Harold fiddled with his transistor radio.

"Picking up a little static," Harvey Wood said. "Small price to pay. I can't have my baseball on radio and eat my cake too."

"This place was designed for the senior citizen," said Mrs. Wood, who looked to be in her 70s. "We, that is, Harvey and I, live in St. Paul. We used to drive our car to the games at the Met with another couple. But now we take a bus, transfer twice and then walk only three blocks. It's so much easier for senior citizens to get to the ball park."

"Most of your senior citizens," Harvey said, "practically live right downtown."

"What do you think of the crowd, Mr. Wood?"

"Tell you the truth," he said, "I'm a little disappointed. Four thousand fans on a night like this is a little disappointing. Seems to me the Yankees used to be a better draw."

Like Harvey Wood, I couldn't figure it out. How could anyone stay away from a ball park on a night like last night?

October 17, 1979

There was some commotion Tuesday morning on the corner of 4th St. and 9th Av. S. in the area of scrub weed and backfill known as Industry Square. The big guy with the beard was Denny Thoreson and he had his ear cocked to the engine of his Koehring 1166E hydraulic back hoe, which is used to move earth in the construction of things like domed stadiums. It's a beautiful piece of equipment with heavy cat tracks and a long, jointed steel arm with a scoop shovel at the end.

Thoreson is the operator. A guy named Scott Brecht, who is only 18, is known as the oiler on the rig. And now there was some trouble because a pump gave out and there was some question about what to do. They shut the Koehring down and jumped to the ground, kicked dirt around with the toes of their work boots.

"We're rerouting a sanitary sewer line for the city," Thoreson was saying. "Have been for three months."

"Probably close 4th St. pretty soon," Brecht was saying.

Maybe you think the domed stadium only became a reality on Monday, when bonds were sold to pay construction costs. Maybe you also think the moon is made of cheese. Down here on the barren landscape of Industry Square, land has been ripped up all summer, a chunk of 5th St. has been closed and a sewer line that once ran 20 feet below ground east to west across the site has been refashioned in a big loop so as not to conflict with the playing floor of Minnesota's new arena, which will be 40 feet below ground level.

Maybe you thought you had a chance against the dome with lawsuits and charter amendments and this bill against that counterbill and your signs that said "Save the Met." You never had a chance.

These guys in the work boots, through no fault of their own, have been moving dirt for months, long before Calvin Griffith ever signed a lease for his Twins, for example, and long before the Vikings forked over more dough to keep the thing alive. Maybe you held out the hope that Minnesota's teams would continue to play their games in the chill of winter and on warm summer nights the way they were meant to be played.

People who like to watch games outdoors never had a chance because some time ago the Big Buck guys put their mark on this development and everything since has been charade. Get ready for an indoor summer, the phony hop, the steel beam-trapped fly ball. Get ready for a clean and sterile game of football. Baby, they are taking your games from you and they are going to play them in a living room.

And now the Koehring was hissing and about to expire because of a problem with an oil pump. It figured. Nothing has gone right. Thoreson, 32, works for the city and lives in East Bethel, 30 miles north of Minneapolis. He fishes and he has a snowmobile and he doesn't much care about the Vikings and the Twins.

"I don't think the dome can hurt anything," Thoreson was saying.

"Yeah," Brecht said, "but if they needed it so bad, they should have built it two years ago. I got friends who drink and they don't like the liquor tax."

"It's a good thing," Thoreson said, "but I can't believe the whole deal myself. Too much politics. Wasn't there a referendum a few years ago that shot the thing down? Anyway, it's being built. I might go to it once or twice, I don't know."

Brecht lives in Maple Lake. He drives motorcycles and snowmobiles and, like Thoreson, he is not a big item on the ticket rolls of the Twins and the Vikings.

"I've been to Kicks games," Brecht was saying. "I think this location here has more streets out than the Bloomington location. This is more centrally located."

"And with an energy crunch on," Thoreson said, "it will be easier for people to get here. Old people walk by here and ask what we're doing. It's like we know something they don't. They seem pleased to get a stadium downtown."

Another guy in the crew, a guy who didn't want his name in the newspaper, was walking circles around the big back hoe and sticking his comments in. The guy wore a hard hat and he was talking about sewer bulkheads and the flow of the lines and geological surveys.

"Too much politics in this," the guy said. "I've seen too much of it in my life. I think it's important to keep a city alive and keep the city growing and I think the dome is good for employing people. But there has been nothing but lies in the entire project. We should have competent people in the legislature to get this done right. I'm at the corner of S. 4th St. and 9th Av. S. You don't think they lied to me about that, do you?"

The guy laughed and walked away. Thoreson and Brecht got back to the business of fixing the busted pump. There was no time for more talk. There was work to do and millions of dollars to be spent before the Big Buck guys could break ground in the ceremony that will take the fun out of big league sports.

13/The Minnesota Vikings

The players

Chuck Foreman

October 7, 1977

Stripped of his football garments, Chuck Foreman could pass for any other successful young businessman, with digs in Edina and two of Germany's finest cars in the garage.

Foreman is as compulsively neat, cool and collected off duty as on. His apartment is decorated sparsely in muted natural-toned furniture, Ho-Chu Oriental prints, a graphic on framed glass and assorted plant life, here a philodendron in a wicker basket, there a fern that seems to have taken root in a tall chrome cylinder.

A bookcase has been ordered as well as additional art for a living room wall. Foreman currently is reading "A State of Blood", written by Ugandan Henry Kyemba, Idi Amin's exiled minister of health. Foreman will read most anything that interests him, including passages from a slim, leather-bound Bible, the only book on display. Foreman is religious, but I have never heard him publicly credit his maker for a 60-yard touchdown run.

"It suddenly occurs to me," I said, "that the greatest part about being a professional athlete is that you don't have to go jogging when you get home from work. I mean, you've worked physically all day so that when you come home you can enjoy yourself without feeling guilty."

"And I do," Foreman said. "I come in that door tired and it's a good feeling to know I can relax. I don't bring football home with me. I stay here alone, clean and cook for myself."

Foreman punched a button on his videotape playback machine and Elvis Presley's final televised concert, commercials and all, appeared on the adjacent television screen.

"That Elvis was a main man," Foreman said. "This concert might be a classic some day."

Elvis was tossing his sweaty scarves to ladies in the audience. They screamed. Elvis smirked. Foreman smiled.

It might astonish some people, while pleasing Coach Bud Grant, that despite his wealth and stature with the Minnesota Vikings and his instantly recognizable features, Foreman rarely leaves this home he has made for himself.

Minneapolis is not his kind of town. On his drives from Miami to training camp in Mankato, Foreman has discovered more night life in rural Georgia than he finds in Bloomington or Richfield or Edina. Foreman rarely sees a black face at Metropolitan Stadium, never sees one at his apartment complex. There are no night clubs here per se, no black night clubs, no favorite hangouts, haunts, restaurants, whatever. There is no corner for Foreman.

Yes, of course, these are small, perhaps even inconsequential agonies to suffer, especially for a man drawing Foreman's pay. But Foreman didn't bring up the subject. I did. Just a little more than a month ago Foreman and his teammate, Ahmad Rashad, were asked to leave their table at Maximilian's in Richfield because a waitress apparently thought they were through ordering refreshments. I asked him about it now but he sighed and spread his hands.

"That incident is done," Foreman said. "Let's speak in general terms. I make the best of the situation here but the lack of night life, not just for black people, but for everybody, is a drag. When you get to be an adult you should be able to stay out till 2 a.m. if that's your thing. We got to step it up a little here. I'm a city person by nature but Minneapolis is very much a country town, very slow."

Foreman likes Minneapolis and likes its people. And when he speaks of night life he is not looking for a place to bang his head on the bar. He doesn't drink, he sips, a distinction all waitresses should be required to make.

The unsaid thing between us was that the black professional athlete in Minnesota might never feel a total part of the community simply for the lack of a substantial and local black audience to appreciate his talents, for the lack of a black audience to embrace the athlete on and off the field.

One of the reasons that Larry Hisle and Lyman Bostock played out their options with the Twins was because they can make as much money or more in a town where their considerable talents can be parlayed into business opportunities, endorsements for and investments in black-owned and operated businesses, for example.

During the time Foreman tried to renegotiate his contract he said he felt it was hard for him to gauge whether he had community backing.

"I don't think people gave me the respect I earned," Foreman said. "I had to speak up for my own talent." Foreman also believes he would have more business opportunities in New York. Minnesota granted him his demands and he said the Minnesota Vikings are an undeniably good team to play for.

But Foreman will not put down roots here. He has lived in five different apartments in his five seasons as a Viking. He keeps his winter clothes in a steamer trunk, the only ill-fitting piece of furniture in his living room because right now the trunk is a table for his television and taping equipment. If the Vikings don't get past the play-offs, he might never have to unpack it.

August 23, 1978

Mankato, Minn.
Last winter Chuck Foreman called his mother from Miami and told her he would drive up in his new car and visit her in Maryland. He made the trip in 14½ hours, in a Ferrari 308 GTB, which is a sports car with the approximate feel of a fighter jet and the power of a nuclear submarine.

"Damn," Janet Foreman said from behind the curtain of her living room. She had heard her son come into the driveway and it was like the sound of an invasion. "Damn."

"Hey," Foreman said. "What do you think?" The car was new, the color of fresh mint. He pulled himself out of it in sections and removed his driving gloves finger by finger.

"Get rid of it right now," she said. "You'll kill yourself." She began crying.

"Come for a ride," he said.

"Get rid of it," she said.

Foreman's father, Francis, walked circles around the car. He looked at the car and then he looked at his son. When Foreman was growing up the family of six had one car, a 1949 Plymouth. Foreman didn't even have a driver's license in high school because he couldn't afford one, but he is a connoisseur of the world's finest automobiles now, or at least the fastest. His current obsession is the product of Italy. He has had others from Germany and America.

Chuck Foreman is consumed by the prospect of speed, as a running back might be, but it worries him. He walks around training camp saying things like, "I can't help it," or "What's wrong with driving fast?" or "I think I'll become a race car driver." He was to have raced the Ferrari in Florida over the winter but Mike Lynn, Minnesota's general manager, made objections.

"I've got to race," Foreman said Tuesday. "I know I'd be good at it and I feel it. I've got to race, as a hobby. I'd never make my living at it but I could win some amateur races. I love speed. Is that wrong?"

"Not if you are good at it," a man said.

"I'm good at it," Foreman said. "There's a time for speed and there's a time not to. I've only gotten two tickets this year and both times I was under the speed limit. People see this car coming and they think I'm speeding. It's so low to the ground and so loud that they think speed right away. But at 55 miles per hour in this car I'm only in third gear."

Foreman is not one of the world's third-gear types. He rides the fast lane, with his cars and his music and his income. His car is an absolutely shocking conveyance on the good streets of Mankato, and it probably will be in Minneapolis. Foreman owns one of only a handful of Ferraris in the country.

"It gives me a thrill," he said. "My Porsche Turbo was faster, but this is a thrill. I had to learn how to drive all over again."

You can tell a lot about a football player from his car. Or a coach. Bud Grant drives a truck, suitable for portaging rivers. Linemen travel in luxury. Tight ends chose strong sedans. The rookie's van is a mural of sunshine.

Foreman is unique. His car is an exclamation point, a possession of such concern that he uses it every day to transport himself the 200 yards or so from the team's quarters to the practice field at Mankato State University. His car is usually visible through the back door of the dining hall. At night, before and after meetings, he retreats to its leather cockpit and accelerates through the hills of Blue Earth County.

"I will definitely race," Foreman said, "but it looks like after my football career. I know the risks and I know the danger, but I am challenged by speed. People might think I'm crazy but the faster I go the better I feel. I'm in control. I'm alone. Very soon now I'm going to begin gathering the parts to build my own race car. A dream. I'll get a Porsche body and a Sebring engine and I'll build my own car. Faster than this."

"How fast is this one?"

"Did 180 m.p.h. so far," Foreman said. He bent down and examined a minute nick in the paint. A crowd assembled. Foreman reached in and pulled on his driving gloves finger by finger. "Need these gloves for control," he said. He climbed in one leg at a time and fired the engine. He was gone in a blur of green.

A man is without his possessions and without his family in a football training camp. Foreman has everything with him right outside his window in the parking lot. Standing still it looks to be doing about 60, which is what a lot of observers have said about its owner.

September 7, 1979

On Thursday, on the first truly crisp day of the new autumn, Chuck Foreman was refining the craft of running fast with the football. This is an employment — as Foreman proves every time he escapes through a sliver of light — that is best left to the processes of natural selection. The grass was firm under his feet yesterday, the sun was bright and Chuck Foreman was reinstalling the *the* in front of his name.

"I don't want to talk to no reporters," Foreman said afterward, walking across the field at Midway Stadium. "I don't want to talk to no reporters who call me fat and slow and put me down."

A man mimed horror at the thought. Foreman laughed. Foreman is 28 now and he is grown into the kind of man who knows how to have fun with his critics. This is a rare quality in athletes, especially gifted and high-strung running backs who are in the prime of their lives.

"I'll talk only a little bit," Forman said, lowering his eyes. "I don't have anything to prove. Callin' me fat and slow!"

"Wasn't me," a man said.

"I know," Foreman said. "I'm kidding. I'm having fun. I'm making the moves again."

"What's the football term for that," Foreman was asked, "the term for making the moves?"

"Going sideways through the hole," Foreman said. "I felt myself going sideways through the hole today. And when I looked at the game films from last Sunday, I saw myself going sideways through the holes."

Against the 49ers Foreman's moves were economical and quick, none of that waltzing with himself that tended to mark his performances last year. But last year Foreman suffered an injury to his right knee that prevented him from achieving a fourth consecutive 1,000-yard season. The knee was often swollen and stiff, so much so that he missed two games and parts of two others and rushed only 237 times, or about 40 fewer times than he wanted to.

Foreman also spent last season caring for his son, Jamal, who is now 3½. As any working parent knows, caring for a child can absorb energy and create tensions of its own kind. This season Foreman has retained live-in help for his son, whose mother lives elsewhere, presumably freeing the father for another of those seasons that will assure Jamal the college of his choice.

"I'm completely recovered physically," Foreman said. "A knee injury is a tough mental hang-up to overcome. That knee hurt me more mentally than any other way because I couldn't do the things I knew I could do, like go sideways through a hole. I'm a 1,000-yard runner. People expect 1,000 yards out of me and I expect it out of myself."

Foreman did not require surgery. Instead, he brought his leg back through weight training. He built up his entire body during the off-season and came to camp heavier than he had ever been, at 230 pounds, most of it newly acquired upper-body strength. More than a few cynics took one look at him, recalled his less than poetic running of last year, and decided that Foreman was not only slow, but fat.

"That's abuse," Foreman said. "I don't need that. If anything I'm faster than I ever was and I doubt anybody can catch me in that 25- or 30-yard burst from the line of scrimmage. My knee is healed. Besides, you get speed from upper body strength. It doesn't slow you down."

"You do look different," a man said, "broader in the shoulders."

"Bud Grant says that greatness comes with durability," Foreman said. "I think I've proven that I'm durable. The extra strength is like insurance for me. I'm different from other running backs because the game hasn't worn me down if I stay strong. We have a young man now named Ted Brown. If Ted Brown is durable he'll be a superstar."

Foreman will not call himself a superstar. He will not mind if others do. With Fran Tarkenton gone, with Alan Page and Carl Eller moved elsewhere, with Mick Tingelhoff and the rest of the legends retired, Chuck Foreman is the team's most public and recognizable figure.

Ahmad Rashad is finally getting his due, but Foreman can be the Reggie Jackson of the Vikings. He can be the straw that stirs the drink. The man is healthy again. He can go sideways through a hole.

December 7, 1979

It's doubtful that fame ever detached itself so severely from a performer as it has this year from Chuck Foreman, out of uniform now and recuperating in Miami Beach from a broken rib.

A man is entitled to a lost weekend now and then, but Foreman misplaced the entire 1979 season, which will enter the books as his worst campaign in seven years as a Minnesota Viking.

It's also entirely probable that when Foreman dived over a left tackle early in the second quarter against Detroit on Nov. 18, and fumbled, he performed his final chore in Minnesota colors. He was hurt on that play. Bud Grant gave Foreman the option of healing in Minnesota or at the beach, and because he has not been conked on the head once too often, Foreman chose the beach.

His final statistics, for he is on the injured list for the remainder of the season, read like the numbers of a fourth-stringer: 215 yards on 83 attempts, with two touchdowns and a longest run of 16 yards. These are the numbers of a man not two years removed from the third of three consecutive 1,000-yard seasons.

It was reported a few days ago in this newspaper that the Vikings attempted to trade Foreman as early as last spring and will attempt to do so again. General managers often engage in speculative and casual hypothetical bargaining, but it's not likely that any specific package involving Chuck Foreman was ever engineered by General

Manager Mike Lynn.

"If it's true that the team tried to trade me," Foreman said Thursday from Miami, "then I've been lied to. They told me they never tried to trade me."

As for attempting to do so, Foreman considers it inevitable. Perhaps it has been inevitable since game four of 1978, when Foreman injured a knee against the Bears. He will insist that he never fully recovered from that injury while continuing to play out last year's schedule. He will insist as well that he was ill-prepared to play second string to rookie Ted Brown when that situation developed in game five this year.

"In 1978 I tried to be a team man by playing with the bad knee," Foreman said yesterday, "and I end up getting the shaft. This year I came to camp and people were on me, the press was on me, said I was fat. I'm tired of this mess; it's been a long year and it's taken a lot out of me."

It was not easy being Chuck Foreman this year, just as it hasn't been easy for contemporaries like Lydell Mitchell and Lawrence McCutcheon to be themselves this year. Running back is such a volatile position that Foreman, and others his age, might have burned out at 29. Notice the hesitation. No one has had the nerve to actually catalog Foreman's demise and it will not be done here. Healthy, and proud once more, Foreman could still be devastating.

"Two or three years left," Foreman said, "I've got at least that."

But where? Foreman began the year as a starter, but after he gained 11 yards on six attempts against Green Bay on Sept. 23, he lost his job to Brown, who gained 77 yards on 15 carries in the same game. Brown started against the Lions in Detroit, became injured and reclaimed the job for keeps Oct. 28 in Tampa Bay.

"If the change had to be made, then fine," Foreman said. "Make it and keep quiet about it. I got tired of reading how washed up I was. I believe in myself and I know all of this is happening for the good of Chuck Foreman. I know what I can do and I can't think of anybody on that team who can play my position better than I can.

"They took me out of the line-up and the running game still went nowhere. There's no running attack at all. There's no way, I've got too much talent to play second behind anybody. I'm not going to play behind Ted Brown — not that he doesn't have talent — but I'm not playing behind anybody."

Foreman is under contract to the Vikings next year, with an option year in 1981. But he can be traded and he could come back and make fools of those who dispatch him. He could come back and make fools of us, who tired of his tread-water spins and doodles that led to nowhere. Chuck Foreman could come back.

"Football is a business," Foreman said. "Everything can't be all wine and roses. They've got to do something. I'd want to play someplace that has an offensive machine, where I can make a contribution. I don't need any more problems but I'll show people I can play.

Alan Page showed people he can still play."

Chuck Foreman is many things, but he's not stupid. Besides, it's hard to doubt a man who maneuvered himself to Florida in the dead of winter.

Tommy Kramer

November 16, 1977

Back home in San Antonio, Texas, Tommy Kramer entrusted his future to his father, retired Col. John Kramer of the U.S. Army. The colonel and his wife, Marie, had deposited their 11 children for brief stops in Seguin, Hallettsville and Kingsville, Texas, before they settled in San Antonio about the time Tommy, the youngest, was ready for junior high and his first organized football.

John Kramer had boxed some and played basketball and coached football at Texas Lutheran for a six-year stretch, but he advised his four daughters and seven sons to approach games casually and only after a proper amount of backyard seasoning. The seventh son had an inclination to basketball, but after a critical appraisal — Tommy hadn't yet reached 6 feet — John Kramer said football might be a wiser choice.

"And there's no use playing football until you're ready," the colonel told his youngest. "Junior high will be soon enough; there's just no sense to starting earlier than that. You can wear one of your brother's old uniforms, and we'll fool around in the back yard."

The colonel hung a tire from a tree in the back yard and rigged up a net behind that. He started Tommy off slowly throwing strikes through the tire until he had him up to 250 passes per day, proving that quarterbacks, good ones, are a little bit born and a little bit made.

Tommy Kramer never played quarterback behind anyone in junior high, and he was the starting quarterback for Robert E. Lee High School's junior-varsity team as a sophomore. As a junior he started for Lee, led the team to the state title and was named Texas high school Player of the Year for 1972.

The team lost out in the semifinals of the playdowns the next year, but Tommy Kramer had made a big name for himself and could have chosen any college in the country. At Rice, where he started all four years, he threw 1,036 passes, or about a week's worth with a back-yard tire.

"My dad knew what it would take for me to be a quarterback,"

Kramer said the other day after Vikings practice, "knew exactly what it would take and then showed me, right down to the agility drills he designed for me. He coached all his life so he also had a good notion of the pressure that exists for a little kid in football, so he kept me out of that and tutored me himself. I was getting enough pressure at home. Being the youngest of 11 you get picked on, might even lose out a little at the dinner table. We weren't poor, but we had to make do with what we had, and it wasn't a lot."

Last spring, after Kramer became the first quarterback ever chosen by the Vikings in the first round of the draft, Bud Grant said the youngster couldn't have chosen a more appropriate time to join the Vikings, given Fran Tarkenton's age and the then-free-agent status of Bobby Lee. Kramer agreed.

Raw quarterbacks, even consensus All-Americans and collegiate passing champions, are expected to serve a reasonable apprenticeship on the bench. John Kramer taught his son that part of the game as well. This was especially true with the Vikings, a team that was quarterbacked exclusively from its inception —except for a five-year time-out on Broadway — by Tarkenton.

Tarkenton achieves immeasurable fame for this community and he manages to paralyze us for six months a year with the kind of drive and intensity that marks his team. He is wealthy, famous, instantly recognizable and loved in the manner of that hot-and-cold romance between clients and the entertainers they pay to see.

But when Tarkenton went down with a broken bone in his leg last Sunday there was only a moment of hushed silence before the roar of welcome for the new kid, Kramer, who was so excited at the prospect of a genuine debut that he forgot to remove one of his warmup jackets.

"What did that moment feel like?" Kramer was asked. "Really feel like?"

"I felt elation," Kramer said. "But I want to clarify that. I felt elation that I would play in a game situation that meant something. I wasn't happy to see Tarkenton hurt, but you take your opportunities where you find them; that's the hard reality of the game. It's a good feeling to play, and I want to play badly. The expedient nature of the game is why it's a business at this level, just a means to some future end."

"Seems like a lot of good players just end up getting carried off the field one day," a man said.

"That's why I opened my books at Rice," Tommy Kramer said. "I got a degree. In business administration."

February 6, 1980

Tommy Kramer, late of Bloomington, Aspen, Colo., and the municipal hoosegow in Houston, Texas, appeared at the Radisson South Hotel the other evening as one of the celebrities at the Pro Sports Banquet. The Pro Sports Banquet allows Minute Men from both banks of the Mississippi to hang their arms around bigshot sport types and there is no bigger shot in sports than the local football quarterback.

"Happy to be here," Kramer told the clan at a cocktail party before the dinner. "Nice place. In jail I had a private suite. It was nice and quiet."

"There will be a run on Kramer jokes now," somebody said at a back table. "Maybe Kramer and Leon Spinks should form a driver's education school."

Kramer did have himself a set-to with the law down in Houston a while back, something about his condition to operate a motor vehicle. But Kramer is playing it smart by not hiding the incident. A man told him as much, but Kramer waved him off. He is under advisement from his attorney not to disclose too much about that night in Houston, so Kramer makes only a few light remarks, as though to put the crowd at ease.

"Shoot," Kramer said, "I ain't got nothing to worry about. I wasn't stopped for driving recklessly. I was stopped for an argument. The court date comes up in March and I'm not worried."

Kramer was in fine health on this occasion, considering the demands that might be made on a 24-year-old bachelor football star who makes a ton of money. After Minnesota's final 1979 game, at New England, he split for home in Houston. He hung around there long enough to heal the bruises and play some golf and then he moved the act to the ski slopes at Aspen.

"The Vikings allow you to ski?" somebody said.

"Intermediate hills only," Kramer said. "I'm afraid of those hills that go so straight down they look black at the bottom."

Kramer is a valuable package of bones and maybe a little sharper than people give him credit for. He owns a piece of a security-alarm system company, a couple of homes, and his mug is featured on the kind of bedroom poster that kids go wild for.

Besides, anybody who doesn't spend any more time in Minnesota during the winter than he has to is a leg up on the rest of us. Kramer was in town in December to sign five one-year contracts but then he disappeared again, presumably to spend the rest of the offseason in peace — until a wire service reporter saw Kramer's name on the Houston police charts.

"Could have happened to anyone else in this room," Kramer said, "and their name wouldn't have appeared in the paper."

Kramer's past performance record isn't long enough to determine if he will be a great quarterback or simply a good one. But last season he did something Fran Tarkenton never did by throwing every pass the team threw and playing in every offensive play save one, a fake punt maneuver in the last game of the year.

"It helped so much to play all the time," Kramer said, "it helped to stay in there even when I was making mistakes. Bud Grant knew what he was doing and I knew what he was doing by leaving me in there so I got the experience."

"What would you like to improve on next year?" Kramer was asked. Kramer threw 24 interceptions in 566 attempts, eight fewer interceptions than Tarkenton threw the previous year on just six more attempts.

"Throw less interceptions," Kramer said. "We need some help. We need some secondary help and we need a big running back, the kind of guy who can hit the line for two or three yards and not fall backwards."

"You'll be the quarterback forever," a Minute Man told Kramer.

"Unless I get traded," Kramer said. "There's no team I'd rather play for. I'd like a different climate maybe, but not a different team." The Minute Man looked shocked. "You won't get traded," he said.

Kramer didn't look so sure. He doesn't take much for granted in this young life, except that maybe no self-respecting football fan of a judge is going to nail a poster boy for arguing with the cops.

Bud Grant

December 7, 1977

Just after his lunch and just before his racquetball appointment Tuesday, Bud Grant was cornered by a man who carried an urgent question from all inhabitants of the seven-county Metropolitan Mosquito Control District: WHAT THE HECK IS GOING ON WITH YOUR BALL CLUB, BUD?

Grant pulled back his sleeve and examined his watch. "I've got 17 minutes," he said.

"How can a miracle like Sunday's happen?" the man said. "What accounts for consistency and inconsistency?"

"In the stands it's easy for people to give up," the Vikings coach said. "The coaches and players are the last to give up on a game. It's like in a fight, when the fighter is the last guy in the place who thinks he's getting beaten. The toughest thing a coach does is try to maintain intensity from week to week. That's the biggest job we have. It's difficult. It's so difficult that there are good football players who can't make the pros because they can't maintain the intensity.

"We are involved in emotional endurance contests. We see many teams come apart at various times during the season. You fight that off. A week doesn't go by that I don't get a call from somebody who wants to come in and do research on players. One week a guy wanted to sell us transcendental meditation. I get calls from psychologists and experts in biorhythms, people, cold and calculating, who want to figure out the emotional levels of the players and the games."

"The Dallas Cowboys use biorhythm charts," the man said.

"They would," Grant said. "After we beat the Cowboys in the playoffs a few years back I got a call from someone in their organization. He wanted to know everything. What kind of strength program we had, did we have psychological training. He said that we were the first team that year to physically manhandle the Cowboys and he demanded some kind of logic for it. I thought the guy was putting me on. I told him we didn't use any such programs, didn't spend $500,000 a year on such stuff."

"What did the guy say then?"

"He was upset," Grant said. "He said, 'Please don't tell anybody I made this call.' "

"You mean," the man said, "that the Vikings of 1977 don't use any of the techniques currently available for developing human potential?"

"Me," Grant said, "I'm all of that. I'm their TM and the biorhythm man. I'm all of it. Not in a cold and calculating way. It's all in my head. It comes from the experience of being in the game for 30 years. Football is a set of the same experiences repeated over and over again. Sunday's game left an indelible mark on the players and the fans. You don't normally win a game 28-27 after trailing 24-0. But it was a great experience and it could happen again."

"Is coaching more difficult toward the end of a season?" Grant was asked.

"No," he said, "but maintaining that intensity gets more difficult. I feel my responsibility more. We maintain the intensity subconsciously. We shorten practices, for example. Players today are very perceptive. You don't tell people to run through walls anymore. They don't buy anything on face value.

"They need proof and reasons for things. They look at you intently. I was brought up under the old-time coaching, you're only as tough as a tough practice, that kind of thing. Doesn't work any more. We've all had to change. We've become salesmen. We sell and the players buy. They'll question us carefully until they know exactly what it is we want so they can know how to deliver," Grant said.

Grant was saying that his football team will win, lose or draw because those are the only options. Victory is a product available to them and they will pursue it in much the same way a consumer goes after something he wants. Sometimes methodically, sometimes irrationally, sometimes spontaneously, but usually, depending on the salesman, wholeheartedly.

July 23, 1978

Bud Grant has a nice office. He has a purple telephone and a picture of a dog with a bird in its mouth. He has a stuffed lake trout on the wall and its mouth was fixed into a permanent scream by the taxidermist. He also has a bust of his old dog, Cork, cast in bronze.

"Old Cork," Grant said.

"Cork," I said.

"Yup," Grant said.

"You start training camp Thursday," I said.

"Umm hmmm," Grant said. Paused. Took a sip of soda pop. Listened to the business of football being conducted in the adjacent offices.

"Old Cork," I said.

"Yup," Grant said.

Look, it was almost that casual with Grant in his office. He is not, as the Viking mystique insists, one-dimensional, stoic or without humor, but he allows that illusion to exist because he is entertained by it. It also helps him to guard his privacy. This apparent dullness or complacency, even Grant's own calm on the eve of another season of condoned violence, might be his truest genius and so subtle as to be overlooked by a majority of local and national clients, not to mention Howard Cosell.

Once again the Vikings report to training camp without one glaring vacancy to fill. Once again the Vikings report to camp following a season of tremendous success. Once again there is no need for hysteria or conjecture or doubt, because the Vikings will need to build only a little bit upon existing strengths. There are people in football who find these conditions absolutely unacceptable, because they conduct the business of their own teams in more uproarious and haphazard fashion. Chuck Noll of Pittsburgh and George Allen of Los Angeles have already been fined, for Pete's sake.

"I still retain some thriftiness from my days as general manager in Winnipeg," Grant said. "We don't have rookie camps, we don't employ three dozen coaches, we don't have the mini-camps. I don't like to waste money or time. Other clubs spend a fortune, and all based on the assumption that the coach knows what he's doing."

Bud Grant won't come right out and admit to genius, but he'll leave crumbs. By making the unsuspecting dodo aware of certain truths — his Minnesota Vikings have more victories, 84, than any other team since the 1970 AFL-NFL merger, for example — Grant effectively destroys the team's myth of antiquity.

When the Vikings report Thursday to Mankato, they will be the last of 28 NFL teams to begin training and for good reason, another crumb. If all goes according to plan, Bud Grant will get his crew cut topped off every three weeks, fill his gas tank every four days and win another Central Division championship by mid-December. It would be the team's 10th title over-all and sixth consecutive in Grant's 12 years at Minnesota.

There's just not much for the guy on the street to worry about. Fran Tarkenton will be present Thursday and if he feels healthy he'll play. Maybe Duck White can win a tackle job and maybe, with a full training camp to his advantage, Bob Tucker can ace out Stu Voigt at tight end.

The Vikings didn't draft a receiver, but they have Bob Grim in backup and some free agents at that position. Who will run in tandem with Chuck Foreman is no big problem because Sammy Johnson, Brent McClanahan and Robert Miller are formidable athletes.

"If we had to," Grant said the other afternoon, "we could line up tomorrow and run a play that could fool the average fan. The season is 5½ months, seven days a week. Why tack on an extra month at the beginning? Time doesn't necessarily equal success. A rookie would go to camp after he signed his contract. The veterans guard the privilege of a late camp judiciously. It gives them an edge, it gives them ammunition when they line up against some guy who has been sweating it out the month of July."

"Training camp is kind of dull anyway," the dodo said.

"It is," Grant said, "it really is. There's not much to see, at least in our organization."

Training camp might be dull, but two players who played out their options with the Vikings, Ed Marinaro and John Gilliam, have called their old boss trying to get back in. Grant doesn't want them, not because of personal reasons, but because in Bud Grant's calm and orderly scheme of things they no longer fit into the system.

"Ed was a New York kid," Grant said, "he always used to go home and say that nobody knew who he played for because he played for the Vikings. He discovered the Vikings weren't so bad. Same with Gilliam. He wanted to live in Atlanta, his home. But suddenly, without Fran Tarkenton, he wasn't the greatest receiver in the world. He was asked to run on the inside for one thing, something he won't do."

Marinaro? He was released by the Jets, finished out the last half of 1977 on Seattle's bench, was not asked to return and has signed with Chicago. Gilliam? He was cut by Atlanta and Chicago, finished out the season at New Orleans and is out of football.

Not only do the Vikings have the most wins since the merger (Oakland has a slightly better winning percentage) but since slipping to 7-7 in 1972, the Vikings have never approached the pit other championship teams have fallen into.

Green Bay, Kansas City, the Jets, Miami, Pittsburgh and Baltimore have all experienced some manner of disaster after championship seasons. About the worst thing that happened to the Vikings recently was sliding last year from second best team in the league to perhaps the third or fourth. And only six starters remain on the squad from the first Super Bowl appearance in 1970 and only 13 from Roman Number 8 in 1974.

"Something snaps in the organizations that fall," Grant said, "and it's hard crawling out of the hole. The challenge for us is to remain on top. Well, that's one of the best accomplishments you can have in this business. It kind of puzzles me why the only news that comes out of Minnesota concerning us is our age."

Bemuses might be a better word than puzzles. Grant is easily bemused. It bemused him why so much fuss was made when Atlanta established the NFL record for fewest points allowed over 14 games with 129 last year. The Vikings had held the old record of 133 since 1969 and he heard nary a word about it. It bemused him that in the mad scramble before this season, 10 new head coaching jobs were filled. It also has bemused him that one of the essential ingredients of the team's success has been overlooked.

"We find a way to win," Grant said. "We're not inflexible. We go into games with preconceptions but we're not inflexible. Somewhere in a game there will be an opportunity to win the thing. You take our 22 and compare them against the 22 of just about any other team and the other team just looks better. But we win because we do it in different ways. Veterans know how to win, they have more avenues to travel. We don't play up and we don't play down and we don't fizzle out. We're emotionally stronger."

It doesn't make for good television, but it's not bad football.

October 24, 1979

Picture it: The Vikings are leading Tampa Bay by a field goal with only minutes to play. The Vikings punt. The Buccaneer return man clearly fumbles the ball, but the referee — that inept amateur! — the referee whistles the ball dead, awarding possession to Tampa Bay.

Bud Grant goes berserk. It's nightmare time. He rips off his cap and throws it on the field. He jumps up and down. He charges onto the field and goes jaw to jaw with the referee. Grant pulls a rule book from his back pocket, tears it apart and dumps the scraps on the ref's head.

Oh, it's all coming out now, 13 years of frustration and holding back, 13 years of hard swallows and wounded pride. That inept amateur! The refs blew another call!

The referee thumbs Grant out of the game, thumbs him right off the field as would a baseball umpire. Grant circles the field. He won't leave. The referee points. Grant walks very deliberately across the field. The fans are screaming for the referee's hide. The noise is like nothing ever heard at Metropolitan Stadium (yes, and the young Bucs are in awe, that's what's important, the Bucs are in awe). Grant stops at midfield. He peels off his headset and hurls it at the referee. The Vikings are so keyed up now, so shocked and angered, that they hold Tampa Bay and win the game.

It could happen. Sometime. Grant isn't saying when. But if the time is right, he could do it, he could pull an Earl Weaver with the best of them.

"Baseball managers get away with it all the time," Grant was saying Tuesday. "Maybe baseball managers don't have much to do during a game. Football coaches are more under control. There is always the implicit threat of a fine if we walk on the field. We're fined to the hilt. But officials will tolerate a certain amount of jostling and if the time was ever right . . ."

Grant was addressing himself yesterday to the practice of having to name his line-up before the start of the game. It irritates him to do so and deprives him, he contends, of strategic advantages. In a roundabout way, he mentioned that baseball managers deprive themselves of similar strategic edges with the tradition of naming starting pitchers in advance.

"Maybe," Grant said, "they do it for the gamblers. But if I was a baseball manager, I'd come up with a blister for my guys, throw the other team off balance."

"By the same token," a man said, "football tradition deprives you of the opportunity to go on the field and challenge officials."

"There's a time for that," Grant said. "From a team standpoint, there will be a time for that. It's still back there in my mind that I could throw the headset at them. Getting kicked out of a game wouldn't be such a monumental thing in our business. Never on the road. But I'd do it at home. You think that might incite the fans? Especially if I haven't done it in 13 years? Maybe it's one of my nightmares."

Look. No football coach has ever campaigned harder, been fined more often or argued more consistently for professional officials than Grant. Amateurism gets under his skin in a game where even the scoreboard operators are professionals. But the referee — *the referee is a schoolteacher from Ashtabula.*

And Grant can't do anything for his own soul, not the way Earl Weaver or Gene Mauch can. An Earl Weaver will lose his argument with the first base umpire, but, hey, just maybe in the later innings the umpire gives Earl a close call just to avoid hearing from him again. It happens. Grant can't play that psychological game, not really, even though he tries to from his boxed lines on the bench, even though he admits it could be of some use.

"The guys who were really hard on referees seem to be out of the game," Grant was saying now. "George Halas and Paul Brown were rough. When Norm Van Brocklin was here, people spent more time listening to him than watching the game. Don Shula was one of the worst. He knew the first names of every official in the league and then he dressed them all down with every four-letter word in the book. Shula doesn't do that anymore. He got religion.

"I've tried to be cool. Where I come from, it was unheard of to swear at an official. In the Canadian league, you just didn't do it, couldn't get away with it. I don't know how the NFL coaches got away with it."

Grant knows which officials will be working Vikings games two weeks beforehand. When drawing certain crews, his antennae go out a little. He gets tight, but still he has been cool, satisfied to get in his postgame rips and digs and slants. He even has the opportunity, as do baseball managers, of grading officials, but he refuses to.

"I've got enough trouble grading my own players," Grant said, "why should I do the league's work? The league figures it's a nice quiet way for coaches to let off steam. The league knows how I feel about officials."

Grant is not advocating the intimidation of officials, he is advocating professionalism and democracy. And on that one occasion when he chooses to exercise his rights under the First Amendment, whenever it happens, the man's nightmare could be our pleasure.

October 29, 1980

It has become the obsession of those listeners who volunteer their opinions to the various call-in radio talk shows around town that the Minnesota Vikings are experiencing dire straits. These are would-be sports oriented call-in shows as opposed to open line shows where listeners engage the hosts in such serious debate as the effect of moonbeams on gasoline mileage.

Interestingly and quite distinct from newspaper accounts of the same subject, the public has drawn its own conclusions for Minnesota's 3-5 record in the worst division in professional football. Many callers, for example, have demanded Bud Grant's hide. Failing that, the hide of Jerry Burns has been demanded, apparently because the public is convinced that Burns, the team's principal designer of the offense, is responsible for Viking play selection.

Other notable though anonymous theories have been advanced, including that old standby, dissension.

"Yes," a caller was heard to say the other night, "dissension is ruining the team. The players are angry because Doug Martin signed such a lucrative contract. I'm telling you there's dissension."

And, conviction growing weaker, the caller added, "Isn't there? Well, isn't there?"

The telephone is a tremendous conductor of venom. Tommy Kramer has been vilified. The public — never mind that the public in talk radio is perhaps the same 12 or 13 people night after night — is convinced that the Vikings have no player capable of emotional leadership. Nor is there a running back of professional caliber. The fault list is so thorough that even the Vikings would be shocked to discover the range of their weaknesses.

"I don't listen to the talk shows," Bud Grant said Tuesday. A few of the more presentable theories of the Viking collapse had just been advanced to Grant. "I don't put a great deal of credence in the people who call in."

Grant probably doesn't put much credence in sports reporters, either, but the man is honest.

"The one thing that has helped make football so popular is the amount of conversation it inspires," Grant said. "But we're a cloistered group. I go to the barber every three weeks, I go to the gas station once a week and I occasionally see my family. I don't confide in anybody."

"What about the public's perception of Kramer?"

"I remember Lynn Dickey saying a few weeks ago that he doubted he was the man to lead the Packers," Grant said. "He was outstanding against us Sunday. I think that kind of statement was forced on Dickey, just as a similar statement was forced on Mike Phipps at Chicago. I think Kramer is too strong to have that kind of statement forced on him. Kramer is the quarterback and I don't think he lacks assurance."

"What about Burns?"

"The plays go through me," Grant said. "Don't people think I have an input?"

"What about the public's perception concerning the lack of leadership?"

"I don't think we have the kind of dominant player we once had," Grant said. "Chuck Foreman was a leader for us for years but he was leading through example, not by anything he did in the locker room or on the practice field. We are lacking the kind of dominant player who leads by example."

Why the Vikings are missing the dominant player who led by example is probably the more interesting question. It is submitted here that Alan Page, regardless of his clubhouse posture, was a player who led by example on the field, but he interfered with Grant's totalitarianism.

Same goes for Carl Eller and Foreman, although they were aging less gracefully than Page. And, because he told us so, we already know that Grant is as much responsible for play selection as Burns, and that Tommy Kramer is Grant's quarterback.

The Vikings are Bud Grant's team, through and through. Discounting his barber and his filling station attendant, the rest of us might never know how he feels about what he has wrought heading half steam into the 1980s.

Jim Marshall

December 10, 1979

Two decades of a certain kind of football brilliance ended Sunday afternoon at Metropolitan Stadium when Jim Marshall played his last game as a Viking before the hometown customers.

Most players do not last long in this brutal game and fewer still come to represent a franchise, so it was with some regret that 42,239 fans watched Jim Marshall revive the Minnesota defense for an old-fashioned 10-3 win over the Buffalo Bills.

Jim Marshall will be 42 soon. It's unlikely in the next decade, with the Vikings moving into the sterile, indoor world of artificial turf, that another Jim Marshall will be produced. He is a unique man and, when he rode in a red convertible parade-style around the stadium before the game yesterday, he was greeted with hesitant cheers, as though fans were witnessing the conclusion to chapters in their own lives.

You can play a number game with Jim Marshall. Yesterday was his 281st consecutive start in the National Football League, an ongoing record that will be topped off next week at New England, by which time Marshall will have played 302 games in the NFL, counting playoffs. All but 12 of those games have been played with the Vikings.

The temperature at game time yesterday was 42 degrees. The sun was shining and there was no wind and Jim Marshall played as though it was the summer of 1961. He wore No. 70 on his back then as well. Presumably, the number will be retired along with his legend of invincibility.

"A typical game that Jim Marshall has been involved in over the years," Bud Grant said, "a close, low-scoring game that we usually have at this time of year. But the weather didn't cooperate. It was the nicest Dec. 9 I can ever remember."

"What was the best play of the game?" Grant was asked.

"Marshall's sack," he said.

Marshall played nearly the entire game. Frustrated in his outside moves against Buffalo's Ken Jones, Marshall cut inside on Jones early in the second quarter and dumped quarterback Joe Ferguson at the Buffalo 5. Like the old days. Marshall got the the game ball for that play — and for his 19 years in Minnesota colors.

"I'd give him a bag of balls," the Vikings' equipment manager, Stubby Eason, was saying afterward, "there aren't enough game balls for a guy like Marshall."

Eason, trainer Fred Zamberletti and team doctor Doc Lannin, along with Marshall, are the only surviving members of Minnesota's first year in the league. During the game, Eason replaced Marshall's locker stool with the padded easy chair that had been presented to Eason during training camp. Because it is so rare, there is nothing trite about genuine emotion when it is expressed in a football locker room. On more than one occasion after the game, Marshall went to the washroom so that he might cry in private.

George Marshall, 65, sat in his son's new chair during those absences.

"I live in Columbus, Ohio," the senior Marshall was saying. "I'm a truck driver, might retire myself next year. My uncle lived to be 107. Jim's grandmother is 82 and gets around better than I do. Jim comes from good, strong people."

"I hate the word retire," Jim Marshall said. "It's just a time for a change for me. I'm a talented man and it's time to put those talents to other uses."

All of Marshall's football talents were tested yesterday. With seconds to go in the game, Marshall was inserted as an offensive tackle, replacing Steve Riley. It was the first time since Marshall played both ways at Ohio State that he had engaged in an offensive play. It was a showcase opportunity to have Marshall on the field for the final play of the game, an opportunity for him to lead the run from the field, with the ball held aloft for all to see.

And it was during his final flight from the field that the fans responded with more enthusiasm than they had given Marshall earlier. The repetition of his name made a cheer that did not stop until he had stooped into the dugout and out of sight for the final time.

"All during the game," Marshall said, "my teammates kept coming up to me and talking to me. They said, 'Let's win this one for the captain.' When I ran out on offense at the end, they said, 'What the hell are you doing here?' I told them I was doing my job."

Marshall leaves an organization that has been good to him, an organization that cared about him in ways we might never know. Not every player gets the chance to appear in 301 games. Marshall earned his trust, but he still had to prove himself year after year.

"The opportunity is there for another player to break my records," Marshall said. "Somebody could make it happen. I feel like I could play another 10 years."

"He hasn't lost any steps that I can tell," said Randy Holloway, the man who will inherit Marshall's defensive end position. "I learned a lot from him and it won't be easy at first for me without him there."

There was a cake to be cut. Jim Marshall passed the first piece along to Holloway. There were interviews to be done. There was Carl Eller to be hugged. He secured permission from Jack Patera, his coach at Seattle, to fly in for Marshall's last game at home. There were friends waiting outside. There was a party last night with teammates. There was a father standing off to the side.

"It was an emotional day for me," Marshall said. "There will be nostalgia tonight. I'm happy and sad. I almost wish that ... I'm a little teary now. I heard Grady Alderman said on the radio that it was one of the top games I played all year."

Paul Krause

September 10, 1978

Paul Krause was a victim of his own spectacular legend for thievery last week during Viking practice. He intercepted two or three passes in the heat and on each occasion was saluted by a chorus of his winded teammates.

"That ties it, that ties it."

Krause tossed the ball back to the huddle and buried a grin in his sleeve. He wonders privately when the real ball will come, the 79th interception of his 15-year career, the interception that will put him in the guide books with Emlen Tunnell.

The ghost of Emlen Tunnell. He was a defensive back out of Iowa, Krause's school, and he played a decade with the Giants before ending his career with Green Bay after the 1961 season. Tunnell died a few years ago of a heart attack at the Giants' training camp. He and Krause rode the same airplane once and concluded that a pass interception defies analysis.

"It's a nose for the ball and luck, isn't it?" Krause said.

"And longevity," Tunnell said.

"I wish I'd hurry up and just set the danged record," Krause said the other day. "It weighs on my mind. I'm not the emotional type, but when I get that 79th interception, I'm running the ball off the field. I don't think anyone will ever break it if I set the record."

"It will be a big deal," Coach Bud Grant said, "if he gets it."

Krause is 36 now, a little slower afoot than most defensive backs, his reflexes beginning to dull after 15 years of pounding. He could tie

Tunnell on Monday night against Denver, or the next week against Tampa Bay. Or it might be months. Three years ago, Krause led the league with 10 interceptions, but then he suffered two seasons of just two interceptions each.

Twelve interceptions came in Krause's first year, 1964. He was with Washington then and he not only became the first rookie to make all-pro but also established the record for intercepting passes in seven consecutive games.

"Interceptions are so danged elusive," Krause said. "There's so many variables, a tipped ball, a dropped ball, the wind. You can't count on anything for certain and lately teams have been running so well on us that they don't need to pass much."

"What's an interception feel like?" a man wondered.

"It's that touchdown feeling," Krause said. "It's a turnover, that big play feeling. Guys play 10, 12 years and don't get any interceptions. To get 78 of them, I don't know. It's not something you can set out to do. You need a sense for the ball."

Maybe you need the nose of an outfielder. Krause played center field and batted .418 his sophomore year at Iowa and was an All-American in baseball. He separated his shoulder playing football the next year, concluding what was to be a certain career in professional baseball.

"I didn't worry about it," Krause said. "I was drafted No. 2 by the Redskins. I watched the Detroit Lions in their training camp a couple of times and I figured football didn't look that hard."

Krause owns the perfect temperament of a Viking — happy, but not boundlessly so; secure, but not too secure; cautious in the appraisal of his fortunes, but not too cautious. There is money in the bank from land investments and sports cars in his barn in Lakeville, good friends, an enterprising family.

He met his wife, Pam, in their hometown of Flint, Mich., when they were both 4 years old. While Krause labored the past month in Mankato, she took their three children on a camping tour of the west.

"Football is a plus now," Krause said. "I don't need it for financial reasons, but I need the competition. Life's a treat. It's a simple thing. I've never worried about anything in my life. With a little dose of faith, you can do anything. I want to play more. I didn't like it when I was taken out of the New Orleans game, but I realize they've got to reduce my playing time. And I realize when I have to get out of the game I have to get out."

Krause will get the record first. He's waiting for it. His teammates are waiting for it. They already know he's the best thief in professional football. It just isn't official yet and practice swipes don't count.

Alan Page

October 8, 1978

The evidence mounts, maybe. The guard is ever changing, maybe. Now there is another Viking awakened to and bruised by the mysterious workings of a secretive management.

Alan Page, 12 years out of Notre Dame and a bar exam short of becoming the area's most formidable-looking attorney, suffers no illusions about his dispensability in the hardened world of professional football.

Loyalty was a word they used in Pat O'Brien movies. There isn't a player alive who can't prepare himself for business eventualities. But if Page is to be dispatched elsewhere by Tuesday's National Football League trading deadline, and General Manager Mike Lynn's refusal to confirm or deny the speculation makes such a deal more believable, then why can't the club tell the man of its intentions?

"Because," Lynn said. "We don't comment on that type of activity. We are constantly talking with 27 teams, constantly, but the end result in 99.9 percent of the cases is bull. Ask me about Fran Tarkenton."

"Is Tarkenton going to be traded?"

"I have no comment," Lynn said. "Ask me about Chuck Foreman."

"Is Foreman going to be traded?"

"I have no comment," Lynn said.

Lynn has no comment, but he volunteered that last year the Vikings were the only NFL club to negotiate a trade right on the deadline, sending a fifth-round draft choice to the Giants for Bob Tucker.

"As strange as this all seems," Page said, "I'm sure that stranger things have happened around the league. If I am to be traded, how complicated would it be to tell me? I've tried to take the speculation lightly but I'm getting resentful and that's not a good position for me to be in. The more I think about it and try to be rational about it, I wonder what my reaction is supposed to be when I'm playing against Seattle. Am I supposed to be in limbo come game time?"

Page is supposed to be a Viking come game time, the way he has been a Viking for 12 seasons as a starter and an eight-time Pro Bowl competitor. But in what Lynn called "an unfortunate development", Jimmy (the Greek) Snyder prognosticated last week on television that Page was regarded as trade material by the Vikings.

The next day it was revealed that Page had filed a grievance with the National Football League Players Association (NFLPA), claiming he shouldn't have been fined $50 for his tardiness at a team meeting. The two events are not necessarily unrelated. The notorious TV gambler stirred the rumors. The filing of a grievance was further demonstration that Page is above and beyond all else an individual in the strictest team game. That can be a crime, punishable by disrespect.

"There is no fine schedule in the current collective bargaining agreement," Page said. "At this stage of my career I don't need the grief. But if somebody in my position doesn't stand up for what's right, who will?"

Page doubts that any trade for his services would be purely a cold business decision. Skepticism may or may not be an inherent part of his character, although the posture of silence the club has taken is beginning to irritate him.

The individuality that sets him apart from his teammates may have set him too far apart from management. Page, for example, is the only Viking to have become enamored with the sport of running. He now weighs 225 pounds, feathery for a lineman, but Page, at 33, remains lightning quick off the ball and this year has blocked a conversion as well as a field goal attempt.

"Running is a very individual thing," Page said. "The management might feel it sets me apart from the team and the team mentality. They don't like individuals, on or off the field. They have a hard time dealing with people on a personal level. But the team man and the individual aren't mutually exclusive.

"Running was a health decision on my part. I'm not going to play football forever and running is something my family and I can enjoy together. Life is too short not to enjoy it. Running has helped me forget the trivial things, the petty and the negative things. Running has become a part of my life now."

"We exercise less control over our players than any club in the league," Lynn said. "We have more individuals on this team than any team in the league. They're branching out all the time."

If Page is to be branched out, if Page is to be uprooted suddenly from his community and separated from his family, he apparently will find out about it as late as the rest of us. He doesn't mind so much being traded as not being given enough time to pack a bag. And in the meantime, the rest of the Vikings can sleep tonight with the comforting thought that Lynn is constantly talking with 27 other clubs about possible deals that the players will remain unaware of.

That's the way they do business.

February 3, 1980

Alan Page put his money where his mouth is Friday morning when he told the senior class of St. Paul Central High School that professional athletics is not a reasonable career goal and that any student who feels victimized by society is needlessly deluding himself.

"I am not here to entertain you," said Mr. Page, who is a barrister in the law firm of Lindquist and Vennum and looked the part in a bow tie, "and I am not here to tell football stories. Football stories don't interest me very much. Education interests me and it should interest all of you, because a good education is the one way any disadvantaged person can overcome disadvantage."

Page is a tall, imposing figure, familiar to all of these kids as a defensive lineman, first with the Vikings and now with the Chicago Bears. Increasingly throughout his career, Page has slipped his cerebral messages of discontent and protest to sportswriters and other unsuspecting souls who didn't know quite what to make of a professional athlete biting the hand that fed him. Page is sharp, sharp enough to quit wasting his breath in the locker room. He decided to take his message into classrooms, preferably inner-city schools where children might be more susceptible to the lure of pro sports as an escape from poverty or discrimination.

"I have selfish reasons as well," Page was telling the assembly. "I have four children and when they grow up, they will be dealing with you in their society. I want society to work and I believe in the system. You cannot fight the system, nor disbelieve it. The system is educational. Use it. Now, take heed of what I say, because there is no other way to make it in this society."

There is no color line in this message. Page told of his own schooling in Canton, Ohio, and how his interest and enthusiasm for study seemed to deteriorate as the demands on his football talents increased. At Notre Dame, Page took a degree in political science. Football seemed like a job to him, he said, a conclusion he reached in retrospect.

"I got distracted from school by football," Page was saying now, "and I didn't study very hard. If you feel you don't study hard enough, you will regret it, believe me. Something happened early in my career to make me realize that football was *just* a job. I went to law school, I went back into the system of education because football will end. The average career in pro sports is something like 4½ years, so I've been fortunate in football."

Page was warming to the central theme of his remarks. A good attorney works a jury and Page seemed to be doing that now, working these kids into a frame of mind for acceptance.

"The odds of becoming a professional athlete are one in 18,000," Page said.

There was a whoop from a kid in the crowd.

"Yeah," Page said. "But one out of 60 kids will go on to graduate school. The chances are 300 times better of going on to graduate school. Those aren't good, but they beat one in 18,000."

There was murmuring in the crowd.

"Professional sports? For you people? The odds are more likely that one of you in this room will be hit on the head by a meteorite in the next 10 years. You don't hear much about getting hit on the head with a meteorite."

Page told the students to use athletics as a means to an end, and that education and study were not only the best, but the only insurance for working well within the system. Not an entirely novel idea perhaps, but unique coming from the mouth of a man who has made a fortune in professional sports. Page will do more of this. He will be back at Central next Friday and the Friday after that.

"And then I'll keep the show moving," he said after the students had returned to class. "I don't know how many, if any, athletes are out doing this. I've been in the game for 13 years and I'm just getting around to it now, but then I'm just getting comfortable with myself now."

"We've got to close the gap," said Central's head football coach, Floyd Smaller, "between the haves and have nots."

Those kids should listen to Page and others like him. Sports hasn't been in the headlines too often lately. But a whole lot of more important matters have.

Fran Tarkenton

October 29, 1978

The hotshot Georgia Peach can wrap his arm around a man, wink, and create the illusion of lifetime friendship. This is a gesture of affected Southern hospitality currently practiced by people like Billy Carter, or to a lesser degree by the hotshot Georgia Peach, Francis Asbury Tarkenton.

Francis Tarkenton is charming, enduring, quotable and perhaps even loveable in his wide circle of pals, to whom he will confide his greatness. But a more arrogant quarterback has yet to surface in the known solar system. And if you and me and the rest of the bleacher bums in town don't throw a pail of gooey slop his way every now and again he takes his ego off the leash and lets it bark.

This past week Tarkenton was still ranting about the Bronx cheers directed his way early in the season. Remember? He didn't get no respect. He pointed out that in other towns veteran players are revered, like public statuary or delicate art. Fans never got on Sonny Jurgensen's back, Francis said, or Bart Starr's ... they didn't want to exterminate the old guys in Green Bay and Washington. But obsequiousness, the hotshot Georgia Peach discovered, doesn't come with the eleven-buck ticket to the Met.

It was unintelligent to criticize Tarkenton's misfortunes or inadequacies in the season opener against New Orleans and in the third game against Tampa Bay, both defeats. It was never argued here that Tarkenton isn't a fascinating quarterback, blessed by improvisation and shrewdness and animation.

It was inevitable that he would shake off whatever lingering doubts he might have had — but refused to discuss — concerning his broken leg against Cincinnati the previous season. He did, and now that he is again accumulating glowing reviews, even his severest critics have been appropriately enlightened.

What Francis wanted, and felt he wasn't getting, was enough credit for 18 years on the job, about 40,000 yards worth of passes and a couple of hundred touchdowns. It was as if his own arrogance motivated him to recover his touch and move him to the top of the statistics.

What else could motivate him? The guy is 38 years old and he is rich and he has done it all. He doesn't need dough or another trophy, he needs credit. There can never be enough of the stuff for a man who has done it all, never.

If Tarkenton has a flaw in his otherwise engaging personality it's that he doesn't realize his arrogance should be compatible with his relative insignificance in matters great and small.

Tarkenton can believe that he does what he does better than any man on earth, but by demanding reverence for being a good quarterback his arrogance becomes insufferable.

All brilliant athletes are arrogant, but some of them just have a deeper perspective of their own worth. Catfish Hunter, after signing for millions with the Yankees in 1975, fell upon hard times and injury last year, was booed and emerged from a 9-9 season with a colloquialism that ultimately endeared him to his constituents.

"My daddy," Catfish said last year, "told me that the sun don't shine on the same dog's ass every day."

Gaylord Perry, two years Tarkenton's elder, was so revered in San Francisco for eight summers that he was traded to Cleveland in 1971. In 1972 Perry won the Cy Young Award after winning 24 games for the Indians. Perry was so revered in Cleveland that he was traded to Texas in 1975. After winning more than 30 games for the Rangers in a little over two seasons, Perry was so revered in Texas that he was traded last winter to San Diego. And this past summer Perry won 21 games, becoming the only man over 40 to win the Cy Young Award as well as the only man ever to win the Cy Young Award in both the American and National Leagues.

"I dedicate the Cy Young," Perry said last week, "to everybody over 40."

Both Hunter and Perry could be hotshots. Both, with a wink and a hug, could make a friend for life. It wouldn't be illusion. The hotshot Georgia Peach is playing so well now he could play forever and he should. And he could polish his act with the kind of class of athletes who can handle their professional arrogance. Just so long as we don't have to bless the ground where Francis Tarkenton stands.

March 7, 1979

Maybe the shell game Fran Tarkenton is playing with his pro football career is more serious than his constituents want to believe. There is enough evidence now — trade rumors and trade demands, thinly disguised jealousies and other unpleasantries — to suggest that Tarkenton's cavalier attitude could be affecting his Minnesota Vikings teammates, from reserve quarterbacks to star linemen.

Many Vikings are worried about Tarkenton, worried that he might show up in Mankato, Minn., come July in spite of his intentions.

The latest Viking to speak between the lines was Ron Yary, who suddenly wants to be traded to a team with a winning attitude, which narrows it down only a little bit. This abrupt request was apparently triggered by Yary's distaste for criticism from teammates last season, and no Viking reviewed his peers more often than Fran Tarkenton.

Yary did not specifically mention Tarkenton as the agent of his distress, but perhaps he was recalling Tarkenton's remarks to a Washington Post reporter. The Georgia Peach said the Vikings were outmanned on the line of scrimmage every game and that they couldn't run if they had to and that, furthermore, the Vikings generally prevailed on the guile of one Fran Tarkenton. These views were probably shared by other Vikings, but they never saw newsprint.

Yary is an offensive lineman and, as the joke goes, at 6-foot-6 and 255 pounds he can say anything he pleases. But he speaks so seldom that he's worth hearing out. Yary watched Ed White break his shackles and embrace a new challenge in San Diego. Alan Page, dumped for scrap in October, rebounded with zest and a new contract with the Chicago Bears.

Yary seems to make himself clear when he insists that his wish to be traded has nothing to do with salary, contract, coaches, fans or climate. That leaves either the freeway system or the quarterback, and the freeway system didn't complain a bit last year.

Yary isn't the only Viking suffering anxiety over Tarkenton's mysterious posture regarding next season. Rumors have had Chuck Foreman being traded to Miami. Interestingly, Foreman doesn't mind the rumor, as he is a back who likes to run the football. In Tarkenton's Rube Goldberg offense, Foreman runs the ball when Tarkenton's arm gets tired.

The club's other quarterbacks, Bob Lee and Tommy Kramer — remember them? — don't have to be poked with a hot stick to concede their own ambitions. Kramer can play. He knows it and he's tired of pacing the sideline, which means Lee must be absolutely mummified by now. Lee threw four passes in all of 1978 and there had to be days when he knew he could move the club better than Tarkenton. There were days when the guy in the end zone seat had the same feeling.

These developments and dissatisfactions haven't exactly caused any emergencies at the Vikings' corporate level. Yary's request isn't being considered seriously, and reserve quarterbacks are nothing if not ambitious and talkative. Still, it's hard to imagine the Vikings continuing a charade for one more season.

Detroit, Green Bay and Chicago are well into solid building processes while the Vikings must now rebuild. You can't rebuild behind a 39-year-old quarterback no matter how charming, daring and innovative he might be. You can try, but what the Vikings could end up with in 1979 is a 39-year-old quarterback trying to do it all by himself. Again. And with fewer believers than he might have had before.

The game

Dec. 27, 1977

Los Angeles, Calif.

Nature never ravaged the lush turf of the Los Angeles Coliseum the way the Vikings and Rams did Monday afternoon during one of the dirtiest and toughest football games ever contested for play-off loot.

It was raining in Los Angeles Sunday night when the Vikings arrived from Tucson and it was raining when they awoke yesterday morning and it rained all day yesterday afternoon on the 62,538 clients who covered their smirks in sheets of plastic. It was 14-7 Vikings and the legend of these fond, and yes, even old, warriors continues to grow.

The line play was furious, according to Bobby Lee, the quarterback, and Alan Page and Jim Marshall, the defensive linemen who each had two jerseys torn from their bodies during the course of the game. Players were mired in mud that was six inches deep and Marshall, who has played pro football for 18 years, said he never saw such a poor field in his life.

"I sunk past my ankles in the middle of the field," Marshall said. "Tough, rotten game. I was held so flagrantly I couldn't stand it. The jersey was ripped right off me and they wouldn't call the holding."

"Actually," Page said, "the field didn't get a hell of a lot worse during the game. It was bad to begin with. Look at Marshall. Look at that 40-year-old man. Look at the way we played. Being physical is mind over matter. I hope people realize now how good we are."

Page didn't have to remove his jersey. It dripped off him like wet tissue and he groaned: "Old and tired and weak and weary," adding "and seven-point victors."

Old. That was the tag that hung over the Vikings yesterday. The bookmakers counted on it and even loyal fans secretly believed that the Vikings needed new youth and new spirit. But there is something stunning about the Vikings when they play in slop or cold weather or when they get caught between a rock and a hard place or when money is on the line.

The Vikings now have beaten the Rams in four play-off encounters and you could almost feel that delicate Los Angeles psyche begin to bend when the Vikings marched down the field on their first possession to score.

"It was unbelievable," somebody said to Bud Grant.

"Maybe there were unbelievers," Grant said, "but it wasn't unbelievable. It was our weather. We got our weather and it was an omen. We're used to bad fields. We play on more bad fields than any other team. We know a bad field gets worse. We know."

They know and the Rams know now, and anybody who watched the game on television knows now. Perhaps television brightened this affair with color and bright lights. But the Vikings stayed on the ground most of the second half and wore a black strip down the middle of the Coliseum.

They punched each other on the back and helped each other up out of the goo. It was gray and the rain, which turned to mist in the gloaming, made the whole scene ugly except for the Vikings, who were beautiful in a spooky sort of way. We will never know if the Vikings could have beaten the Rams in sunshine, but in the rain they acted as if they had been delivered into a situation in which the outcome was inevitable.

"Why?" Another question for Grant.

"Because football teams can't play at the same level all year," he said.

You could say the Vikings have a jinx on the Rams, at least in playoff games, but the team doesn't want to hear that. What this team had Monday transcended jinxes. It could have been any team on that field. The Vikings delivered big plays and it was hard to tell which one ultimately broke the hearts of the Rams.

The Vikings held the Rams on fourth down early in the game. Nate Allen intercepted Pat Haden when the Rams had a first down on the Vikings' 5. Neil Clabo punted the ball out of trouble. Paul Krause intercepted a ball. And there was luck to be had. Fred Cox's kickoff in the fourth quarter never quite got off the runway and bounced off the legs of Rick Nazum. Wally Hilgenberg covered the loose ball.

"Not a planned play," Grant said. He almost smiled. "If you need a turning point, I think it was Allen's interception (in the second quarter). It took the confidence out of the Rams' passing game."

Bobby Lee was sought by multitudes who would have him thankful for some kind of redemption from the bench.

"I didn't have to redeem myself," Lee said. "This team would have had trouble adjusting to Fran Tarkenton if he would have replaced me. No redeeming. I know what I can do and what the team did today was beautiful."

"It made it sweeter to win without the greatest quarterback in the game," Chuck Foreman said, "but Lee is steady, stays with his game and calls a good game. We're good. People can see that now."

One of the last men to change into his fresh garments was Marshall. He was angry about offensive holding in the game and said he'd mail a $5,000 check to the NFL right now for complaining about it.

"I played against a man that weighs almost 300 pounds (Doug France)," Marshall said, knotting his tie in a mirror. "He ripped two jerseys off me and tried to throw me around like a rag doll. He was holding me. They have to call that. One time the official said he realized I was held but I wasn't involved in the play. Well, if I was an offensive player I'd hold all the time. If it's gonna be a free-for-all they should tell us, so we can deal with that."

Marshall took his hat from his locker, placed it on his head at an appropriately jaunty angle and checked his image once again.

"Yeah," he said, "they should tell us if it's a free-for-all."

He was smiling when he left, a man oblivious to his 40th birthday this Friday. He will be back again next year, he said. Age knows no boundaries on a ball club built of legend.

Dec. 27, 1978

This is the time of year when seemingly fanciful theory can be advanced as law to predict the outcome of divisional playoff games in the National Football League.

Reputation and legend come full flower now with bonus cash on the line and it says here that the Los Angeles Rams haven't a prayer of a chance to beat the Vikings Sunday in the Coliseum. Most of the Rams already are defeated in their own minds and it wouldn't be surprising to discover that they have their bags packed and the motor running come Sunday.

You can completely disregard the previous Rams victory over

Minnesota this year. Last season, as the entire state watched in Monday night horror, Los Angeles ripped the local forces 35-3, which set up quite a few bettors for the tumble when playoff time rolled around. You'll recall that Minnesota came back to beat the Rams 14-7 on the day after Christmas in steady rain.

Theory No. 1: *Any climatical aberration whatsoever immediately makes Minnesota the favorite in any game they play.*

This is the oldest playoff law applicable to the Vikings. Like the sentient engineer in Walker Percy's "The Last Gentleman", the Vikings find it absolutely impossible to be happy when everyone else is. Earthquakes, tidal waves, rain, fog, even an obscure canyon fire in Santa Barbara will make the Vikings happy, wise and ultimately victorious.

Remember that the Vikings were 0-3 in domes this year and that they were mounting a terrific comeback in a rainstorm in Oakland when the sun broke through and made them sad.

Last year's 14-7 victory over the Rams in the rain was a delightful exercise in chicanery. It apparently never occurred to the Rams to score early and hang on through the mudslide. The Vikings scored early and slopped it out, happy as pigs in a trough.

Theory No. 2: *The Vikings, hardy, law abiding and conservative, cannot lose any game in which they are opposed by freaks who live on the beach and drive open roadsters.*

That the Rams have never beaten the Vikings in four playoff games is all the proof you need. Sometimes this is also known as the Chatsworth Osborne Jr. theory of football.

Poor, simple Dobie Gillis always won his small struggles against the hoity-toity Osborne who lived in a mansion on the hill, and so it is with the Vikings.

The Vikings represent working stiffs all over the world. They come from a humble and outdated home and carry their lunches in paper sacks. They practice on vacant lots and frequently ride buses. Stubby Eason, the team's equipment manager, darns socks and scrubs the uniforms on a washboard. On game days many of the Vikings do not shave and this tends to create the impression, particularly to a bright and shiny crew like the Rams, that the Vikings have just emerged from an open pit mine.

Theory No. 2 was evidenced this year as well. The Vikings beat the Cowboys in Dallas. Uncomfortable in the presence of so many comfortable clients, the Vikings performed a gauche display of shocking sight gags, something akin to the rube who palms a joy buzzer to shake the city slicker's hand. The Rams cannot become poor enough fast enough to equal the gutty fires of the repressors.

Theory No. 3: *Every dog not only has his day, but every dog gets a year thrown in once and a while.*

This is the year of the dog. The Atlanta Falcons won four ball games in the final 10 seconds of each game and just a few days ago beat Philadelphia in the final moments of play. By playoff standards the Vikings are a dog team and with theories one and two already making them overwhelming favorites there is no way they can lose with dogism in their favor.

Dogism bespeaks a higher order, an all encompassing theory that forgives a variety of ills; the absence of a running game, too many men on the field, interceptions, fumbles, injuries, things like that.

These theories point so conclusively to a Minnesota victory that there is every assurance the Vikings will advance to a fifth Super Bowl appearance. Keep in mind that should Atlanta beat Dallas Saturday, the Vikings would play host to the NFC championship on Jan. 7. Theories two and three might cancel each other out in such an affair but theory No. 1 would guarantee the Minnesota title. Even a good winter day in Minnesota is a climatical aberration, thereby making the Vikings boundlessly happy.

Jan. 1, 1978

If love is measured in weight, about five tons of it pulled into Dallas late Saturday night aboard a refrigerated fruit truck dispatched Friday from the "Detroit" lot at Metropolitan Stadium.

It was there yesterday morning that Viking fans assembled, with shovels, to feed snow into the truck's cargo hold. Snow presumably will set an emotional fire under the Norsemen when deposited in modest and containerized allocations behind the visitor's bench in Texas Stadium. The Vikings can freeze their hands over it, you see.

Bud Grant may or may not have inspired this gesture of good will when he wished out loud that it would snow in Dallas so the Vikings could have their weather. This is the same Bud Grant, remember, who occasionally delivers a lecture explaining why Eskimos can work harder and longer outdoors than their Yankee counterparts.

Vikings weather, as we have come to understand the legend, is any weather that produces mudslides, blocks freeways, closes schools, halts air traffic and inspires the continuing search for Bigfoot. Unfortunately, Dallas climatologists have soured the script by predicting fair skies and warmth for this afternoon, a bad omen.

"What we want to show people around the country," said Brian Wadnal, one of the college-aged shovelers at the Met, "is the fine quality of life we have here in Minnesota."

"Yeah," said his buddy, Rick Renner, "we don't have anything to do except shovel snow."

"And if the Vikes win," said Dave Bernlohr, "it will be because of us. We've read all week long how the Vikes will get killed in Dallas. When they see snow, they'll win. Because of us."

Vikings fans may have a lock on this kind of activity. After all,

Minnesotans were the first to prove that man could eat and drink in the relative immobility of snowmobile garments. Pushed by the elements, our loyalty knows no limitations.

I have an uncle who used to drink his beer in continual salute to the Green Bay Packers. He lived in Stevens Point, Wis., from about 1959 to 1964, and he remembers that every Sunday after a Packers road game he and the rest of the inhabitants in that corner of Wisconsin were urged to turn on their porch lights to "guide the Packers safely home". But he never packaged snow for delivery.

Thousands of Denver Bronco fans turned out one autumn day in 1962 for a public burning of the team's old brown-and-yellow vertically striped socks. But they never shoveled snow. A man in the Chicago Bears office, Pat McCaskey, said, "I've been around the Bears all my life, and I never heard of our fans doing anything as crazy as loading snow to send someplace. We're sane by comparison."

A call to Dallas was far more disturbing. Doug Todd of the Cowboys' public-relations staff said he had heard about the Viking snowlift.

"They have two chances of getting that snow into the stadium," Todd said, "slim and none. Why, our fans have never done anything like that."

Pay him no mind, ye who struggled to fill the fruit truck. Like a useless Christmas gift, it's the thought that counts. Lord knows the Vikings need every edge in today's tournament, and I imagine the veterans Marshall, Page and Eller will sense the presence of snow even as it remains on board the truck in the Dallas parking lot, dripping, dripping away onto the hot macadam. Perhaps they will go and touch the melting stuff as it seeps from the truck, the water of Lourdes.

A couple of guys in the persuasion business, Rob Brown and Dick Rainbolt, take credit for the snowlift. They represent a hotel chain that happens to house the Vikings in Dallas.

"We were going to send a cake," Brown said, "but why not snow?"

"And call it Viking Turf Conditioner," Rainbolt said.

According to Prof. Greg Stone of the University of Minnesota, there are sociological explanations for this kind of behavior.

"First of all," Stone said, "our community has snow. Right? What better way to remind the Vikings that their roots are back in Minnesota? The Vikings represent the community, and the fan feels an identity with the community through the Vikings. It's a very serious business. Fans want credit for victory. My guess is that the fans shoveling snow into the truck are very sports-minded people, not TV watchers. Very active people. They would have to be. It takes a lot of gumption to get out and shovel snow."

July 29, 1979

Mankato, Minn.
Serious young men of grim countenance are gathered here in institutional formality for the purpose of becoming entertainers. Afraid to smile, afraid even to grunt for fear of revealing a character flaw, most of the prospective Vikings live for those rare and judiciously timed signs of approval from an assistant coach. What this camp needs, before it collapses under the weight of its own exhaustion, is a Dale Hackbart to step forward in his flowing cape and World War I aviator helmet.

"As your launch commander," Hackbart told the troops one day after practice, "I am advising you that we intend to rocket a live frog, Astro Frog, over the skies of Mankato."

But wait. Before we get to the frog and the snakes and the bowling tournaments and the dormitory track meets, a crew-cutted man of model sternness wishes to speak.

"Comedy ain't easy," Bud Grant said the other day. "Timing is important around here. From a coaching standpoint there's even a right time and wrong time to give a kid a lift. As for characters, we don't have as many as we used to have. Every team will develop its own characters but it takes time. These kids today are more serious than the old gang. Hackbart, Bill Brown, Karl Kassulke, Paul Dickson—those guys had perfect timing. Those guys knew how to lighten the atmosphere."

Dickson, a defensive tackle, was not obsessed with his agent or tax shelters or his image so much as he was obsessed with philosophy, reality in particular. And it was Jim Lindsey, a running back, from whom Dickson sought counsel.

"Jimmy," Dickson said one night, listing to port in Lindsey's doorway. "I found it."

"What?" Lidsey said.

"Reality," Dickson said.

Dickson's discovery was coincidental to the introduction of the Harvey Wallbanger in Mankato taverns. Down the hall on what might have been the very same evening, Gary Larsen lit a fire under Oscar Reed's door. Reed doused the flames and went immediately to Larsen's room, convinced that Larsen was the culprit and equally convinced that Larsen deserved a face full of water. Reed had the decency to knock first.

"Who's there?" Larsen said.

"It's da coach," Reed said.

"Keep in mind," Grant was saying now, "that today is the good old day 10 years from now. It's easy to highlight a year with a paragraph or an incident. You can't always do it."

Grant looked around the dining room and the prospect of looking back on this day 10 years hence might have troubled him.

Would a fellow named Arthur Meadowcroft conduct a dormitory

track meet? Kassulke routinely did. Would a youngster named David Stephens or Bob Winkel or Sammy Steinmark ever bring a snake to camp? Clint Jones brought live snakes to camp, his pets. He use to put a rubber snake on a sleeping Jerry Burns's chest and Burns, upon awakening, would fling the gag item into a corner of his room. The maid got used to this. The maid was not prepared for the day when the snake she picked up in a corner of the room wrapped itself around her hand. She could be running still.

Childish pranks perhaps. But does there breathe life in the sweaty brows of a Jerry Lawrence, a Keith Nord, a Perry Kozlowski, or a Steve Gortz, a Cecil Overstreet, a Paul Litwicki? Aspiring professional entertainers, all of them, but bring on Dale Hackbart to paint this bald and sunburnt hilltop with color.

The frog launch occurred in the days when model rocketry was the rage at football camp. From empty tape cannisters a two-stage rocket was constructed, with engines and nose cone purchased commercially. Jim Marshall, entrusted with recovery, decided that Astro Frog needed a trial run. Marshall fitted a little parachute to the frog's back and carried Astro Frog, hereafter known as Astro Frog I, to the roof of the Gage Center dormitory. A sensitive man, Marshall, while on the roof and unseen by the entire team below, sedated Astro Frog I with half a grain of phenobarbital.

Marshall leaned over the roof and dropped Astro Frog I. The little chute opened perfectly and the frog floated gently to earth. Astro Frog I was pronounced dead at the scene. He had died of a drug overdose while in flight.

"Secure another frog," Hackbart said, "and this time no test flights. No sedation."

Betting was quickly established as to whether Astro Frog II would survive real flight in his little nose cone. Hackbart hooked up a car battery to the rocket engines. Marshall loaded the astronaut into the nose cone. Three, two, one, blastoff. The first stage went perfectly. The rocket lifted smoothly but then began to roll in flight so that the nose cone was pointing earthward.

"No," screamed Hackbart.

But too late. Second stage ignited with the effect of driving Astro Frog II into the ground with the force of a thrown spear. Mourning was brief. Bets had to be settled. It was finally decided that Astro II, unlike his predecessor, had died of a broken back and would have lived under the circumstances of normal re-entry. Now, on this recent evening at dusk, there wasn't a sound coming from anywhere.

Aug. 22, 1979

Mankato, Minn.

Customers of the Minnesota Vikings apparently have a new body language with which to communicate across Metropolitan Stadium.

You could see them here and there and across the way the other evening in the gloaming when the Vikings actually scored a touchdown, the team's first in three practice games. Rather than stand with uplifted arms in conventional exuberance, the fan now clamped his nose between thumb and forefinger and rolled his eyes in the swoon one usually associates with the discovery of sour milk.

This curious signal might be so foreign as to need translation. The Vikings stink, or at least have stunk so far this season. There are probably more diplomatic ways to suggest the team's shortcomings after three test matches, but stink is close to the mark and so shockingly novel to local professional football that the fan cannot resist laughing up his sleeve.

And what a stink it is, a team stink, a cooperative stink. From the general manager, who seems only to get along with himself, to the last rookie, this is a big stink.

Now, you might think stink is too strong a word for a team that has won 10 Central Division titles in the last 11 years and visited itself upon four Super Bowls. But this stink has nothing to do with the past. This current stink has everything to do with the future and the really bad thing about this stink is the timing.

This is a bad time to stink because not only do the Vikings need to retain the loyalties of old fans, but they need to make new ones to follow them into their covered playground three years hence.

If the current trends continue — the lopping off of high-salaried veterans, for example, and the failure of many of the third- and fourth-year men to achieve anything short of their own perspiration — the guy on the street will be able to rent one of Mike Lynn's private dome boxes for a song.

Officially, the Vikings are in a rebuilding year and beyond that they are tooling up for the kind of fast and durable club that the artificial turf in the dome will require. But with parity becoming a reality around the league, no team can be hurt more by a dull and spreading mediocrity than the Vikings.

By playing outdoors the Vikings at least retain a legend of cold-weather invincibility and a sense of individuality that sets them apart from other mediocre teams. Once the Vikings move indoors and this legend is lost forever, the shock of just how mediocre the club can be will finally hit home.

We, of course, have been spoiled by the Vikings, who have always managed to rebuild on the sly, slipping in outstanding rookies like Sammie White and waiting patiently for others, like Mark Mullaney, to plug the holes left by legends. We are only now beginning to experience the kind of wholesale rebuilding undertaken by other clubs and realizing, for the first time in Bud Grant's tenure, just how bad a team can stink when it doesn't score points.

To his credit, Grant has always discovered ways to win with the talent available, and encroaching parity doesn't necessarily frighten him, but then Grant is not likely to respond to a clamped nose, either.

"What is parity?" Grant said Tuesday. "It doesn't really mean every team will go 8-8. It could mean that teams will no longer win 12 games in a row. It also could mean more games will be decided by one touchdown, or a lucky bounce."

By various shrugs and head feints Grant allowed as how the Vikings might be experiencing an inevitable downturn in the fortune department, partly because of the parity he questions and partly because of the tremendous turnover in personnel. And as much as he will miss coaching outdoors — "It gives me an extra dimension to work with," he said — he can't see a shift to the dome causing any alienation of affections.

"It might have been more detrimental to us, after the kind of success we have achieved here," Grant said, "if the stadium had been defeated. We anticipate a new era. It's something to look forward to. Most teams that have moved into new facilities have seen their fortunes rise."

Most of us are more fickle than Grant. The once-mighty Vikings now comprise anonymous clusters of players who have only one more chance to win a practice game. If they don't, look for 45,000 right hands going to the nose.

Aug. 6 1980

Mankato, Minn.

Like the annual dispatches from Australia featuring girls on the beach, or the yearly reports that swallows have returned to Capistrano, it is common in these parts each summer to reveal the imprisonment of those 75 or more souls who hope to become Minnesota Vikings. No newspaper is complete without a grotesque photograph of a football player about to faint dead away in the searing heat.

We — the customers — fall for this perpetuated myth with varying degrees of sympathy and concern, but if truth be known, there isn't a breathing body among us who wouldn't like to get away from the telephone for a month. Or the wife and the kids and the neighbors and the errands.

Training camp is an escape for most players, about as hard as the country club prison time served by Watergate conspirators. For the very best of players, those who come to camp in confidence, training camp is the most enjoyable season on the calendar.

"It takes a few camps to know how to feel about it," Bud Grant said Tuesday after his lunch, "but once a player is here and confident that he has a job, this can be a delightful time. It's unique. It's a time away from responsibility. We set the schedule, prepare the food, take care of the everyday things. All the player has to do is play football, and that can be a genuine relief for a lot of players."

You can fall for this prison stuff, this military-like atmosphere. You can weep for the barren landscape of Mankato State University and you can thirst for a player who misses his beer, but there are worse ways to make a living than running around in your shorts all day. Ahmad Rashad, perhaps more than any other Viking, actually looks forward to training camp, and this is a guy who tools around Beverly Hills in a Rolls Royce on his days off.

"It's my job," Rashad said, "my sharpening-up period. This is great. Fran Tarkenton once told me that if I couldn't make it at this camp, I couldn't make it anywhere. I'm a football player and down here, twice a day, I get to do what I do better than anyone else in the world."

James Garner was once asked why an actor of his stature and talent would rent himself out to perform in advertisements for a camera company.

"Because," Garner said, "I'm an actor. It's what I do."

Somewhere along the line we have been led to believe that professional athletes are absolved from perspiration, and that toil is necessarily evil. Tell that to Bill Brown or Jim Marshall or even Fran Tarkenton, even though at the end of his career he thought it pointless to spend so much time perfecting what to him was already perfect.

It feels good to sweat or to hit somebody or to feel a ball in your hands. On feeling the ball, incidentally, Rashad has lain in his bunk and analyzed the role of the little finger in the catching process. Because Rashad had a lightweight cast on the little finger of his left hand, the result of a minor injury last week, he finds it difficult to anticipate the feel of the ball.

"The little finger is the radar finger," is what Rashad determined. "It lets the other fingers know that the ball is on the way into the hand."

For the very best of players, then, training camp is also a time for deep mental exercise.

"O.J. Simpson loved training camp," Rashad said. "I'm convinced that the very best athletes love training. Reggie Jackson loves to go to spring training. I feel like I fill some kind of void while I'm here; there's kids waiting for my autograph, there's people watching me. It's like playground time for me. And my time is limited, I don't know if I can do this when I'm 40, so I might as well enjoy it."

It would be impractical to suggest that all prospective Vikings can share a similar ebullience. The ball club is suffering from progressive transformation from age to youth, and there is reason enough to veteran and rookie alike to be looking over their shoulders.

"It's the player who isn't sure of himself who suffers the worst," Grant said. "He's going through his pecking orders, trying to figure out what's what and who's who. The rookie isn't prepared for the intense competition."

Yeah, but in the meantime the rookie can eat like a veteran and his phone isn't ringing and kids who don't know any better still ask him for his autograph. Football players need to play football just the way writers need to write and lawyers need to argue and politicians need to kiss babies.

"It's a great time for positive reinforcement," said Fred Zamberletti, the trainer. "If you're a doctor and you go away on vacation, you love to hear how you were missed and how you were needed. It's the same with football players."

None of this will change anything for next summer, of course. The Vikings will come to camp again in chains and complain of the heat and photographers will be sure to capture the death crawl to the water bucket. It makes for a good legend.

Dec. 15, 1980

Maybe we have become too cinematic with this game of football and all its pretensions, but Sunday afternoon at Metropolitan Stadium the ball seemed to travel its arc through onrushing dusk as though in slow motion.

There aren't many moments like it, when the season is on the light end of the scale and the football is sailing through the air to upraised hands in the end zone and thousands of cold and disbelieving fans have stopped in their tracks to the exits.

The Vikings trailed Cleveland by a point, 23-22, and Tommy Kramer has just launched a pass from the Browns' 46-yard line into the right corner of the end zone, with four seconds showing on the scoreboard clock. Terry LeCount, Ahmad Rashad and Sammy White had been deployed to the right corner, LeCount in the middle as if it had been a wing formation. The clock ticked down to zero with the ball in flight. The Browns had responded by sending out a fleet of six deep backs, most principally Thom Darden, the eight-year safety out of Michigan.

"I chose to stick with White," Darden said later in his locker room. "I am sure the ball was intended for White to tip to Rashad. In my mind White was the tip man and I wasn't going to permit it."

"Where was Rashad?" somebody asked.

"At that point I was between White and Rashad," Darden said.

"Suddenly, White stopped. When he stopped, I stopped. And when he went into the air I went with him. I did get a hand on the ball."

"Where was Rashad now?" somebody said.

"By now he was in the vicinity," Darden said.

Rashad caught the ball, on what the Vikings insist was a tip off White's fingers. Rashad was near the 2-yard line and he backed in, victorious in this astonishing and totally unlikely game of volleyball that had given the Vikings a victory and yet another Central Division championship. It was almost a replay of the ball Drew Pearson of the Cowboys caught in the shadow of Nate Wright at the Met in a 1975 first round play-off game.

"I wasn't going to allow Sammy to tip the ball, much less catch it," Darden was saying. "And I ended up tipping it to Rashad. It did not occur to any of us — me or Rashad or White — what had happened until we heard the crowd reaction."

In the Cleveland locker room later there was an occasional curse. Dirty laundry was flung this way and that. A television newsman discovered Cleveland coach Sam Rutigliano in the corner of the bathroom.

"Can we get a live interview?" the TV man said.

"How can you?" Rutigliano said. "I'm a dead man."

Rutigliano was more than gracious, almost bemused by what had just happened. He couldn't for the life of him remember Darden as his primary defender on the miracle catch.

"It was great concentration by a great player," Rutigliano said of the catch. "It was a 30-foot putt and he'll never make it again, but it was memorable. Neither team got much pressure to the quarterback today and the quarterbacks proved resourceful, didn't they?"

"Are you as cool on the inside as you appear on the outside?" Rutigliano was asked.

"I don't know," he said. "You'd have to perform an autopsy."

As interesting as the miracle catch — or more accurately, as astonishing — was a Brian Sipe pass intercepted by Bobby Bryant minutes earlier in the fourth quarter. Cleveland held a 23-15 lead with nearly five minutes left in the game and the Browns were cruising upfield when Sipe chose to pass on a second-and-nine from his own 41 yard line. The pass was intended for Reggie Rucker.

"That was an option screen play," Rutigliano said. "It worked well for us earlier in the game. We were thinking first down, we were thinking ball possession. I had warned the team at half time that the Vikings were an extremely patient team."

"Were you surprised that Sipe passed at that point?" Bud Grant was asked.

"Not at all," Grant said. "They've always used the short pass as a form of ball control. Bobby Bryant just cheated a little. He knew that Sipe wouldn't throw deep and he moved in front of Rucker."

"Rucker was the intended receiver," Sipe said over in his quarters. "But in retrospect I wish I would have dumped it off to Cleo Miller, which was my option on the play. But hey, even after that I didn't think we were in trouble."

But the Vikings struck quickly with a touchdown to Rashad, Cleveland got the ball back and they eventually punted, giving Minnesota its final possession at the Minnesota 20-yard line with 14 seconds left in the game. The play that moved the team downfield was a pass to Joe Senser and the subsequent lateral to Teddy Brown, a play that moved the ball from the Viking 20 to the Cleveland 46, from where Kramer struck with the miracle throw.

"A flea flicker is what beat us as much as anything," Calvin Hill said afterwards. "A damn good flea flicker, that Senser-to-Brown play."

But it was the catch that people will remember, one of those great moments in sports that can be called up in the mind and played over and over again. It did take the chill off a winter day, all that heat and passion boiled down to the final play of a football game.

14/Around and about sports

Bobby Hinds and his violin case

August 14, 1977

A guy named Bobby Hinds hit town Friday, and the only thing he carried off the airplane was a violin case.

Bobby Hinds rode a cab downtown with his violin case on his lap, then he checked himself into the Leamington Hotel and took a corner room on the 10th floor with two street views.

"I want this town," Bobby Hinds said. He loosened his tie as he went to the window, and then he drew open the curtains on Minneapolis. "This town is on my list."

The violin case was on the bed. He unlatched it in three places, laid the cover back and took out his jump rope. He held the rope in his right hand and twirled it until it swung with no discernible movement of his wrist. Bobby Hinds got his feet going then, just little pitty-pats, maybe three-quarters of an inch off the floor. Then Bobby Hinds put it all together.

The rope cut a song in the air. He accelerated, and his hands crossed in front of him in a blur. He downshifted into a pretty boxer's shuffle then threw in a crossover then looped the rope. Then he threw his head back and laughed from down deep in his throat. If a shark could laugh he would sound like Bobby Hinds.

He cut the laugh. Bobby Hinds said he was upset, and it all came back to him. Some kid out of Bloomer, Wis. — tough kids are always coming out of Bloomer with a jump rope and a dream — some kid from Bloomer had just tied the Bobby Hinds speed record, 63 revolutions in 10 seconds.

"He wasn't even using my rope," Hinds said. "If the kid was using my rope he'd have that record to himself. Youth is important in this game, kid. I'm 49 years old. Don't look it though, do I? The kid from Bloomer should get one of my ropes. Hey, I don't mean to hurt anybody in this town, kid. You got a five-dollar bill?"

For a five-dollar bill Bobby Hinds will sell you life. He is the jump-roping king of the world, and he can prove it. He carries his clippings in a black case: Rave notices from doctors, lawyers, judges; good reviews from Time, People and newspapers from across the land.

Bobby Hinds invented an adjustable jump rope and for the fee he includes a book with scientific data that boiled down to this: Ten minutes on a Bobby Hinds "Lifeline" is worth 30 minutes of hard jogging. The jump rope is cheap, convenient and easy, and that's the same logic that these days makes tennis more popular than golf.

None of this "sailor, sailor, do your duty, here comes Jennifer the bathing beauty" stuff for Bobby Hinds. His rope is a piece of silence. It's nine and a half feet long, a foot longer than traditional ropes. And it isn't a rope really, but sections of plastic tubing strung like beads over nylon cord with a tapered handle that acts as a ball bearing and perfect ratios of weight and density and 66 moving parts, for God's sake.

Rope too long? Remove equal numbers of tubes from both sides and burn off the excess nylon cord. Facts and figures rush from the mouth of Bobby Hinds uncontrollably. His mind must look like a ransacked room. He admits it. "I get too worked up," he said. "But this thing is incredible."

Bobby Hinds went to the window. "I've got work to do here," he said. "I have a booth at the hockey equipment exhibit at the Convention Center. They'll go nuts over this rope and my other stuff. And then, kid, I've got to visit the stores and see how the product is moving."

All right, so the guy is hustling a jump rope. His claims are real. You don't fake articles from The Research Quarterly, and those people said 10 minutes of rope skipping is worth 30 minutes of jogging. You must believe that. If you sit in a room with Bobby Hinds for one hour and weed through his imaginings, you will be converted. You will rise out of your chair in a trance, do the boxer's shuffle and throw your head back and laugh.

Bobby Hinds has a story. It is disjointed, like searching through a box of color slides for chronological order. He comes out of Kenosha, Wis., he said, and by the time he was 9 he was sent to a reformatory for a two-year stint for armed robbery.

It didn't start with a gun. It started when he stole milk off porches. His father was an alcoholic, and his mother had polio. Bobby Hinds had his own brand of responsibility. He became a Golden Gloves boxer and got a scholarship to the University of Wisconsin when boxing was a big intercollegiate sport. He couldn't read a book in high school, he said, but he graduated from Wisconsin with a double degree in art and criminal psychology and became an art teacher.

He got fired. It doesn't matter why. He sold encyclopedias door to door, then sold life insurance for the General Life Insurance Company of Wisconsin. He said he sold a million dollars worth, then two, and in 1973 he sold 20 million dollars worth, more than any other agent in the country. He has the numbers on a piece of paper.

Seven years ago Bobby Hinds was sitting around his house in Madison, Wis., when the idea of the rope came to him. He wanted one that was virtually indestructible and perfectly suited for indoors or out. He went to physicists, doctors, lawyers. He checked everything out and got himself a trademark.

He made them at first in his basement. He hired the neighborhood. He hired handicapped. Finally he had to get his own plant because he said he is currently turning out 50,000 ropes a month and can't keep up with the demand. His wife handles the phones; his four kids model for the sales brochures, and he hits the streets with his violin case to attract attention.

Bobby Hinds said that he didn't have the proof but that all the stores he stocks say he is far outselling everybody else.

"But I'm selling a concept with my ropes — strong hearts and flat bellies," Hinds said. "Muhammad Ali came out with a rope after he saw mine, but my sales are leading his. Ali is good with a rope. I'm a pro with a rope, maybe the only one. I mean I was on the Walter Cronkite news and that's about as heavy as you can get."

Jump ropes are only half of Bobby Hinds's dream. The other half looks like a hunk of garden hose with stirrups attached. The Bobby Hinds portable gymnasium! Yes, of course it's the greatest thing in the world. Hinds put his feet into the stirrups and strained against the rubber. He was rowing a canoe, throwing uppercuts, throwing a baseball, all against the strain of the rubber tubing. He ran to a door and stuck the gizmo into a doorjam and tried to pull the wall down. He was huffing and straining, and the words came tumbling out.

"This thing isn't even isometric," Hinds said. "I've gone beyond that. The thing is isokinetic. It's better than barbells."

Hinds inserted a plastic bar in the rubber, slid his feet into the stirrups and strained as if lifting weights. Isokinetic excercise is that which makes every muscle carry maximum load through its full range of movement. The pull up equals the downward release.

"Isn't it great?" Bobby Hinds said. "Wait till the people see this and the football teams and tennis players. Wait till every American has the Bobby Hinds gym in his home. I want this town."

Billy Carter at his best

December 16, 1977

Cable, Wis.

The brother of the president of the United States held a beer in one hand and in the other a cigarette that he smoked so long and hard the filter began to burn at his fingers. He lit another, pausing to dab sweat from his brow and from around the region of his open and perpetually grinning mouth.

"I ain't ever seen this much snow before," Billy Carter told officials and competitors of the Gitchi Gami Games at Mount Telemark, "and I ain't never skied before and I sure as hell ain't gonna. I'm not too sports-minded. I can barely walk."

Still, Billy Carter was the honorary starter Thursday for the men's 15-kilometer World Cup cross-country ski race, the prestigious main event of the games. It was a first for Billy, who never had set his pointy-toed boots down in deep snow before. And it was certainly a first for the competitors, many of whom were Scandinavian.

"Hew is dis shubby guy?" they asked.

On the night before the race, when most of the contestants were in bed dreaming of new snow and perfect wax, Billy did what he does best. He went straight for the bar with a wad of cash in his fist and bought for anybody who could get close, making no bones that he earns twice the salary of his brother.

Billy, a professional one-in-the-hand-one-waiting drinker, said he's had some of his best drinks with athletes.

"Stock car racers mostly," Billy said. "I went to 22 NASCAR races last year. Man, I love that sport. I don't know what the hell I'm doin' here. I ain't never seen a pair of skis. Down in Atlanta the other day I stopped a guy on the street to ask him what he was carrying. They was ski boots. Craziest looking things I ever saw."

A man came up from behind and spun Billy around by the shoulder. This happens frequently to him at supermarket openings and ribbon cuttings. Billy turned slowly, shaping his grin so intently that he had to wrinkle up his nose to keep his glasses from sliding off his face.

"Hey there, Billy," the man said, "I know your brother, whatshisname. Ha. Ha. Ha."

Billy's own laugh was longer and louder, a night laugh full of booze and smoke. Oh Lord, what a joke Billy Carter is having on us all.

Yes, Billy Carter, nationally famed erstwhile peanut farmer from Plains, Ga. The Billy with the red neck. You figure it out. He reportedly gets $5,000 per appearance and is booked solid through July of next year. There is nothing he will not associate with or preside over or mix and mingle around or drink at.

"I won't go out in the snow and get nekkid is what I won't do," he said.

Tony Wise, the proprietor of Telemark, wants Billy to spread the gospel of cross-country skiing to Southerners. Tony Wise is a gambler. He's betting that Billy Carter will remember where he was three days after he leaves.

Billy hasn't really tapped the sports market. He has flagged a stock car race or two and judged a water skiing contest, but he has yet to throw out a first ball or take over the Super Bowl hustle. Like he said, he's not sports-minded.

The impulse to figure out the why of Billy Carter is about as strong as the impulse to reach out and slide his glasses back up his nose. He is no funnier than any other guy from the back of a gas station in rural Georgia, but he must be sharper than most. If somebody wants to give him five grand to drop a flag at a cross-country race or to judge a belly-flopping contest, he doesn't ask why. He just shows up and says, "Hi-yall, my name's Billy," and aims for the bar.

"The press made me," Billy said, examining an ash that had landed on the lapel of his green leisure suit. "The press wrote down all the lies I told them when they were down in Plains for the campaign and didn't have anything else to write about. Jimmy helped make me a little. But man, it was the press.

"I was saying the same bullshit I been saying all my life, but nobody ever printed it before. And I didn't start selling Billy Carter till Plains went all to hell. I'll keep selling Billy Carter till I get good and tired of it."

"Does it bother Jimmy that you make more money than he does?" a man asked.

"I work harder than Jimmy," Billy answered.

Into the night he "yessired" and "nomammed" his way around his staked-out corner of the bar.

"Yessir, I lie a lot, so don't believe a word I say. Yessir, I like Wisconsin because there's more taverns per capita here than any other state in the union."

"Nomam, I don't want to run for political office. I ran five times and won only once and only because I didn't have any opposition."

"Yessir, I brought my son Buddy with me and he's gonna try and ski. He breaks a damn leg, though, and he's gonna pay his own way out of the hospital."

"Nomam, I'm not the president and I lie a lot about the guy who is."

On and on and on and on into the night the round-faced man from Plains told his stories and smoked his butts and drank his booze and laughed his laugh and spent his cash. Early the next morning, for if nothing else Billy puts in an honest day's work, he wrapped his big hands round what looked like a Bloody Mary and started in again on the act that isn't an act.

"Mr. Carter," called out one of the few people to recognize him at breakfast. "Mr. Carter, can I have your autograph?"

"It's Billy," Billy Carter said, "just call me Billy."

Dan Ford forgets to touch home plate

September 8, 1978

That anything can happen in baseball, to anyone, at any time, was demonstrated again the other night at Metropolitan Stadium when Dan Ford neglected to cross home plate in the prescribed chronological order.

Inexplicably, Ford stopped at the perimeters of the dish to guide the trailing runner, Joe Morales, to a safe standup landing before Ford himself sheepishly touched the plate. Morales was called out.

Minnesota's manager, Gene Mauch, walked cautiously to the scene, his eyes ever-widening at the enormity of the mischance. Right then it became a two-man melodrama and there couldn't be two more dissimilar men in all of baseball.

Ford, for better or worse, is the essence of new baseball chic, the cool, spirited individualist who is often befuddled by the complexities of teamwork and occasionally remiss in baseball geography. Ford was astonished once when he slid into third and came up a good five feet east of the bag.

He also may be incapable of embarrassment — Ford would not elaborate on his mistake to local journalists, but explained the affair in hilarious fashion to Harry Caray the next night during a pregame television interview broadcast back to Chicago.

"Well," Caray said at the conclusion of the interview, "it takes something for a man to come on the air after missing home plate."

"Yeah," said an observer on the spot, "a free wristwatch."

Contrariwise there is Mauch. A wiser and more articulate baseball ambassador the game has never seen. Mauch, incidentally, turned Caray down for the same interview because he could not discuss the incident with the level of jocularity Caray thought appropriate.

Mauch suffers his embarrassments deeply and he mentioned, on the occasion of Ford's mistake, that portions of his innards began to churn. Few players measure up to Mauch's perfectionist standards but he rolls along with this hard old game and adapts. In fact, just as Ford seems incapable of embarrassment, Mauch seems incapable of enforcing the discipline which made him legendary in 16 years of National League managing. Mauch is neither soft nor uncaring. He is resigned that today's ballplayer has a loose hold on the virtue of sincerity.

"If I were to bet on one play never happening again in my lifetime," Mauch said, "Ford's play would be it. As far as I know it has never happened in the history of the game."

Errant base running is not unusual. Tony Oliva, his head lowered into the home run trot position, once passed Cesar Tovar after Oliva hit a home run in Detroit, a ball that Tovar did not advance on because he thought it had been caught.

In 1931 Lou Gehrig lost the home run title after a home run he had struck in Washington bounced out of the pavilion and into the glove of a Senators outfielder. The runner at second, Lyn Lary, set sail for third at the crack of Gehrig's bat but turned to the outfield in time to see the ball being caught. Lary gave up and went to the dugout, where he was finally thumbed out after Gehrig rounded third and was held there on a triple. Gehrig and Babe Ruth each finished the season with 47 home runs.

It was Ford's complete breakdown under such routine circumstances that startled Mauch as much as anything. Mauch alluded to the career of one Bob Dillinger, which was terminated in 1951 when Dillinger failed to score for Pittsburgh on a sacrifice fly before a teammate at second was thrown out at third.

"Branch Rickey had the Pittsburgh club then and he was in the stands that day," Mauch said. That concluded his retrospection. The implication that things were different in a different time was clear. Dillinger resurfaced in the Coast League and hit .366 for Sacramento but he never made it back to the bigs.

Ford was back in the lineup Wednesday night suffering from no more than the effects of a 90-minute conversation with Mauch.

"We talked baseball," Ford said. "Gene plays to win and it's hard for him to accept mental mistakes, especially when a player he thinks shouldn't make them, makes them. He doesn't ask that much, he asks 100 percent. Just get down and play. I don't expect these things happening to me next year or the years after that. And if I worry about mistakes they'll just get worse so I'm not going to worry."

Ford recently turned 26. His .281 average and 73 RBIs are hallmarks of great hope and promise in his career. Some of the goofiest characters in sports have become prominent team men once they were willing to be cool and spirited for only 22 hours a day.

"Well, I learned something, Harry," Ford told the Chicago broadcaster. "Get to the next base before the guy behind me does."

Joe gets robbed

Sept. 17, 1978

New Orleans, La.

"I didn't take your wallet, sir."

His long hair was knotted. His T-shirt advertised his most recent meal. Maybe 19 years old...tops. He came out of the dark in a corridor under the Superdome.

A mob was crowding the escalator that led to the room where Muhammad Ali was holding a postfight exhibition. Certain laws of physics were being violated on that escalator. The police remedied the situation by indiscriminately shoving people, so that suddenly hundreds of bodies were adrift in collision. Panic was like a faint smell on the air.

"Bull," I said, surprising myself. His angular face was accented by a wisp of goatee, in the manner of a guerrilla thug. My hand had fashioned a noose from his shirt collar and I had him up hard against a plate-glass door. I had felt his hand go into my back pocket, but by the time I spun him around, he had dropped the wallet — and not on the floor.

"This guy took my wallet," I said. The people adrift studied their shoes. A cop heard my accusation and took the kid into the adjacent room. I followed.

"It's not the money," I said, saying all the ridiculous things that people say when their wallets are misappropriated. "It's the pictures and cards."

"Well, you ain't gonna see them again," the officer said.

"Yeah, but," I said.

"Your wallet is in the street or in a toilet by now," the cop said, as if I should have been aware of those eventualities.

"I didn't take your wallet, sir," the kid with the wisp of goatee and stained T-shirt said. The cop prodded him and they moved to a security office. They fastened cuffs to his wrists and, when they asked for his identification, he gave his mother's name and an apartment number.

"He's going to jail whether you press charges or not," the cop said.

"I'm not going to press charges," I said. "But I want to say something."

"Say it."

"Nothing," I said.

I figured I might make a speech, but the room came into focus then. Two previously apprehended characters were asleep on a bench and my guy was beginning to look amused.

It was not a financial catastrophe. Besides, I've beaten the odds for five years. It was no big deal and nobody lost any blood. My time was due and I always knew it would happen at a fight.

The fight crowd is populated by representatives from the entire socio-economic-political spectrum, a phenomenon due in large part to the charismatic Ali.

He is a world figure. Governors appear for him in contrived situations. Movie stars, presidential mothers and other well-heeled boxing clients make his scene to justify their own worldliness.

The staple of the gang is the guy who saves a month's pay so he can rent a Cadillac for the night of the big fight. He totes a dame on his arm like a new piece of luggage and she wears a dress she can't afford.

And on the perimeters are the muggers and pickpockets and saps who have their own torn statements to make.

The pickpocket, although poorly dressed, is an agile and sometimes polite bum. He steals popcorn and sits in a seat other than his own and looks offended when told to move. He doesn't drink, not because he can't steal a beer, but because liquor could ruin his timing and mobility. If he drapes a woman on his arm, she is an accomplice and they are practiced in the art of deceitful collision.

The pickpocket can't read, but he can count a fight house in 30 seconds and his eyes light up at the prospect of unruliness. He moves in then, as he did on me. But my guy was dumb.

There were 70,000 people in Ali's arena and 60,000 of them carried more cash than I did. Worshipping at the feet of Ali is a powerful and necessary ritual for some people, even if it means spending $200 for a ringside seat that puts a customer as far as 100 yards from the ring.

Ali brings them all together. That Ali has to beat up somebody to gain such a grip on us is a matter for sociologists to debate. No doubt they will get another chance. Ali will fight again and, when he does, all of us, the bums and thieves and working stiffs and movie stars and politicians, will be differentiated only a little bit by the liberties we take when the lights go down.

Secret Service at Duff's tournament

June 24, 1979

I was at Duff's Celebrity Golf and Tennis Tournament on Saturday afternoon waiting for Vice President Walter Mondale to play tennis when a very nice thought came over me. I was thinking how glad I am to be covering figures in sports as opposed to figures in politics, although I used to consider this was a distinction without much merit.

As this tournament is also the largest collection of expensive blue jeans on expensive legs, there was plenty of opportunity to roam around and think these thoughts. I was wandering absently toward the Rolling Green clubhouse when a German shepherd, and I am talking dog here, strained against its chain and made an unfriendly sound. I came to attention and discovered that I was inside a roped-off area of greensward. Attached to the dog was a policeman.

"You are inside the ropes," the cop said. "You should be outside the ropes."

I saw other dogs and these were not the kind of dogs who fetch the newspaper off the stoop. And then I saw dozens of gentlemen standing around in the shadows with wires coming out of their ears. These were Secret Service personnel, which I could tell from their brown shoes and nice haircuts.

"This must be for Mondale's arrival," I said.

"It ain't for Bill Brown," a cop said.

You do not see this kind of security in the ball parks or fight arenas. Everywhere I looked I could see a Secret Service employee who tried to pretend he was a regular person. When you are covering a baseball team and you want to talk to a player, you might, as a courtesy, seek permission from the manager. The manager might spit something brown at your feet and say, "What do I care? Go talk to the guy."

When you are covering political guys, I guess you go up to the Secret Service employees.

"Could I speak to Mondale when he gets here?" I asked a Secret Service employee.

"I am unaware at this time if that opportunity will become available," he said.

In the meantime, if you were waiting for Mondale, all you could do was walk around and study the rolling scenery of Hamel. Celebrities were playing golf and celebrities were playing tennis, including Harvey Martin of the Dallas Cowboys. Harvey Martin could pick up three Secret Service guys in one swoop and Harvey Martin can crush quarterbacks. But Harvey Martin cannot hit a tennis ball. Not on purpose. Harvey Martin got hold of a tennis ball on a lucky swing and they had to bring a new ball into play because Harvey destroyed the one he hit.

"I have watched Harvey playing tennis here," Ahmad Rashad was heard to say, "and I am glad that I am not a quarterback."

Rashad is a good tennis player. Rashad would team with Dr. John Najarian against Mondale and a player from Los Angeles named Nils van Patten, who might or might not have been an actor but who was certainly presentable enough for a screen test.

Suddenly there was a commotion near the entrance to the tennis courts and all the sportswriters who were waiting for Mondale rushed over to the commotion. It turned out that Loni Anderson of television fame was standing there and she stood there for so long that all the sportswriters missed Mondale's entrance. He had arrived in a motorcade and was trying to move past Loni Anderson and get onto the court where his opponents were waiting.

It is not easy to play tennis in public if you are the vice president of the United States. People yell things before you even get to hit the ball. One guy yelled, "Hey Fritz, get us some gas." Most people figured this was in reference to the energy crisis.

And when play started, and the Mondale-van Patten team jumped off to a quick domination of the Rashad-Najarian team, the same character yelled, "Hey, Rashad, play like you owe back taxes."

This van Patten fellow was so good that his team beat Rashad-Najarian 6-1. The vice president even got to hit a few balls but displayed the good sense to let van Patten run the show. It was all very nice and the dogs never had to be turned loose and all the guys with wires hanging from their ears seemed relieved that the match only took 30 minutes, tops.

Now in the sports world you go up to an athlete after the game and ask him a leading question and chances are you will get a clever reply. For example, you could ask a pitcher who just threw a no-hitter what the strongest part of his game was and the pitcher could reply, "The other team's bats."

"Mr. Vice President," Mondale was asked, "what was the strongest part of your game?"

This was a wide open chance for Mondale to say, "Nils van Patten." But Mondale considered this question to be right up there with questions about SALT.

"My over-all strength?" Mr. Mondale replied. "My backhand and forehand. And my strategy."

This stunned more than a few listeners. It took a sporting figure to come up with a clever line. "Yeah," Rashad was saying. "Doctor Najarian here promised me the operation of my choice if we would have won."

Rodney Dangerfield looks at sports

March 28, 1980

One of the truly bright moments in television, discounting a broken set, is not a show, but a commercial for low-calorie beer that features a bacchanal of those celebrities who, either alone or in pairs, have done commercials for the same beer on their own.

This is the spot where Bubba Smith rips the top off a beer can with his bare hands and Don Carter, the bowler, tries to. Happy Hairston fools around with a plate of peas and Boom Boom Geoffrion is trying to order a meat loaf sandwich and a beer.

But Rodney Dangerfield turns the moment to gold in the role of master of ceremonies. He is completely ignored. His pathetic face collapses on at least two occasions, once when the giant Ben Davidson reaches across Rodney's lectern for more food and again when Jim Honochick, the former umpire apparently suffering from myopia, wraps his arm around Dangerfield and proclaims him to be

Boog Powell.

"I don't get no respect in that commercial either," Rodney Dangerfield said the other night backstage at the Carlton Celebrity Room, where he had just performed a dinner show. "It's good exposure, it's good exposure. I like those fellas, I like those athletes and I hold my own pretty good in that crowd. I get the ballplayers in my joint in New York — Joe Namath, Too Tall Jones, a lot of the ballplayers. It's a good crowd."

Rodney was glistening with sweat. Like a fighter after the bout, he had changed into a bathrobe, royal blue, and flimsy bedroom slippers. Slowly, his eyes went back into his head and he calmed down and he started breathing normally again. A show takes something out of Dangerfield — Karen Olson, a co-owner of the Carlton, was backstage trying to repair the star with mineral water and fresh fruit.

"I like to baby him," Karen Olson was saying. "He comes to town all alone. He doesn't travel with 12 people and his poodles."

"That's fine, baby," Rodney was saying.

"You hang out with a sports crowd, Rodney?" a man asked.

"The sports crowd hangs out," Rodney said. "I don't have time to hang out. I'm here. I'm there. I'm in my club, I'm in Vegas, I'm here. I've got things going, you know, I'm busy, you know, I don't have time to hang out."

"I've seen you at fights," the guy said.

"I like a fight, I like a fight," Rodney said. "I don't know, maybe man is an animal to watch two men fight, but I love boxing. I know a lot of fighters. I was here last August. I saw Scott LeDoux fight Ken Norton. I had 12 of those fight crowd guys over here for a show, a party of 12, yeah. Yeah. So how's life?"

Dangerfield is a New Yorker. He was made for the big town. Damon Runyon would have made a star out of a guy like Dangerfield because in Runyon's day, Runyon was television. These days we get our characters from beer commercials and People magazine.

But that beer banquet of Rodney's was so cleverly filmed and so well scripted that it was a classic, backwards glance at professional athletes and friends of professional athletes, when a beer was a beer and a doll was a doll and you didn't get in trouble for drinking the former and looking at the latter. The athletes who hang out at Dangerfield's in New York would never engage in such behavior in public. An accountant or an attorney might be watching.

"They were athletes acting the way athletes are supposed to act, or the way we want them to act," Rodney said. "It was biff, bam, guys raising hell in a good-natured way. I don't know if you would ever see athletes acting like that in public nowadays. It took 176 takes just to make that commercial. It took a whole, long day because, because athletes aren't actors."

It was filmed at the Lotus Club in Manhattan. It was Dangerfield's sixth or seventh spot for the brewery. On Monday he will return to

New York to film two more. He will portray a photographer at a reunion of the beer's 40 spokesmen, Mickey Spillane, Bubba Smith, Billy Martin, the whole crowd. At the conclusion, Rodney looks up from his camera and says, "O.K. boys, be yourselves." Everybody in the joint breaks out fighting.

"I'm the kind of photographer," Rodney said, "who wears a beret."

But the truth is, Rodney is not a character. A ringside seat is about as close as he gets to a fight and he watches his football on television and he thinks baseball is too slow. He doesn't drink much and he quit smoking.

He brings his own toaster oven with him on the road and he always orders a refrigerator for his suite so that he can stock the food he prepares for himself in the toaster oven. He takes care of himself to prolong his career.

"But if I take perfect care of myself," Rodney said, "I've still got sickness and death to look forward to."

The kids are being organized to death

June 11, 1980

Major research conducted by me has revealed that kids are now out of school for the summer and that they are being organized to death on the playgrounds. Playground and Little League coaches are well-meaning men and women and they are trying so hard not to organize kids to death that they nearly have organized informality.

Organization is a worthwhile virtue at places like the bank or the car wash, or any place that carries on with the business of life. But organization is a dumb thing in sports played by kids, a kid being any boy or girl not yet old enough to drive the car or mow the lawn or get a job for the summer.

These are kids who should be playing pickup games in the vacant lot, but as soon as they gather with a bat and ball, a well-meaning coach pulls up and begins to arrange them in such a way that they become informally organized. There are squads of these coaches who patrol our streets so that children may not gather to play a game without advice.

Kids don't ride bikes any more with playing cards in the front wheel. They ride dirt bikes over motocross courses. A kid picks up a tennis racquet to swat a ball against the house and his mother swoops him up in mid-swing to enroll him in a tennis school. This is perverse, but well-meaning. One of the great pleasures of parenting, apparently, is to give your kid everything, whether he wants it or not.

Soccer comes about as close as any activity to defying the intrusion of well-meaning coaches and playground directors. The natural dumbness of little kids really shines through in soccer. After a kid soccer game, most of the participants have to ask somebody who won.

This is beautiful, even though it causes heart palpitations among well-meaning coaches and playground directors. Soccer does require some minimal organization, such as putting eight children into the same color shirt and then pointing them in the right direction, but after that, the kids are on their own. A soccer coach can't tell a kid a thing because soccer is full of words that don't make sense to adults, words like bloke and header, striker and hand ball.

"Kids don't need a lot of coaching," said Geoff Barnett of the Minnesota Kicks. Three years ago, Barnett opened up a youth soccer camp called Camp Kicks. The club now sponsors four of the camps and they could have dozens more, but someone in the Kicks organization has shown signs of intelligence and they are leaving well enough alone.

"In England," Barnett said, "the kids were organized, but they weren't coached. When I was a kid, I played pickup games all the time. I pretended I was Bobby Charleton or Jimmy Graves. When I was about 14, I saw a guy named Lev Yashin do a drop kick. I went home and practiced it. It took me three years to get it right. When I see kids playing sports now, I wonder if they even use their imaginations to help themselves improve."

Barnett was told that in modern America it is not customary for a child to use his imagination as a coaching tool because it might require permission from a well-meaning playground director. Barnett restrained himself from blowing soccer's horn, but soccer does allow a kid a great deal of imagination because he is out there alone and doesn't understand a thing. He makes up the game as he goes along, at least at the very young levels of play. So even despite minimal organization, kid soccer resembles vacant lot activity without advice.

According to some figures supplied by the Kicks, 2,100 kids played soccer in Edina last fall, including 800 girls, as opposed to 600 girls in a softball program. In Burnsville, 1,500 boys and girls between third and ninth grades play soccer, as opposed to 200 in the football program. The Minnesota Junior Soccer Association represents 5,000 players in the metropolitan area, up from six teams total in its initial 1969 season.

"It's undeniably a good game for kids," said Marian Portesan, secretary of the Minnesota Junior Soccer Association. "A kid who isn't a very good athlete stands out in other sports. In soccer, that kid can run with the mob and not be noticed as much."

"A kid should be a kid," Barnett said, "a kid shouldn't be a robot. A kid's natural ability will take over for him if he is just given the chance to be himself."

This is also true in tennis or baseball or softball or throwing a ball against the house. But the well-meaning squad is out there trying to round the kids up and give them some advice on how to be organized and well-coached. So far, this has been very hard to do in soccer, so the game keeps attracting more and more kids who conclude each exercise by wondering who won and probably not caring very much either way.

Trouble in Paradise, Garvey style

August 13, 1980

Filling this year's literary void in the department of the Gothic romance has been the steamy, pulp-level tale of Steve and Cyndy Garvey, one of whom plays for the Los Angeles Dodgers.

Now instead of lugging "Ashes in the Wind" by Kathleen Woodiwiss out to the beach, or "Scruples" by Judith Krantz, the lovelorn can take along the latest copy of Inside Sports, which, under the title "Trouble in Paradise", contains a disheveling of the Garvey marriage. Come to think of it, the Garvey caper is juicier and better written than "Scruples", and besides, even a Calvinist can haul around a sports magazine if it's hot stuff he's after.

Right off the bat I must exhume an old prejudice and admit that I distrust any bleached blonde of Czechoslovakian descent who spells Cyndy with a y where the i should be.

Aside from that, I feel embarrassment for both the Garveys for allowing a magazine of such spreading appeal to perform what turned out to be an autopsy on a such a splendidly perfect marriage.

At least the Garvey marriage was thought to be perfect until Pat Jordan invaded the suburban Garvey home with his microphone and Mrs. Garvey responded with such thoughts as, "I need to be cuddled, tested, talked to, made love to, and if I don't have those things I turn into a stone princess. I'm very sexual looking but I can be like ice when I'm near someone who doesn't give off a sexual aura. I'm much more sexual than my husband. I need a man more than he needs a woman."

And so on. That selection was not necessarily out of context, as the entire article focuses on the difficulty Mrs. Garvey has experienced with being Mrs. Garvey. Steve is never home, you know.

The two of them met on the campus of Michigan State University and in practically no time at all Garvey had established himself as a star with the Dodgers. Mrs. Garvey now realizes that she existed principally to deliver children and appear at Dodger games looking desirable, which she managed to do in a kind of nouveaux, let-me-slide-into-my-Jordache-Jeans kind of way.

Well, she was playing a supplemental role, at best, in her husband's success, the kind of anxiety-ridden state of the 30-year-old woman that columnist Ellen Goodman so often addresses.

At the age of 29 — she is 30 now — Cyndy Garvey went out on her own to seek work. She landed a spot as a co-host to Regis Philbin on a Los Angeles television talk show, which reminds me of a joke about the shovel-carrying man who follows an elephant around the circus. Ah, but never mind. It is a thick enough web these Garvey souls spin for each other.

It came out over the weekend that the Garveys have filed an $11.2 million suit against Newsweek, Inc., alleging that the article was libelous, malicious and contained quotes out of context. Furthermore, the Garveys have won at least a temporary delay in the publication of excerpts of the article by the Los Angeles Herald Examiner. About four hours worth of tapes will presumably be turned over to the judge and Newsweek's attorneys are planning their own appeal.

All of this was to be expected, I suppose, once the Garveys sat down and actually read what it was they said about each other. Sports fans, as opposed to the thrill seekers who enjoy troubled romance, recognize that Garvey is regarded with some suspicion by his teammates and by ballplayers generally.

Garvey is a nice man, but seems possessed of a smile made of poured concrete. His wife insists that he has not changed one whit emotionally since the day she married him in 1971, but then, too, she may be discovering that time is probably the only real enemy of any marriage, even between Ken and Barbie. Garvey has traditionally been so protective of his image that he comes off in the piece as the less volatile of the two. But he does face his wife's dissatisfactions, however clumsily, as though he were awakening from a bad dream.

"We're not so different from most people, really," Garvey told Jordan. "People would see that if they didn't take into account our appearance. We're just two people who love each other and who have gone through a lot ... I hope ... maybe ... it's just a cycle she is going through ... What do you think?"

I think the title of the article could probably be inscribed over the clubhouse doors of just about any team. In any league.

Sports after tragedy?

April 1, 1981

There seems to be at issue among well-meaning people a question of propriety regarding the carrying on with national sporting events following national tragedies, or, in the case of Ronald Reagan, near tragedies.

Ever since the messenger dropped dead after delivering the news of the victory at Marathon man has debated whether to conduct his sporting events in the wake of tragedies, be they large or small.

The National Football League conducted its full Sunday schedule within 48 hours of the murder of John Kennedy. The summer Olympic Games of 1972 went on in Munich as smoke from the weapons of terrorists drifted over the compound. Robert Kennedy and Martin Luther King went down dead with assassins' bullets in them and games went on.

And Monday evening, about six hours after President Reagan and three other people were shot in Washington, the National Collegiate Athletic Association held its basketball title game in Philadelphia and the National Hockey League carried on with its schedule, as limited as it happened to be.

Was it right for the games to go on on Monday? Probably. By 8 or so that evening television network news persons had undeniably revealed themselves as the buffoons that most of them are, and the entire nation was in danger of terminal redundancy just listening to these talking dogs.

Talking dogs, incidentally, is the Texas appellation given to members of the electronic media. But that is a cavalier way of addressing the real issue of Monday evening. For dozens of reasons the games went on Monday: Business, political, television scheduling and because of a word from the president himself, who, if we are to believe the talking dogs, advised those about him in the hospital that, all things considered, he'd rather be in Philadelphia.

But was the presentation of the NCAA basketball championship, to pick an event, proper in light of President Reagan getting shot, to pick a fallen leader?

"I watched the basketball game," Dr. James Butcher said Tuesday. Butcher is the director of the Clinical Psychology Department at the University of Minnesota. "I do not think there is anything in my training that could provide me with a case for or against showing the basketball game. I suppose having watched the game answers for my personal opinion. If you talk to a hundred psychologists, you'll get 100 different opinions."

Talking to just a couple proved Butcher's point.

"I think maybe propriety is the wrong word," Dr. John Brantner said yesterday. Brantner is a psychologist in the University of Minnesota's medical school. "Whether the showing of a game is proper after tragedy is really a question of manners. It's probably a question best answered by Amy Vanderbilt or Miss Manners. It's a question of etiquette, much like the question of whether two people should get married soon after the death of one of the partner's parents."

"Then is it psychologically helpful for people to see a basketball game after they have just seen the president get shot at?"

"Following catastrophe or tragedy," Brantner said, "the best psychological advice is to return to normal as soon as possible."

Butcher was asked the newly slanted question.

"The best psychological advice after tragedy is to return to normal," he said, "following a period for grief. Because grief is usually reserved for loss, or death, grief wasn't really operative Monday night."

I don't know how far you would have to go back in this country to find an example of time standing still so that we all may dwell on a tragedy — maybe all the way back to the gunning down of Abe Lincoln. But this country has grown so busy and become so complex that its wheels cannot stop even if we wanted them to.

Leader after leader has gone down and there is killing in the streets and at times it seems as though nothing will stay rooted in the ground.

The question of our becoming dulled by these sadnesses is a larger and more frightening question than the carrying on with games. Sports is just one of the wheels that cannot stop spinning.

Joe Louis and Stubby Eason

April 15, 1981

God must have been lonely. He took Joe Louis and Jimmy Eason out of life in the same week, probably to set up a card game or to tell stories.

Jimmy Eason, called Stubby for reasons that had nothing to do with his wooden leg, was the equipment manager of the Minnesota Vikings until he died Monday at the age of 59. Joe Louis was the heavyweight champion of the world longer than any man in the history of the sweet science. He died Sunday in Las Vegas at the age of 66 from a bad heart, maybe a broken heart.

Louis was especially larger than life during World War II, when Jimmy Eason was serving with the army's 34th Division in Italy.

Eason was a little guy with an expressive face. He could have posed for either Willie or Joe, the Bill Mauldin cartoon characters. And because he had done some fighting himself he was a Joe Louis fan, could appreciate what Joe Louis accomplished against the odds of his color.

"We used to kid Stubby about Joe Louis," Fred Zamberletti, the Vikings trainer, said Tuesday. "We'd tell Stubby that Joe Louis had a few set-ups in his day, that he wasn't that great of a champion. Stubby would drop down into a stance. He'd just as soon come to blows over the defense of Louis."

Joe Louis and Stubby Eason didn't have anything in common except that they were characters. And sports is running through its characters at a terrible pace, leaving us with guys who wear masks where their faces should be. How can you tell if a guy is a character?

One small indicator concerns the use of money. Joe Louis made a fortune and went through a fortune. He was always reaching into his pocket and pulling out crumpled wads of cash. Stubby Eason didn't get rich off the Vikings, but he knew how to use money.

"Stubby and I and our wives went to the Super Bowl in Miami in 1968," Zamberletti was saying now. "It was Oakland and Green Bay. We were there for 10 days and it was a party every minute of every night and day. Stubby was wild. The night before the game we all had dinner with Tom McCormick, an assistant coach with Green Bay. He used to be an assistant coach with the Vikings.

"So we go to the Mai Tai, big, fancy place. Stubby tells McCormick, 'Look, you're coming into the dough tomorrow, you pick up at least the hors d'oeuvre part of the check.' It came to $114 and then we ordered dinner. Stubby is flying now, so he goes out into the lobby of the place and buys perfume and Hawaiian leis for all the women at the table.

"Now we're leaving the place and I ask Stubby, 'How can we justify spending $387 in this place?'"

"Make it $389," Stubby says, "I just tipped the guy in the bathroom $2."

When he returned home to northeast Minneapolis from the war Eason became a health inspector. Then he opened a joint called Jimmy Eason's at Broadway and Lincoln where the freeway now runs. When that didn't work out, Eason began a career at the University of Minnesota administering to the dirty linens of 11 athletic teams. But for some reason the Gophers could not find it in their budget to take Eason to the 1961 Rose Bowl. Eason then wrote a letter to the brand new Minnesota Vikings.

"I know every equipment guy and sporting goods dealer in town," Eason wrote in his letter of application. "I can do good work for you."

He was called Stubby because of his 5-foot-4 build, not because of the wooden leg he acquired in 1969. He caught a bullet in his leg in Salerno, Italy, in 1943 and the leg had always bothered him. Norm

Van Brocklin named Eason Stubby when the two one day found themselves on an elevator with a blonde who was built like a public landmark. Van Brocklin looked at the woman and then he looked at Eason. Eason stood only as high as her most interesting points.

"Stubby," Van Brocklin said, elbowing Eason. "You're Stubby."

Stubby always liked to get one thing right out front. He was a Viking. He wasn't some guy who kept his mouth shut and picked up the dirty socks. He counseled Fran Tarkenton. He sparred with Joe Kapp in a mock fight before every game because if Kapp didn't box he wasn't ready to play. He smoked and played cards with Bill Brown. He watched Carl Eller demolish a blackboard at half time of the playoff game with Washington in 1973. Jim Marshall was his pal.

"This is a rough time for me to talk," Marshall said Tuesday, "maybe later."

There is something else about Eason that made him a special man. It was an openness to all people, a kind of natural warmth that Joe Louis was said to have possessed as well. Stubby Eason made people feel at home around the Vikings, which was not an easy task given the suspicions and the pretensions and the politics of the sport of football.

Stubby Eason was a Viking. But he should be remembered as the Viking who didn't let it go to his head.

About the author /

Joe Soucheray arrived at the Minneapolis Tribune in July, 1973, after first investigating and revealing new information about a 50-year-old murder case in St. Paul, in order to prove to those who might hire him that he was capable of newspaper journalism.

In each of his previous attempts to secure a reporting job he had been told that his experience as a writer of magazine articles — for the Webb Company in St. Paul — was not sufficient to ensure his employment in the newspaper business.

It was never Soucheray's intention to become a sportswriter, but when that opening presented itself at the Tribune, Soucheray spoke immodestly of his own accomplishments around the ballparks.

In truth, the first Twins game he covered as a reporter was the second professional baseball game he had ever seen in person.

Soucheray worked at a brass foundry, as a rock musician and as a delivery truck driver for a florist during his studies at the College of St. Thomas in St. Paul. He graduated in 1971 with a degree in journalism.

In 1976 Soucheray became a sports columnist with the Minneapolis Tribune.

In 1975, 1976, 1979 and 1980 his work was included in E.P. Dutton's Best Sports Stories anthologies, and in 1979 Soucheray was voted one of the outstanding sports columnists in the country by the national Associated Press Sports Editors Association.

Soucheray and his wife and two children live in St. Paul.